KINGSWAY WEST

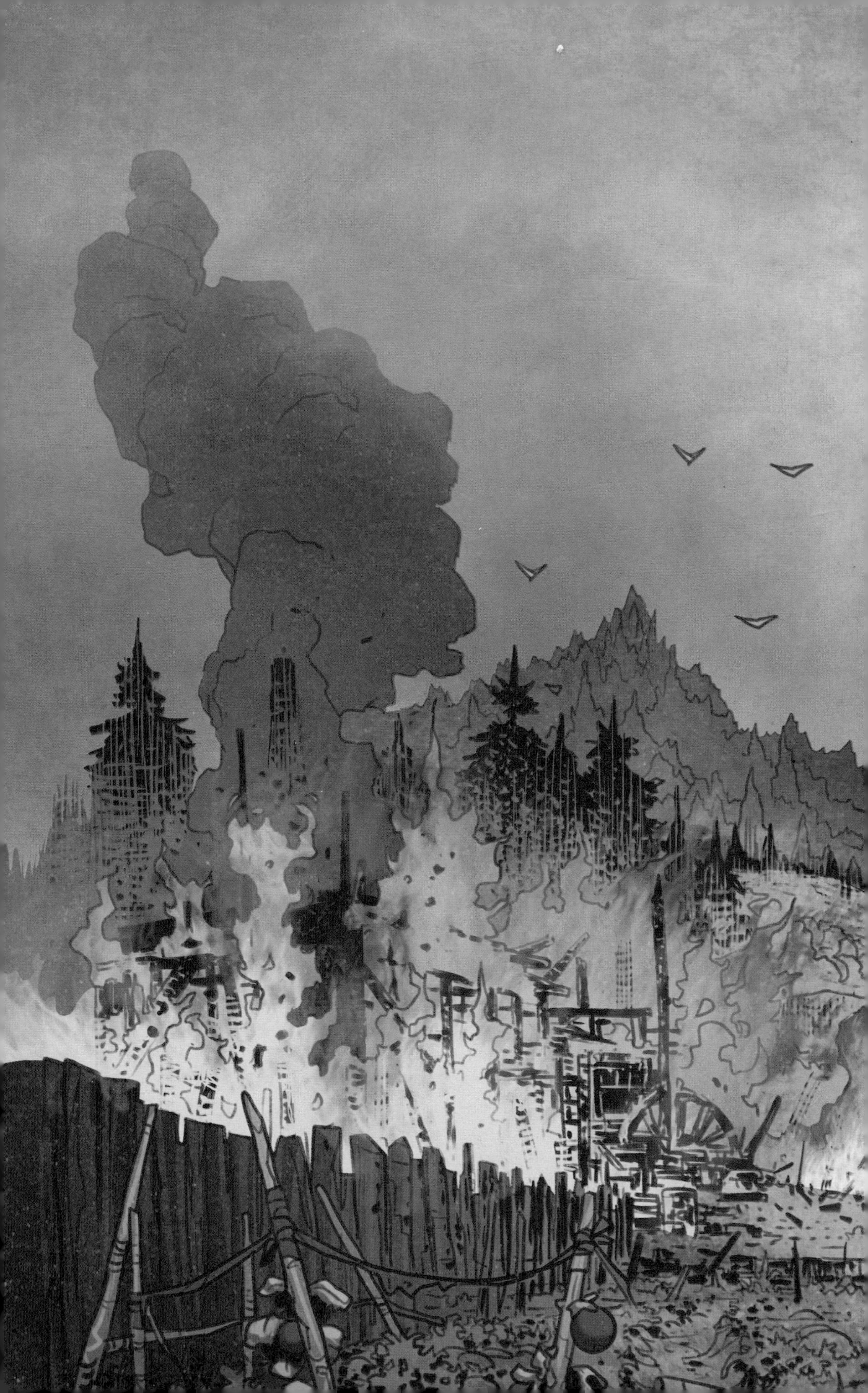

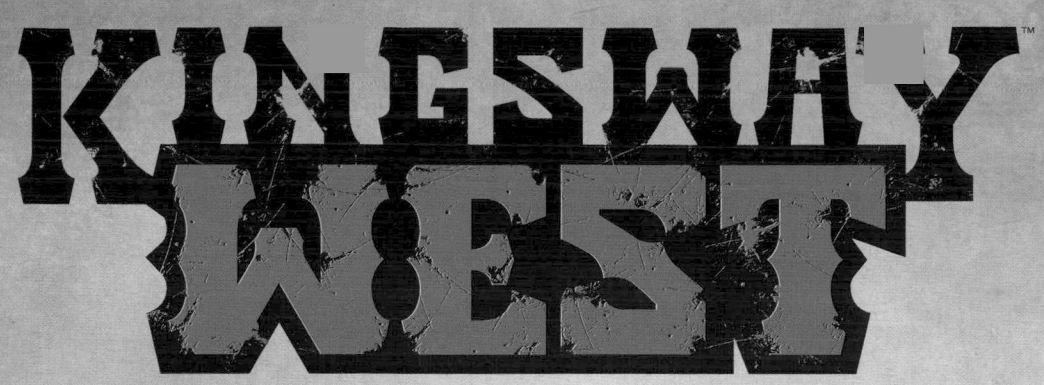

KINGSWAY WEST™

SCRIPT
GREG PAK

ART
MIRKO COLAK

LETTERING
SIMON BOWLAND

COLORS
WIL QUINTANA

COVER ART
MIRKO COLAK AND WIL QUINTANA

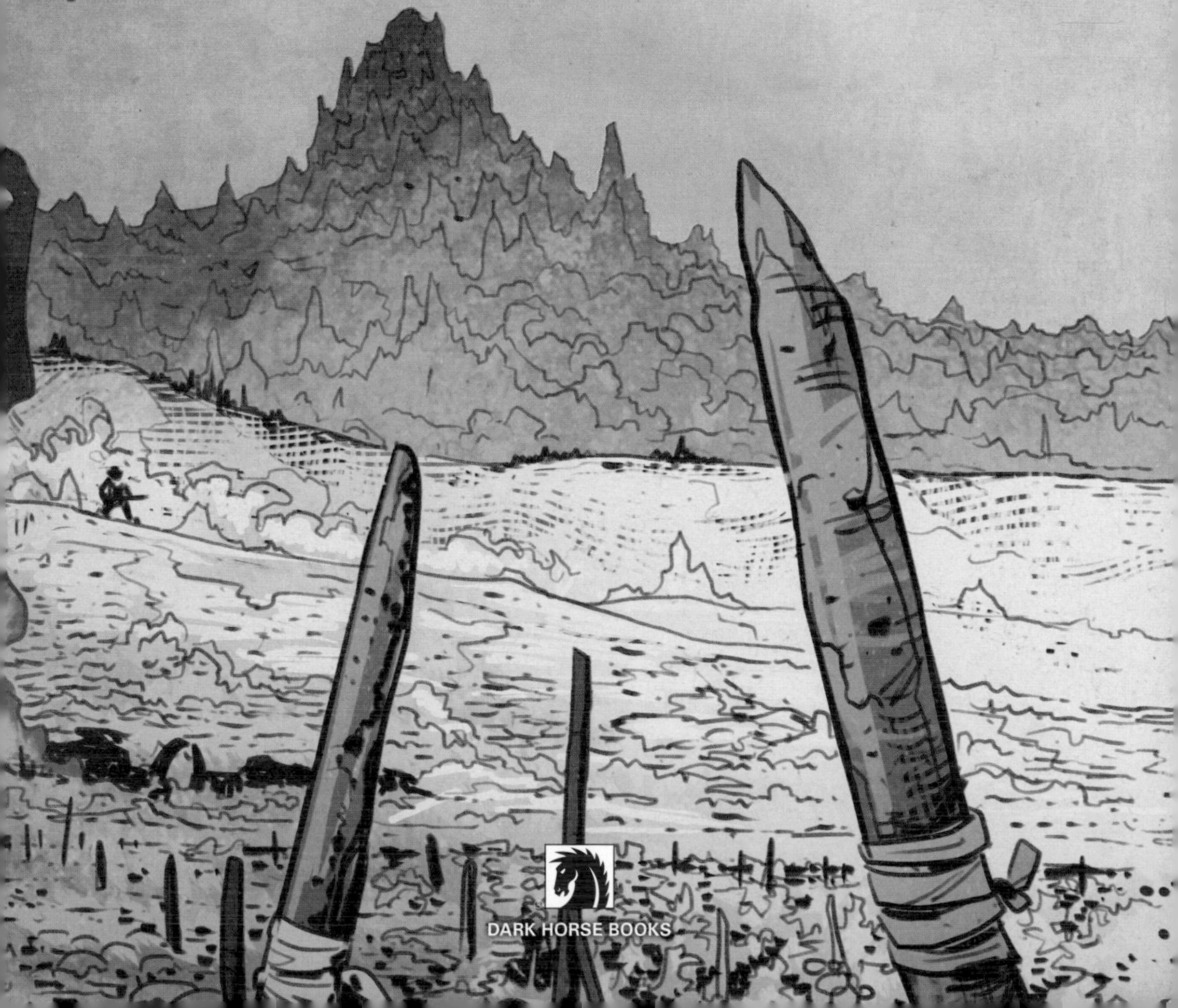

DARK HORSE BOOKS

PRESIDENT AND PUBLISHER
MIKE RICHARDSON

EDITOR
SPENCER CUSHING

ASSISTANT EDITOR
KEVIN BURKHALTER

COLLECTION DESIGNER
ETHAN KIMBERLING

DIGITAL ART TECHNICIAN
CHRISTINA McKENZIE

Neil Hankerson, Executive Vice President • Tom Weddle, Chief Financial Officer • Randy Stradley, Vice President of Publishing • Matt Parkinson, Vice President of Marketing • David Scroggy, Vice President of Product Development • Dale LaFountain, Vice President of Information Technology • Cara Niece, Vice President of Production and Scheduling • Nick McWhorter, Vice President of Media Licensing • Mark Bernardi, Vice President of Digital and Book Trade Sales • Ken Lizzi, General Counsel • Dave Marshall, Editor in Chief • Davey Estrada, Editorial Director • Scott Allie, Executive Senior Editor • Chris Warner, Senior Books Editor • Cary Grazzini, Director of Specialty Projects • Lia Ribacchi, Art Director • Vanessa Todd, Director of Print Purchasing • Matt Dryer, Director of Digital Art and Prepress • Sarah Robertson, Director of Product Sales • Michael Gombos, Director of International Publishing and Licensing

Kingsway West

This volume collects the Dark Horse comic book series Kingsway West #1–#4, originally published August 2016–January 2017.

Published by Dark Horse Books
A division of Dark Horse Comics, Inc.
10956 SE Main Street
Milwaukie, OR 97222

DarkHorse.com

International Licensing: 503-905-2377
To find a comics shop in your area, call the Comic Shop Locator Service toll-free at 1-888-266-4226.

First edition: April 2017
ISBN 978-1-61655-976-2

10 9 8 7 6 5 4 3 2 1
Printed in China

Library of Congress Cataloging-in-Publication Data

Names: Pak, Greg, author. | Colak, Mirko, 1975- artist. | Quintana, Wil, colourist, artist. | Bowland, Simon, letterer.
Title: Kingsway West / script, Greg Pak ; art, Mirko Colak ; colors, Wil Quintana ; lettering, Simon Bowland ; cover art, Mirko Colak and Wil Quintana.
Description: First edition. | Milwaukie, OR : Dark Horse Books, 2017. | "This volume collects the Dark Horse comic book series Kingsway West #1-#4 originally published August-November 2016"--Title page verso.
Identifiers: LCCN 2016044133 | ISBN 9781616559762 (paperback)
Subjects: LCSH: Comic books, strips, etc. | BISAC: COMICS & GRAPHIC NOVELS / Fantasy.
Classification: LCC PN6728.K5746 P35 2017 | DDC 741.5/973--dc23
LC record available at https://lccn.loc.gov/2016044133

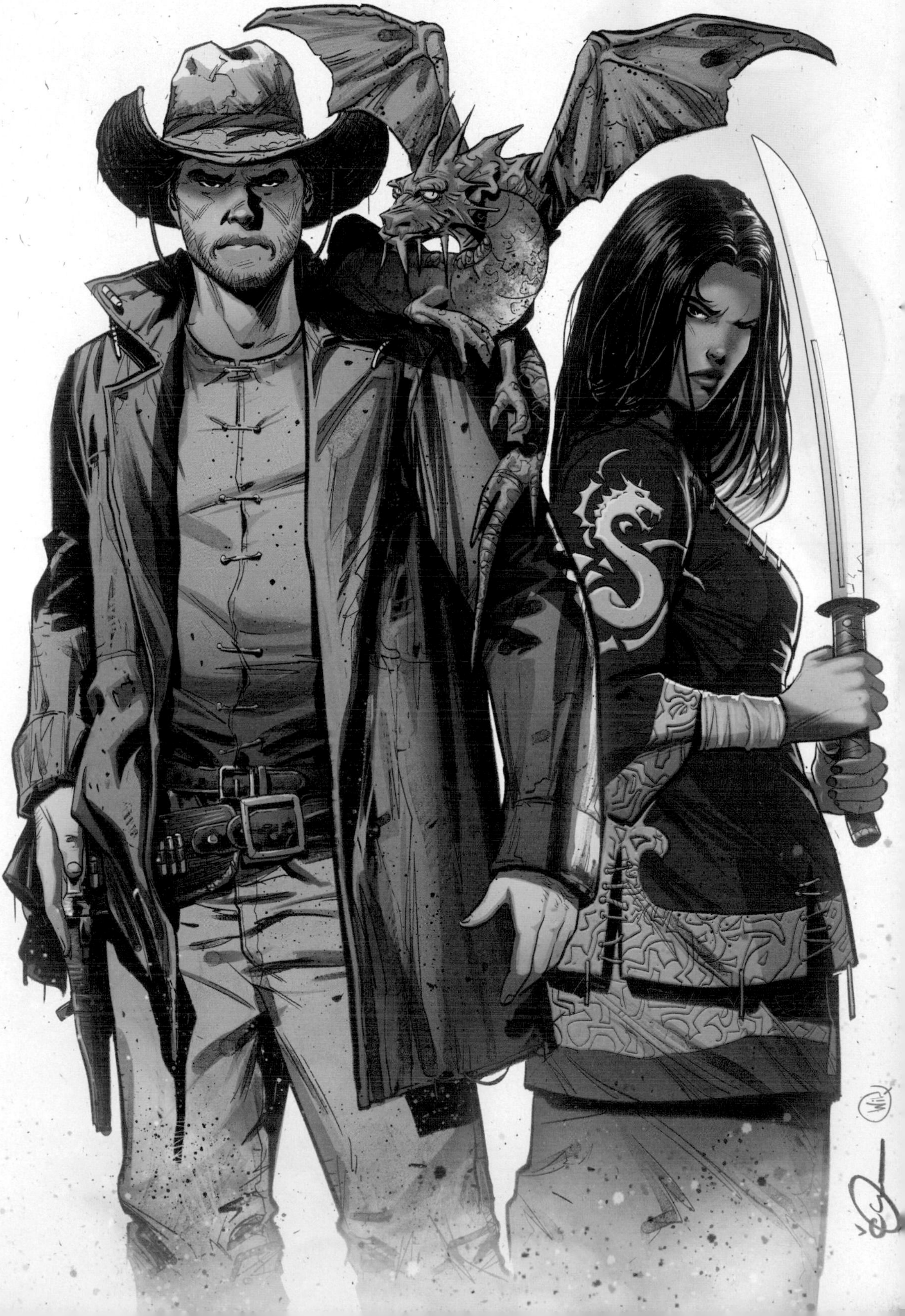

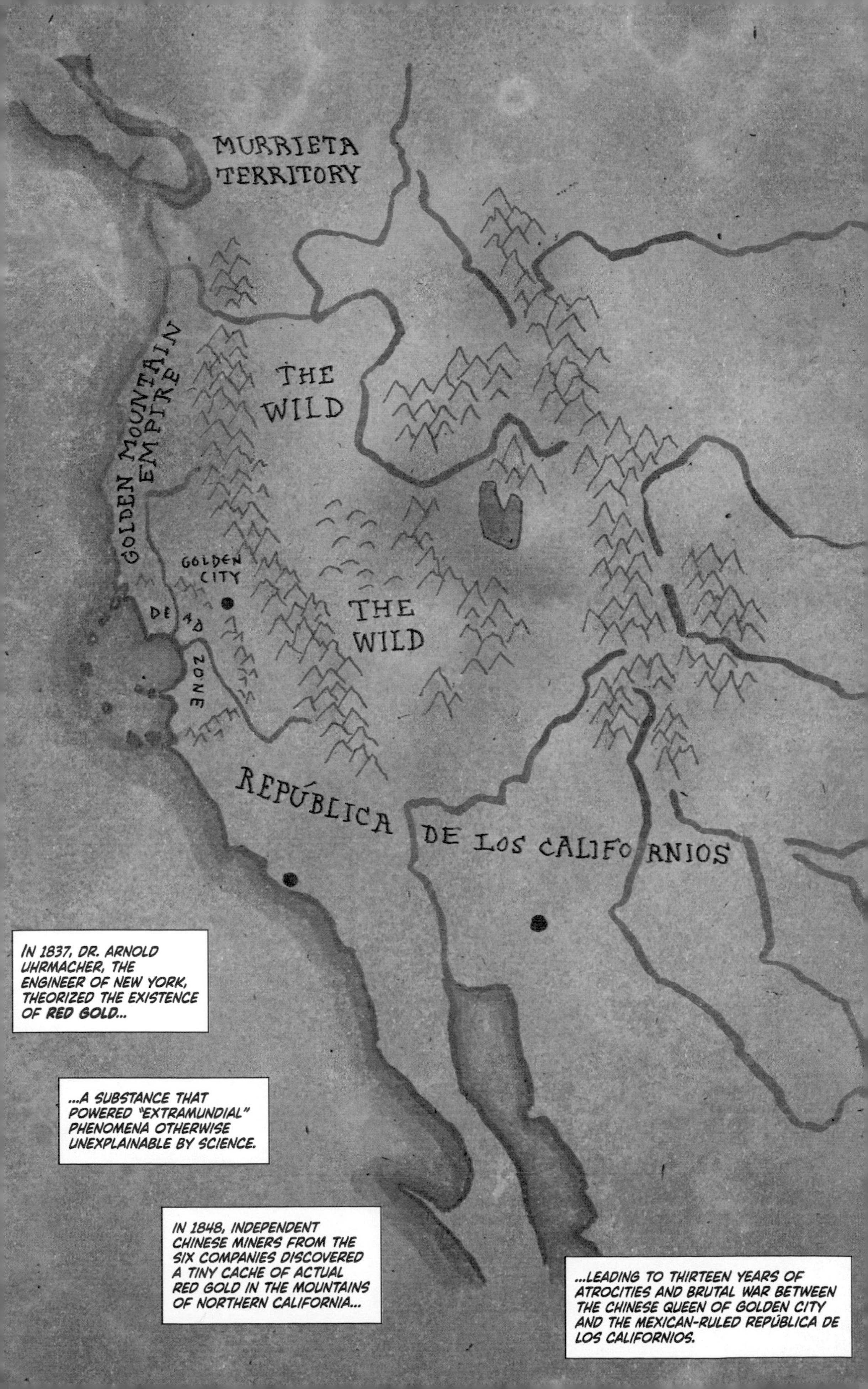
MURRIETA TERRITORY
GOLDEN MOUNTAIN EMPIRE
THE WILD
GOLDEN CITY
DEAD ZONE
THE WILD
REPÚBLICA DE LOS CALIFORNIOS
IN 1837, DR. ARNOLD UHRMACHER, THE ENGINEER OF NEW YORK, THEORIZED THE EXISTENCE OF RED GOLD...
...A SUBSTANCE THAT POWERED "EXTRAMUNDIAL" PHENOMENA OTHERWISE UNEXPLAINABLE BY SCIENCE.
IN 1848, INDEPENDENT CHINESE MINERS FROM THE SIX COMPANIES DISCOVERED A TINY CACHE OF ACTUAL RED GOLD IN THE MOUNTAINS OF NORTHERN CALIFORNIA...
...LEADING TO THIRTEEN YEARS OF ATROCITIES AND BRUTAL WAR BETWEEN THE CHINESE QUEEN OF GOLDEN CITY AND THE MEXICAN-RULED REPÚBLICA DE LOS CALIFORNIOS.

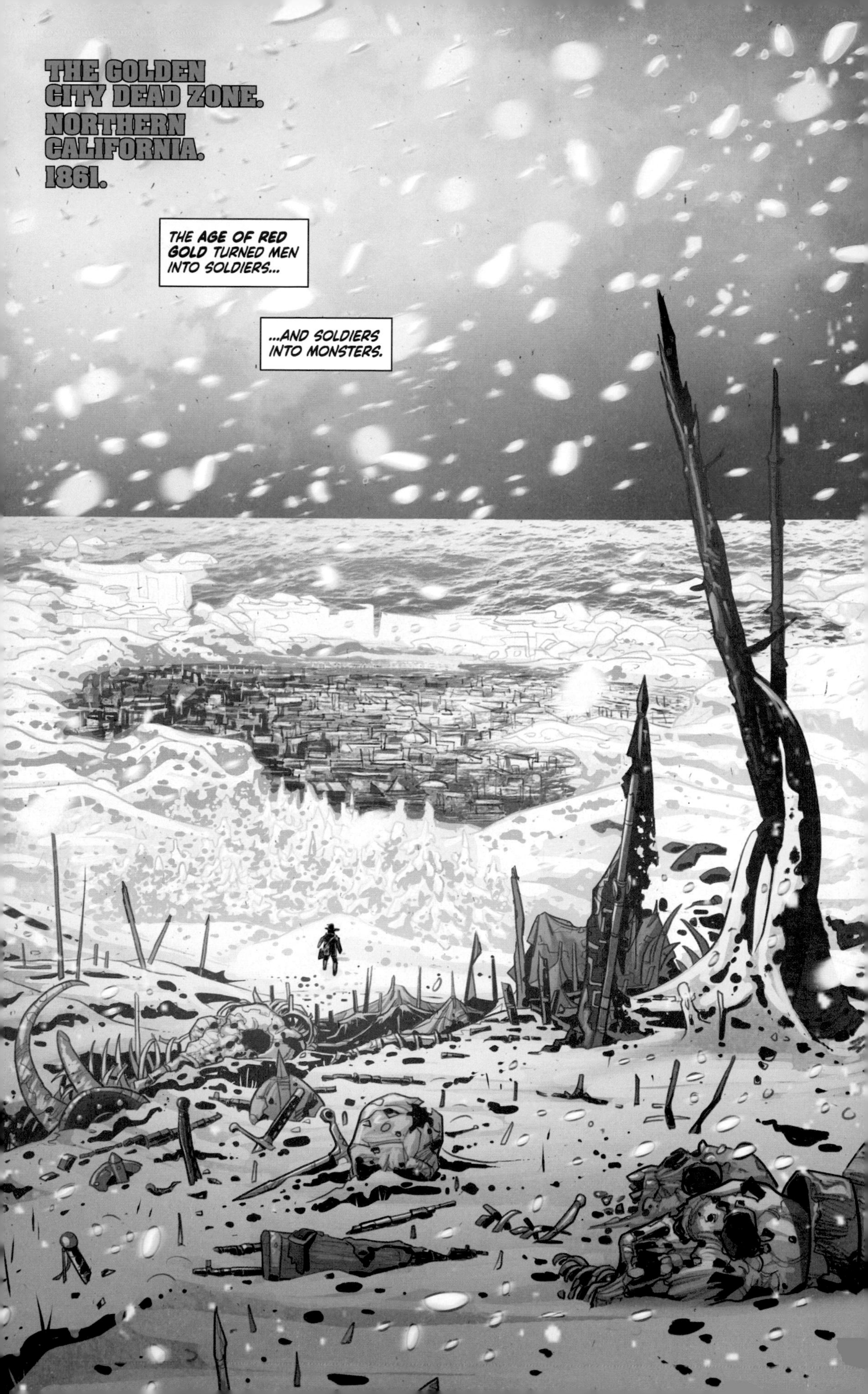
THE GOLDEN CITY DEAD ZONE. NORTHERN CALIFORNIA. 1861.
THE AGE OF RED GOLD TURNED MEN INTO SOLDIERS...
...AND SOLDIERS INTO MONSTERS.

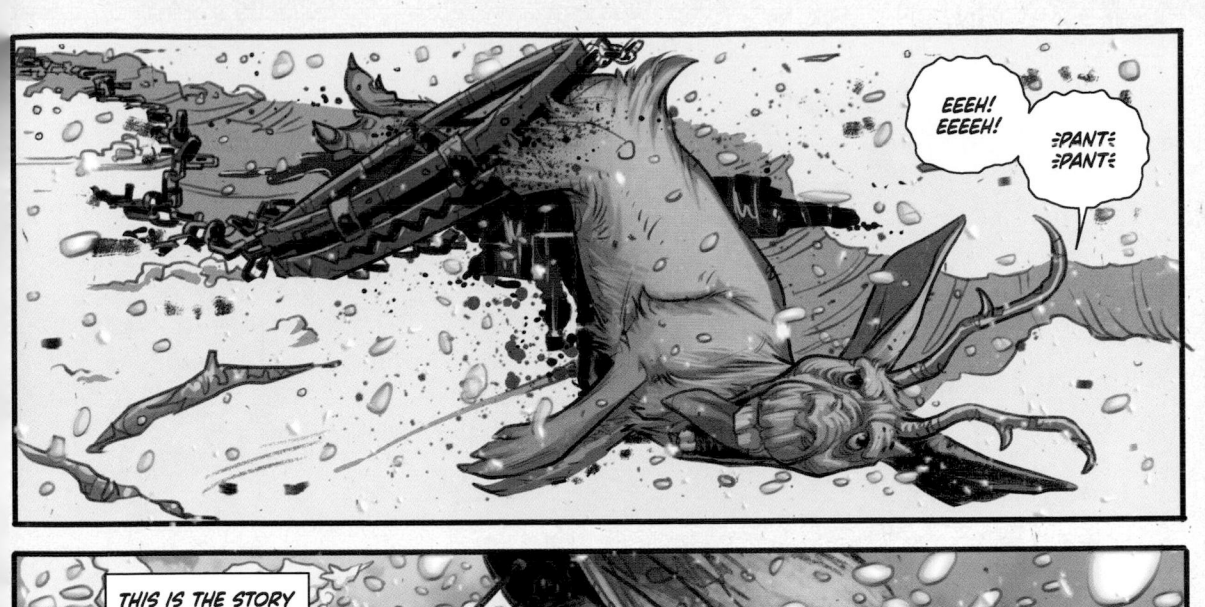

EEEH! EEEEH!

≡PANT≡ ≡PANT≡

THIS IS THE STORY OF A MONSTER...

EEEH! EEEEH!

EEEEEH!

KINGSWAY LAW!

...WHO TRIED TO BECOME A MAN AGAIN.

WE GOT A THOUSAND-DOLLAR *BOUNTY* ON YOU FROM THE *QUEEN* OF *GOLDEN CITY!*

YOU'RE WANTED FOR DESERTION, TREASON, CONSPIRING WITH *FREELANDERS*, AND *MURDER!*

THROW YOUR GUN ON THE GROUND!

WAR'S OVER. JUST WALK ON.

SORRY, OLD MAN.

YOU'RE WORTH TOO MUCH.

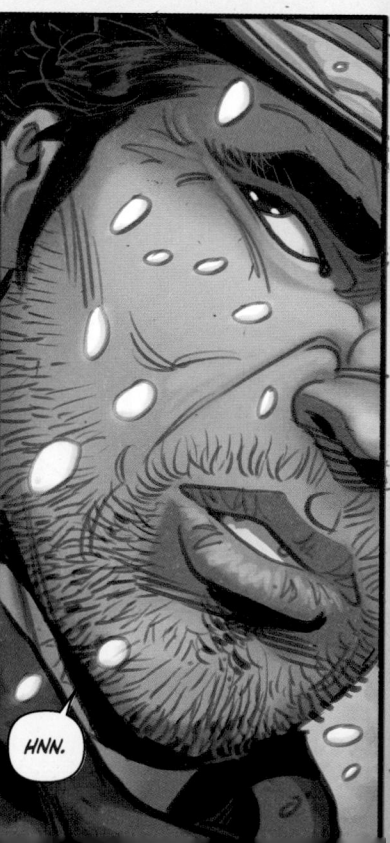

HNN.

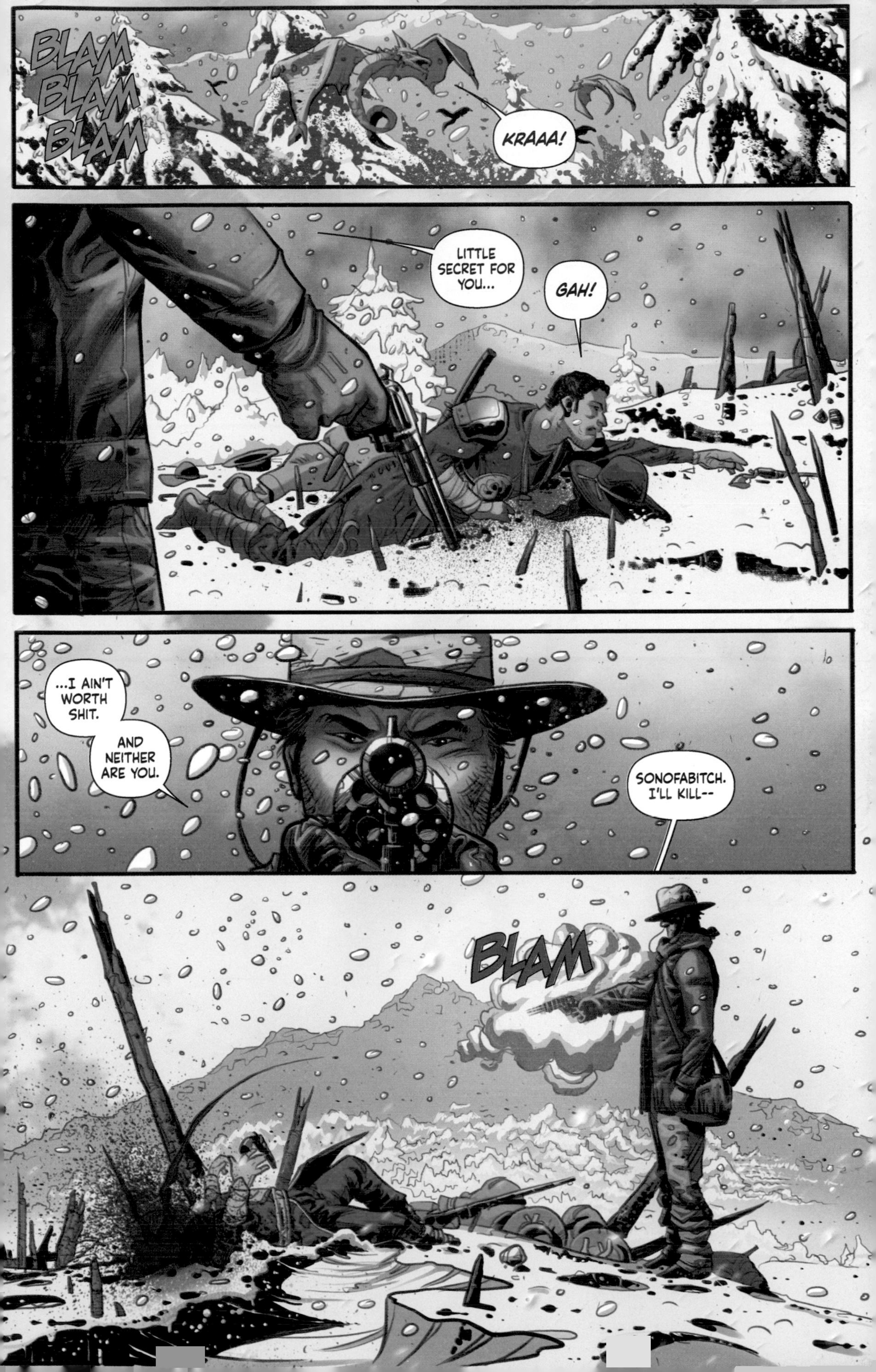
BLAM BLAM BLAM
KRAAA!
LITTLE SECRET FOR YOU...
GAH!
...I AIN'T WORTH SHIT.
AND NEITHER ARE YOU.
SONOFABITCH. I'LL KILL--
BLAM

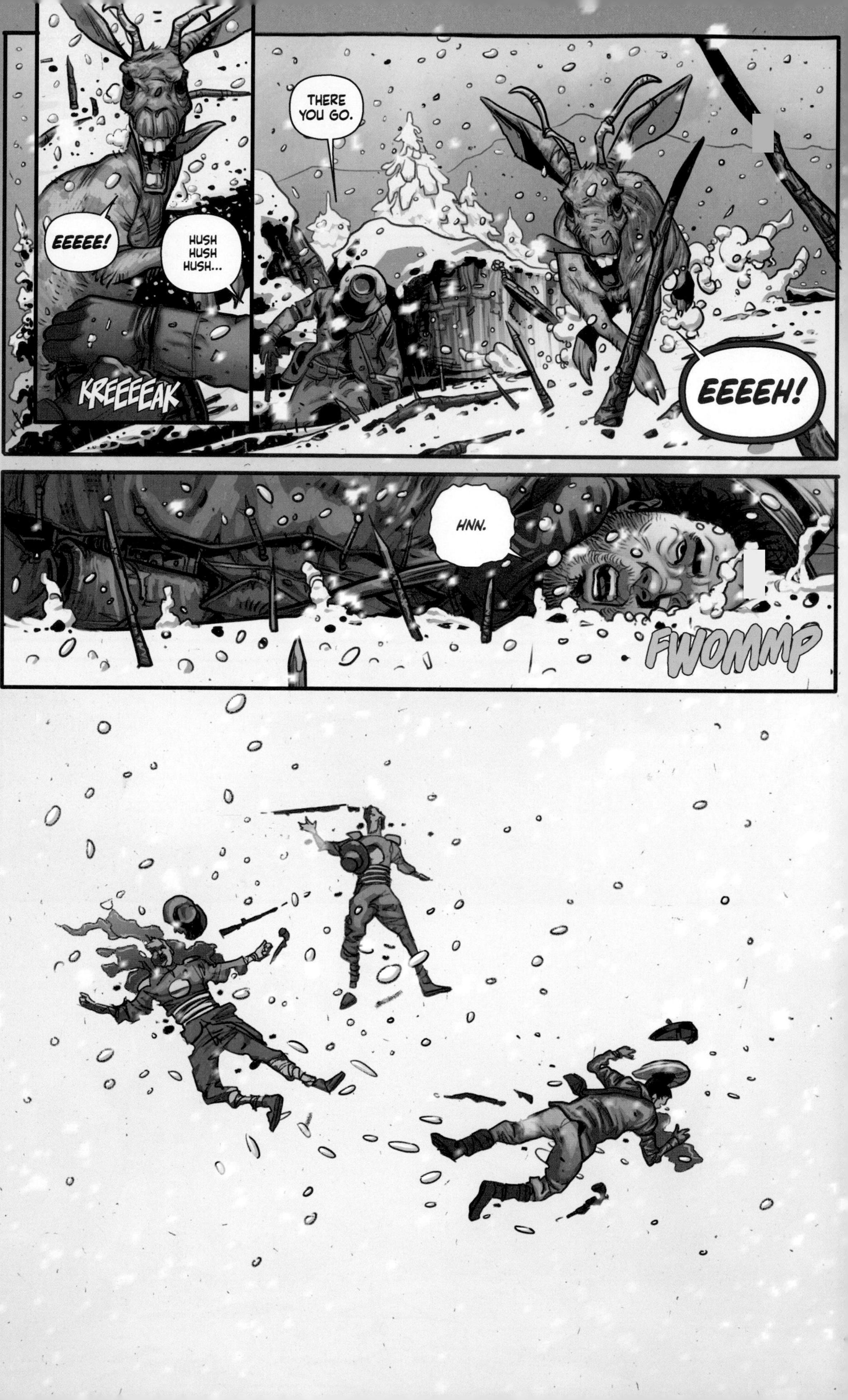
EEEEE!
HUSH HUSH HUSH...
KREEEEAK
THERE YOU GO.
EEEEH!
HNN.
FWOMMP

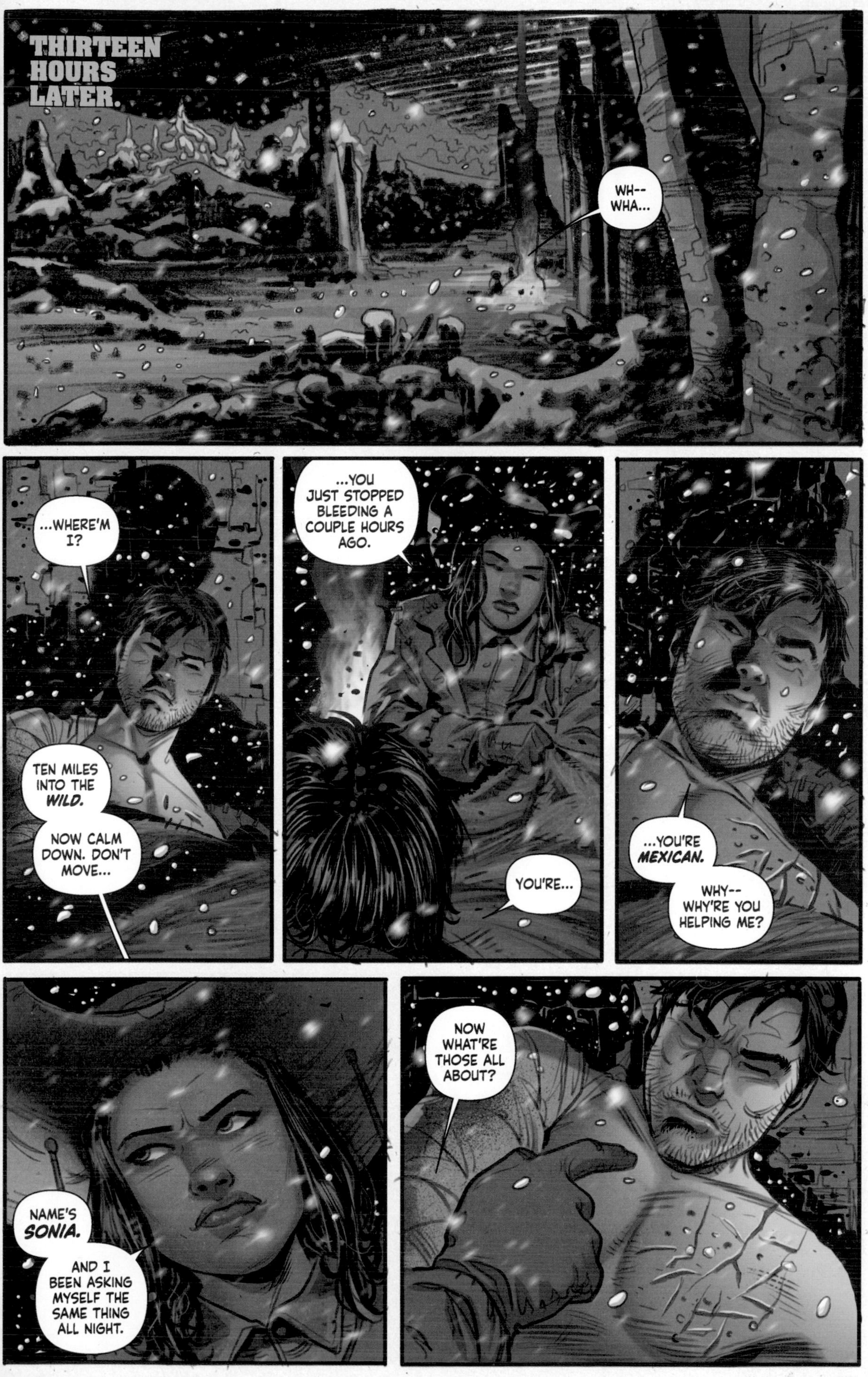
THIRTEEN HOURS LATER.
WH-- WHA...
...WHERE'M I?
TEN MILES INTO THE WILD.
NOW CALM DOWN. DON'T MOVE...
...YOU JUST STOPPED BLEEDING A COUPLE HOURS AGO.
YOU'RE...
...YOU'RE MEXICAN.
WHY-- WHY'RE YOU HELPING ME?
NAME'S SONIA.
AND I BEEN ASKING MYSELF THE SAME THING ALL NIGHT.
NOW WHAT'RE THOSE ALL ABOUT?

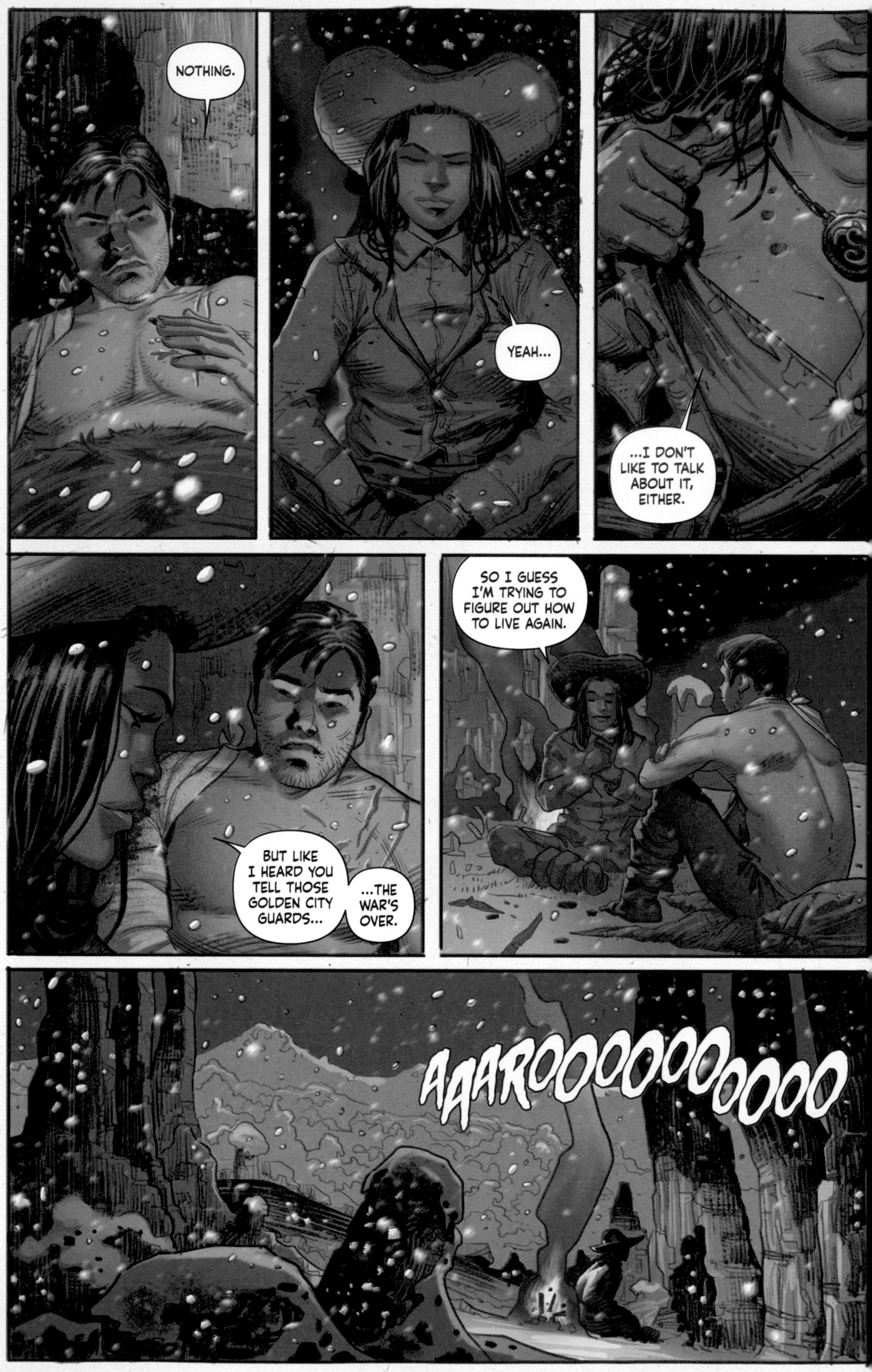
NOTHING.
YEAH...
...I DON'T LIKE TO TALK ABOUT IT, EITHER.
BUT LIKE I HEARD YOU TELL THOSE GOLDEN CITY GUARDS...
...THE WAR'S OVER.
SO I GUESS I'M TRYING TO FIGURE OUT HOW TO LIVE AGAIN.
AAAROOOOOOOOOO

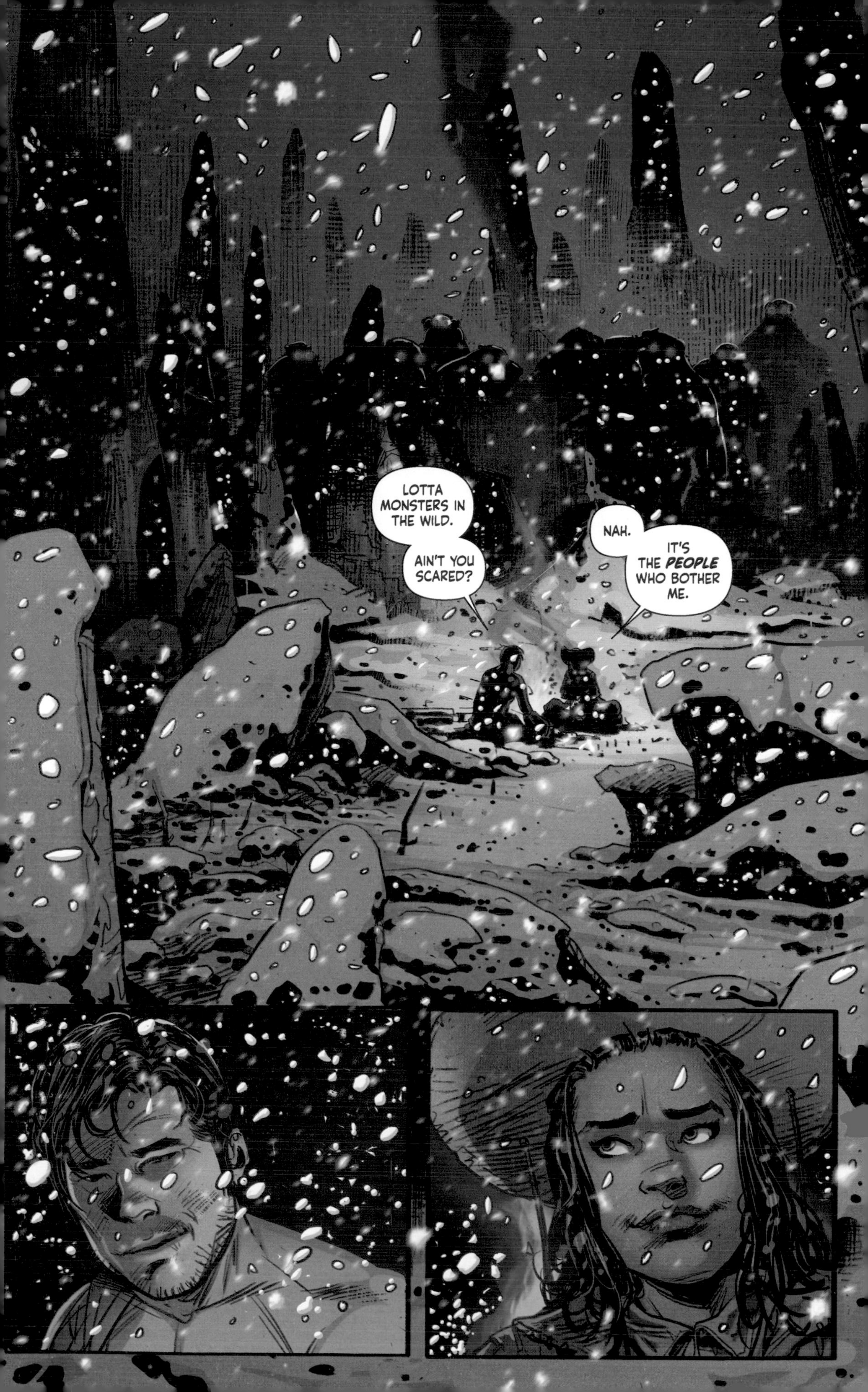
LOTTA MONSTERS IN THE WILD.
AIN'T YOU SCARED?
NAH.
IT'S THE *PEOPLE* WHO BOTHER ME.

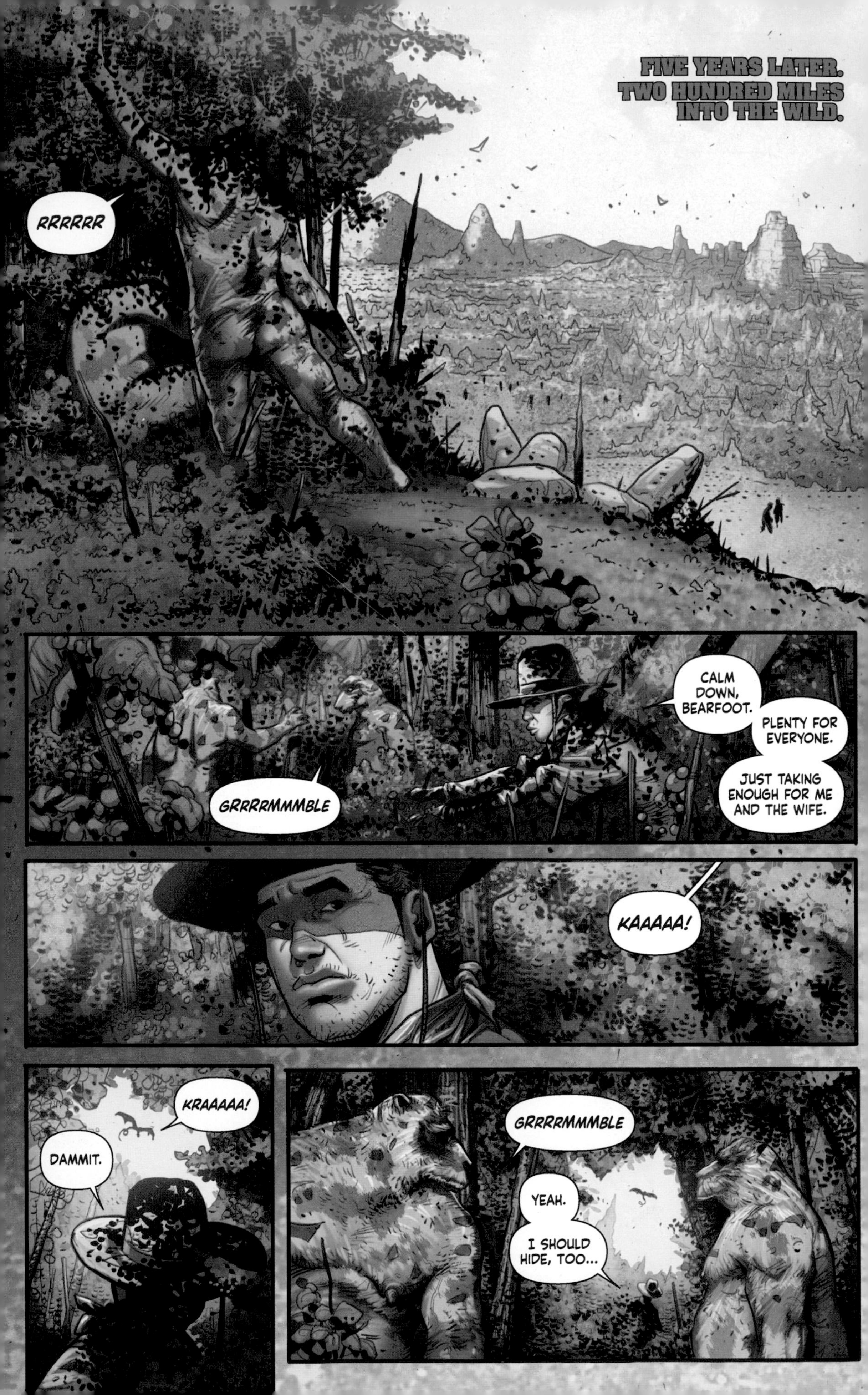
FIVE YEARS LATER. TWO HUNDRED MILES INTO THE WILD.
RRRRRR
CALM DOWN, BEARFOOT.
PLENTY FOR EVERYONE.
JUST TAKING ENOUGH FOR ME AND THE WIFE.
GRRRRMMMBLE
KAAAAA!
KRAAAAA!
DAMMIT.
GRRRRMMMBLE
YEAH.
I SHOULD HIDE, TOO...

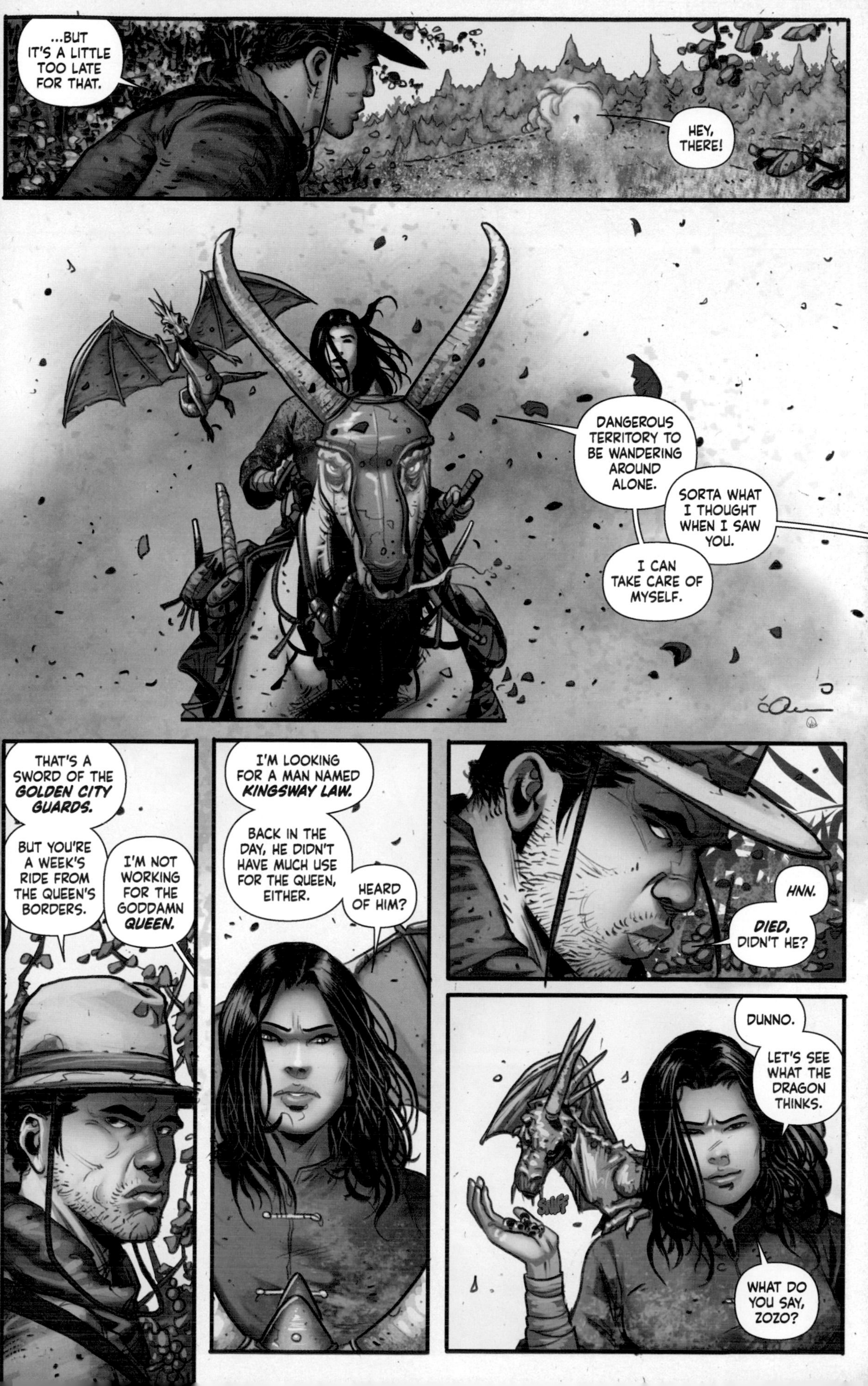

...BUT IT'S A LITTLE TOO LATE FOR THAT.
HEY, THERE!
DANGEROUS TERRITORY TO BE WANDERING AROUND ALONE.
SORTA WHAT I THOUGHT WHEN I SAW YOU.
I CAN TAKE CARE OF MYSELF.
THAT'S A SWORD OF THE ***GOLDEN CITY GUARDS.***
BUT YOU'RE A WEEK'S RIDE FROM THE QUEEN'S BORDERS.
I'M NOT WORKING FOR THE GODDAMN ***QUEEN.***
I'M LOOKING FOR A MAN NAMED ***KINGSWAY LAW.***
BACK IN THE DAY, HE DIDN'T HAVE MUCH USE FOR THE QUEEN, EITHER.
HEARD OF HIM?
HNN.
DIED, DIDN'T HE?
DUNNO.
LET'S SEE WHAT THE DRAGON THINKS.
SNIFF
WHAT DO YOU SAY, ZOZO?

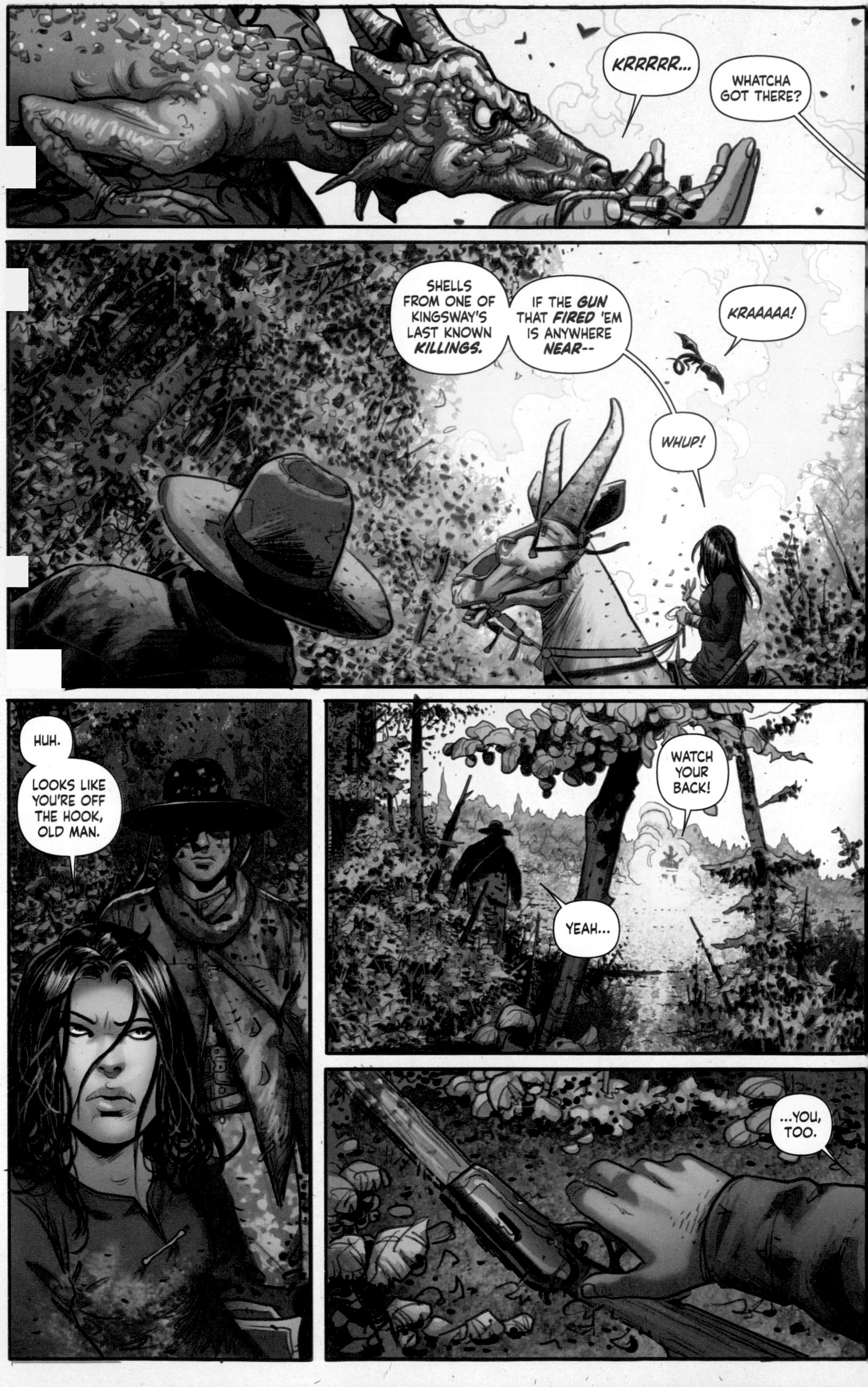
KRRRRR...
WHATCHA GOT THERE?
SHELLS FROM ONE OF KINGSWAY'S LAST KNOWN KILLINGS.
IF THE GUN THAT FIRED 'EM IS ANYWHERE NEAR--
KRAAAAA!
WHUP!
HUH.
LOOKS LIKE YOU'RE OFF THE HOOK, OLD MAN.
WATCH YOUR BACK!
YEAH...
...YOU, TOO.

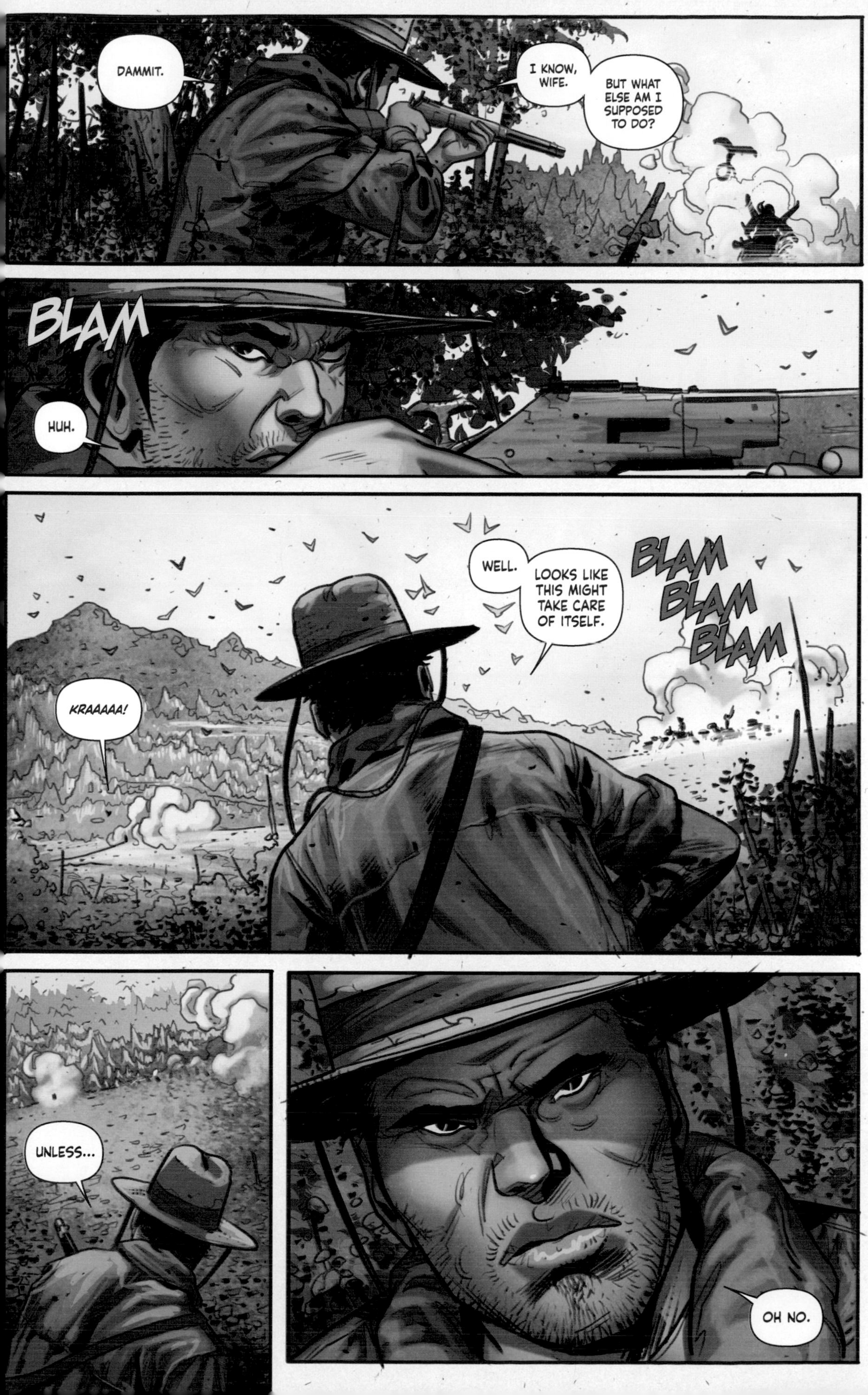
DAMMIT.
I KNOW, WIFE.
BUT WHAT ELSE AM I SUPPOSED TO DO?
BLAM
HUH.
WELL.
LOOKS LIKE THIS MIGHT TAKE CARE OF ITSELF.
BLAM BLAM BLAM
KRAAAAA!
UNLESS...
OH NO.

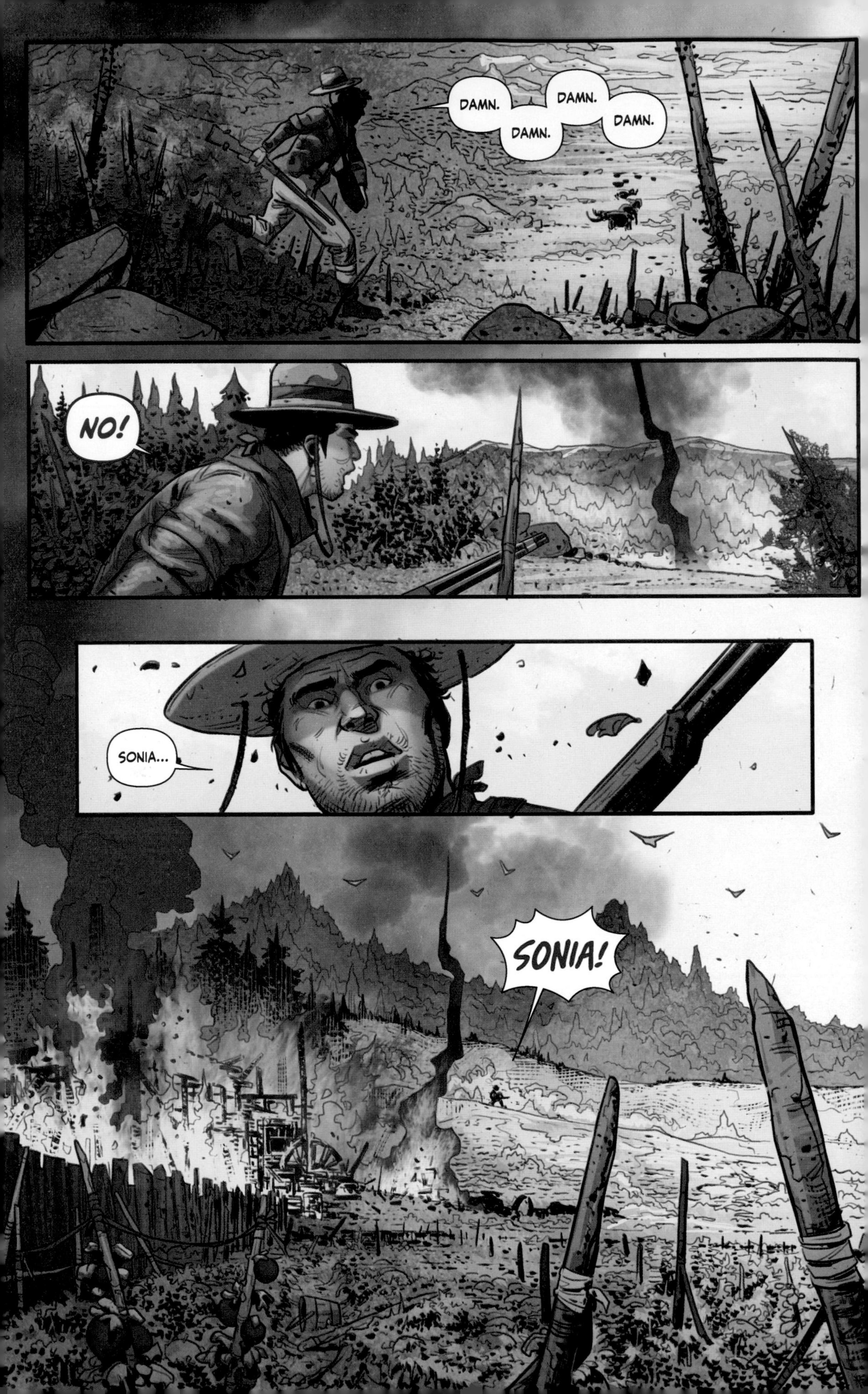
DAMN.
DAMN.
DAMN.
DAMN.
NO!
SONIA...
SONIA!

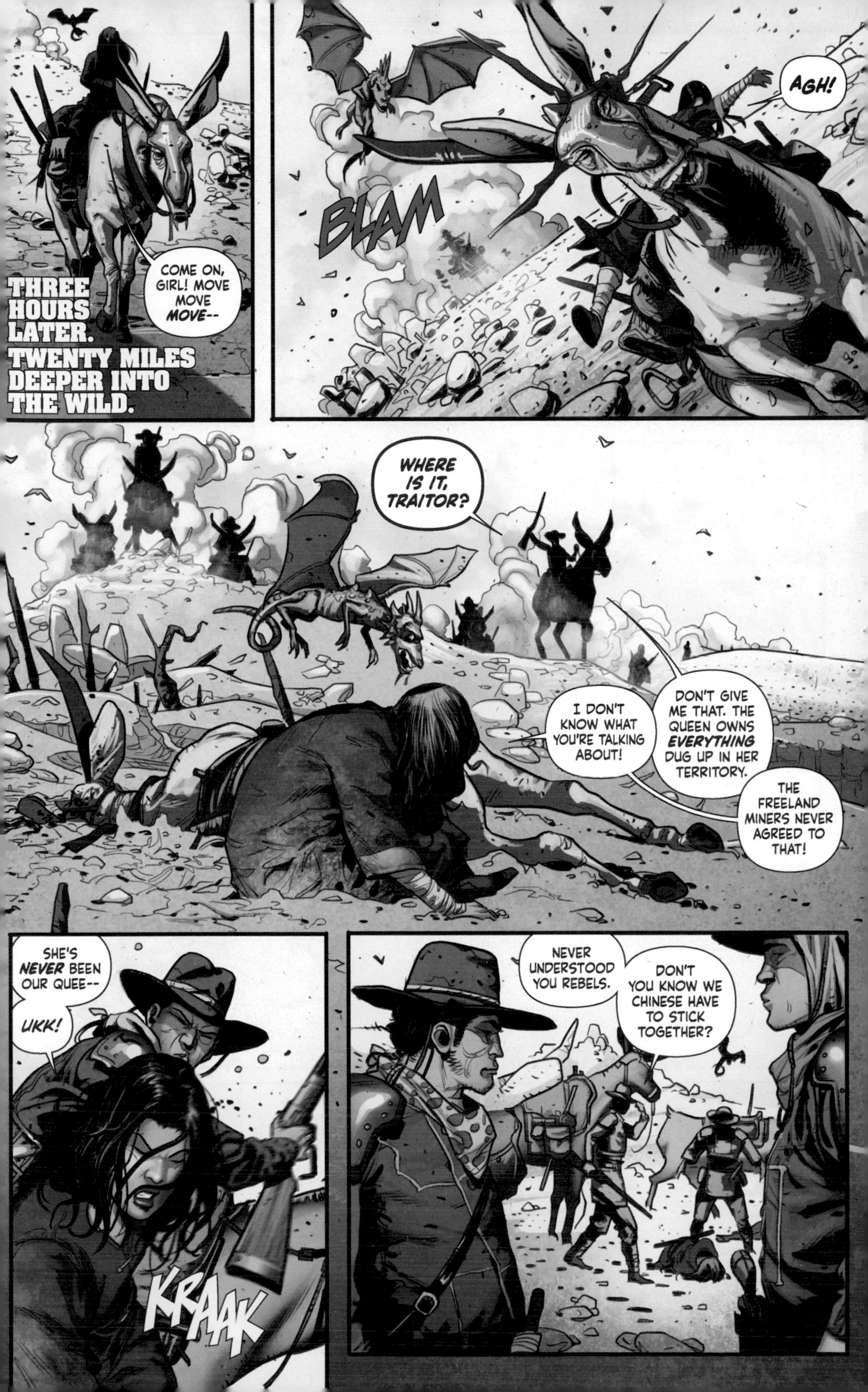
THREE HOURS LATER.
TWENTY MILES DEEPER INTO THE WILD.
COME ON, GIRL! MOVE MOVE *MOVE*--
BLAM
AGH!
WHERE IS IT, TRAITOR?
DON'T GIVE ME THAT. THE QUEEN OWNS *EVERYTHING* DUG UP IN HER TERRITORY.
I DON'T KNOW WHAT YOU'RE TALKING ABOUT!
THE FREELAND MINERS NEVER AGREED TO THAT!
SHE'S *NEVER* BEEN OUR QUEE--
UKK!
KRAAK
NEVER UNDERSTOOD YOU REBELS.
DON'T YOU KNOW WE CHINESE HAVE TO STICK TOGETHER?

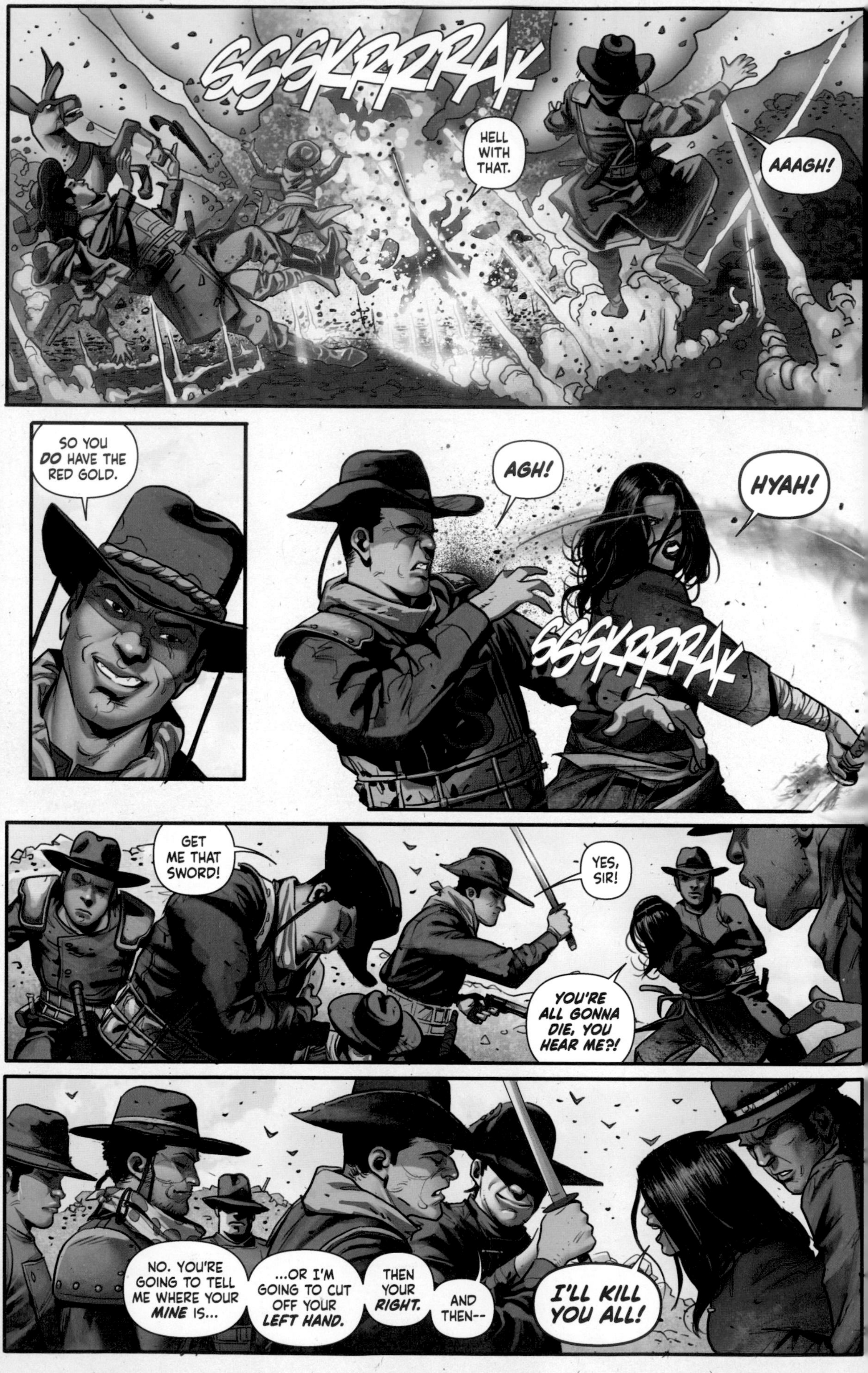
SSSKRRRAK
HELL WITH THAT.
AAAGH!
SO YOU DO HAVE THE RED GOLD.
AGH!
HYAH!
SSSKRRRAK
GET ME THAT SWORD!
YES, SIR!
YOU'RE ALL GONNA DIE, YOU HEAR ME?!
NO. YOU'RE GOING TO TELL ME WHERE YOUR MINE IS...
...OR I'M GOING TO CUT OFF YOUR LEFT HAND.
THEN YOUR RIGHT.
AND THEN--
I'LL KILL YOU ALL!

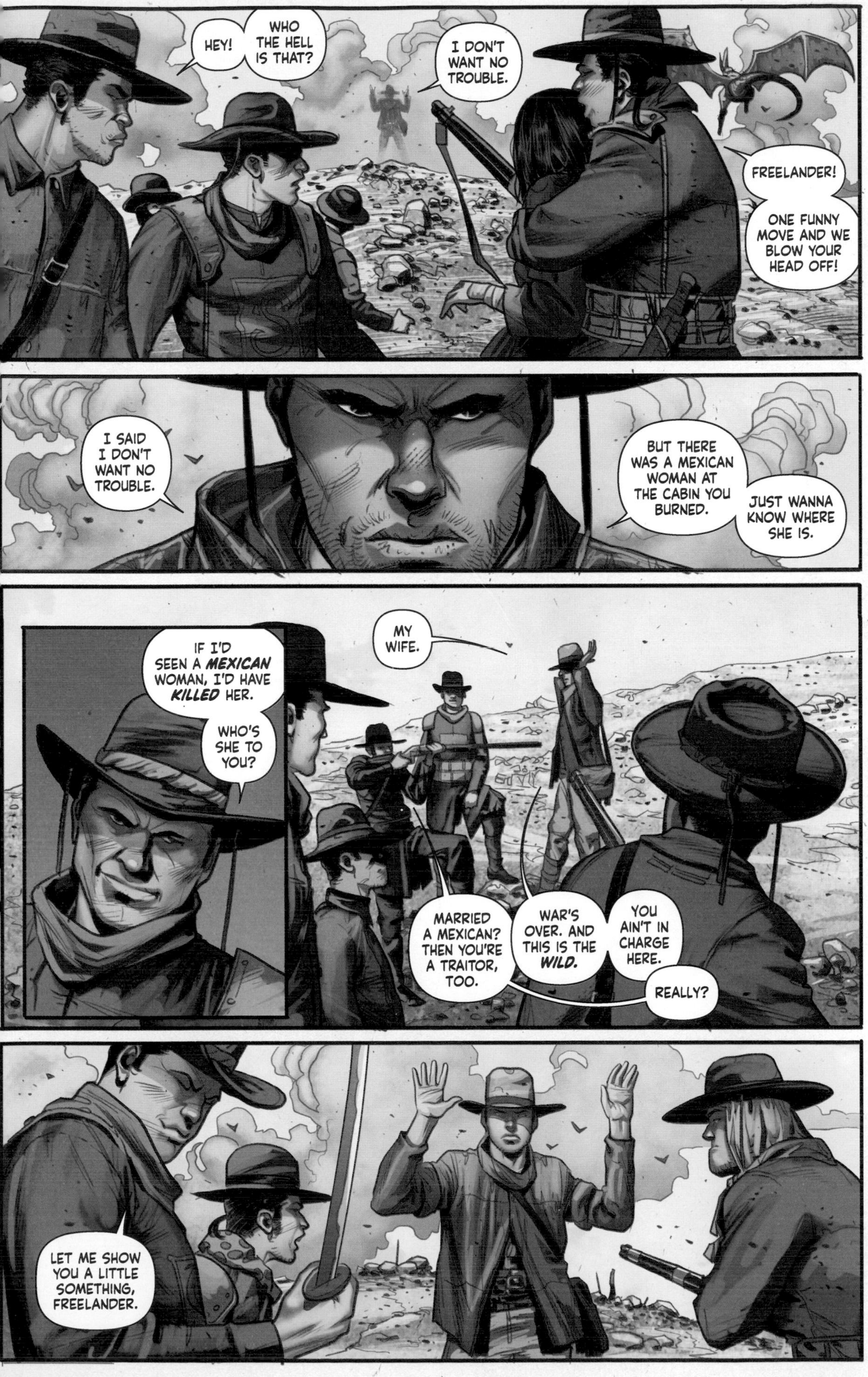
HEY!
WHO THE HELL IS THAT?
I DON'T WANT NO TROUBLE.
FREELANDER!
ONE FUNNY MOVE AND WE BLOW YOUR HEAD OFF!
I SAID I DON'T WANT NO TROUBLE.
BUT THERE WAS A MEXICAN WOMAN AT THE CABIN YOU BURNED.
JUST WANNA KNOW WHERE SHE IS.
IF I'D SEEN A MEXICAN WOMAN, I'D HAVE KILLED HER.
WHO'S SHE TO YOU?
MY WIFE.
MARRIED A MEXICAN? THEN YOU'RE A TRAITOR, TOO.
WAR'S OVER. AND THIS IS THE WILD.
YOU AIN'T IN CHARGE HERE.
REALLY?
LET ME SHOW YOU A LITTLE SOMETHING, FREELANDER.

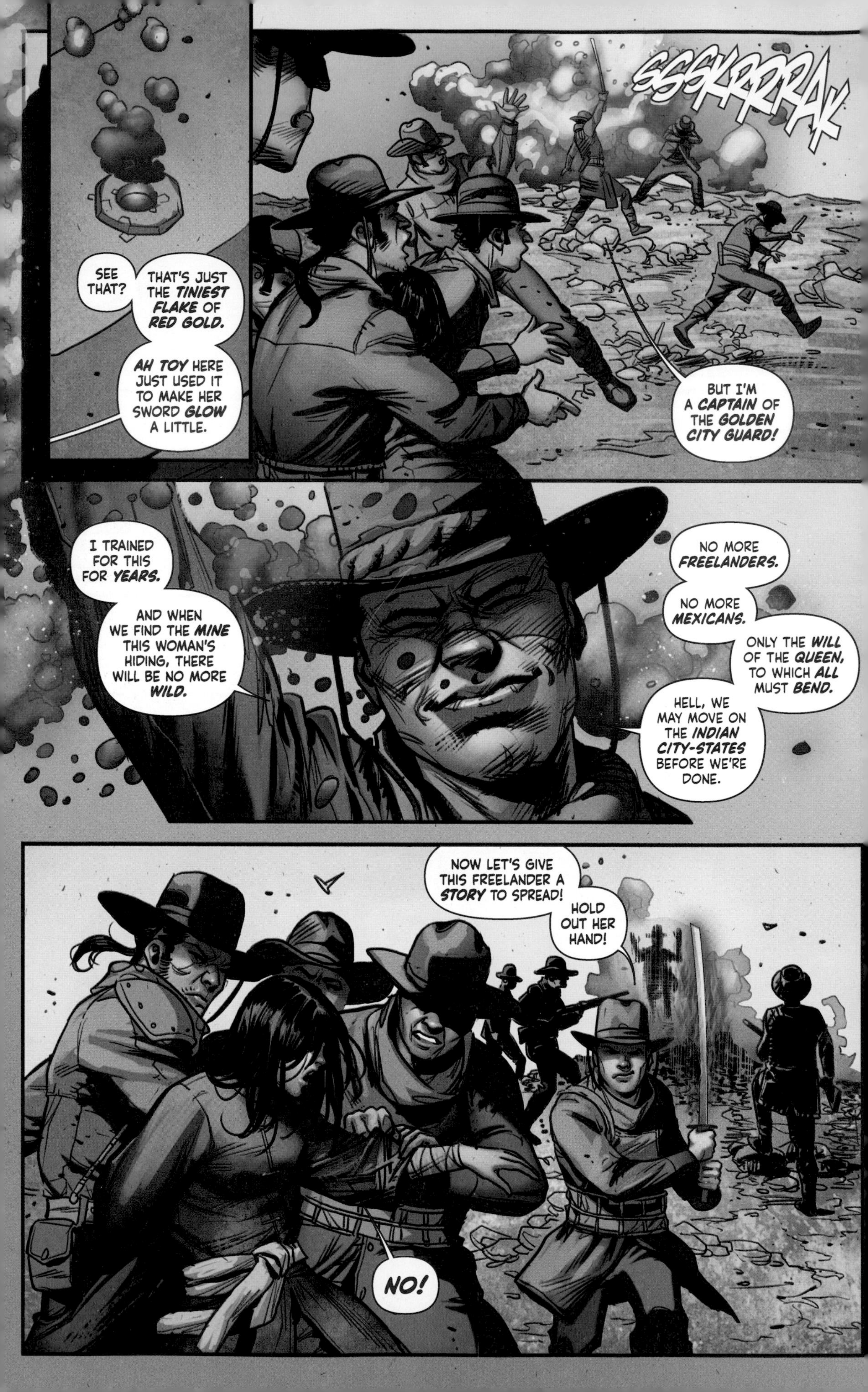
SSSKRRRAK
SEE THAT?
THAT'S JUST THE TINIEST FLAKE OF RED GOLD.
AH TOY HERE JUST USED IT TO MAKE HER SWORD GLOW A LITTLE.
BUT I'M A CAPTAIN OF THE GOLDEN CITY GUARD!
I TRAINED FOR THIS FOR YEARS.
AND WHEN WE FIND THE MINE THIS WOMAN'S HIDING, THERE WILL BE NO MORE WILD.
NO MORE FREELANDERS.
NO MORE MEXICANS.
ONLY THE WILL OF THE QUEEN, TO WHICH ALL MUST BEND.
HELL, WE MAY MOVE ON THE INDIAN CITY-STATES BEFORE WE'RE DONE.
NOW LET'S GIVE THIS FREELANDER A STORY TO SPREAD!
HOLD OUT HER HAND!
NO!

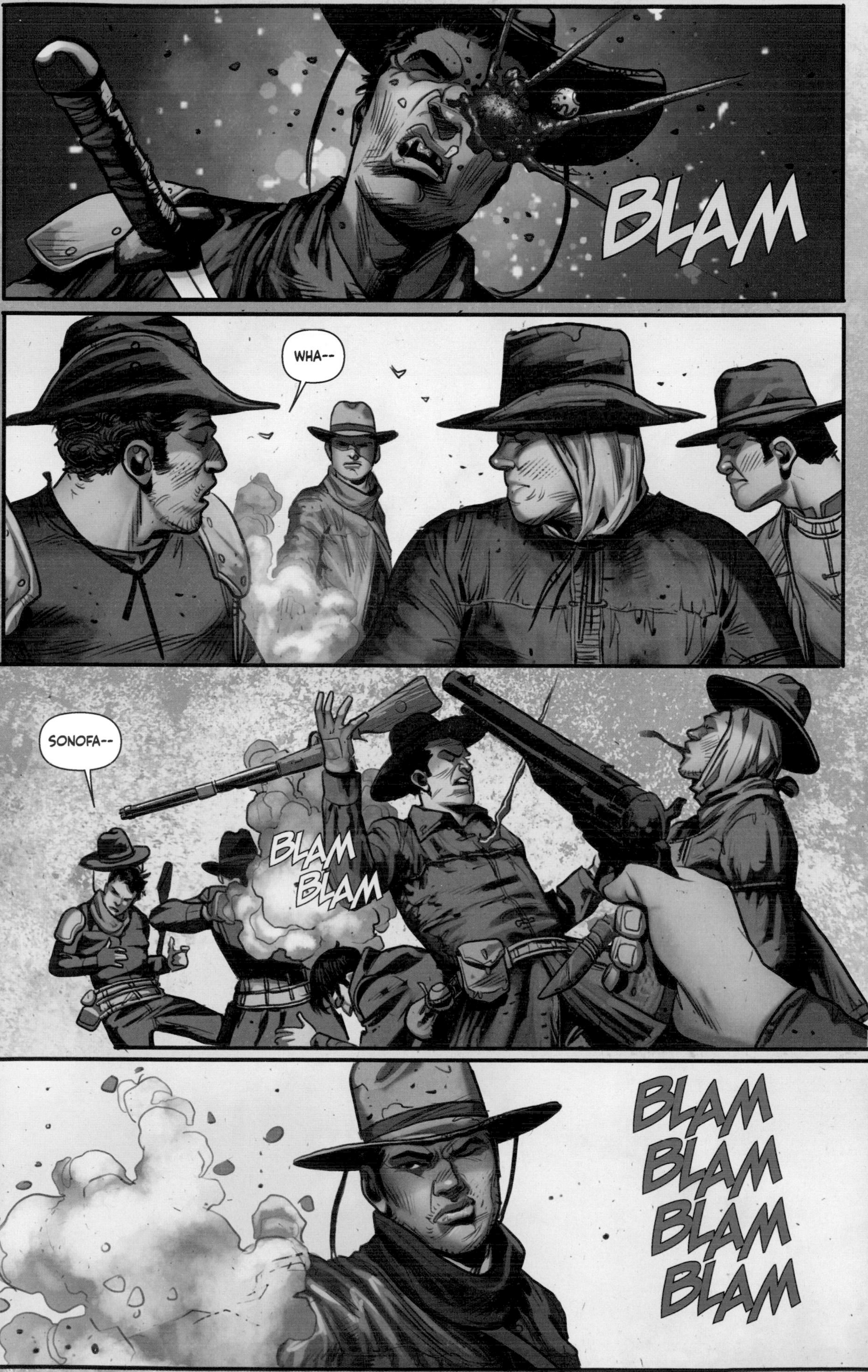
BLAM
WHA--
SONOFA--
BLAM
BLAM
BLAM
BLAM
BLAM
BLAM

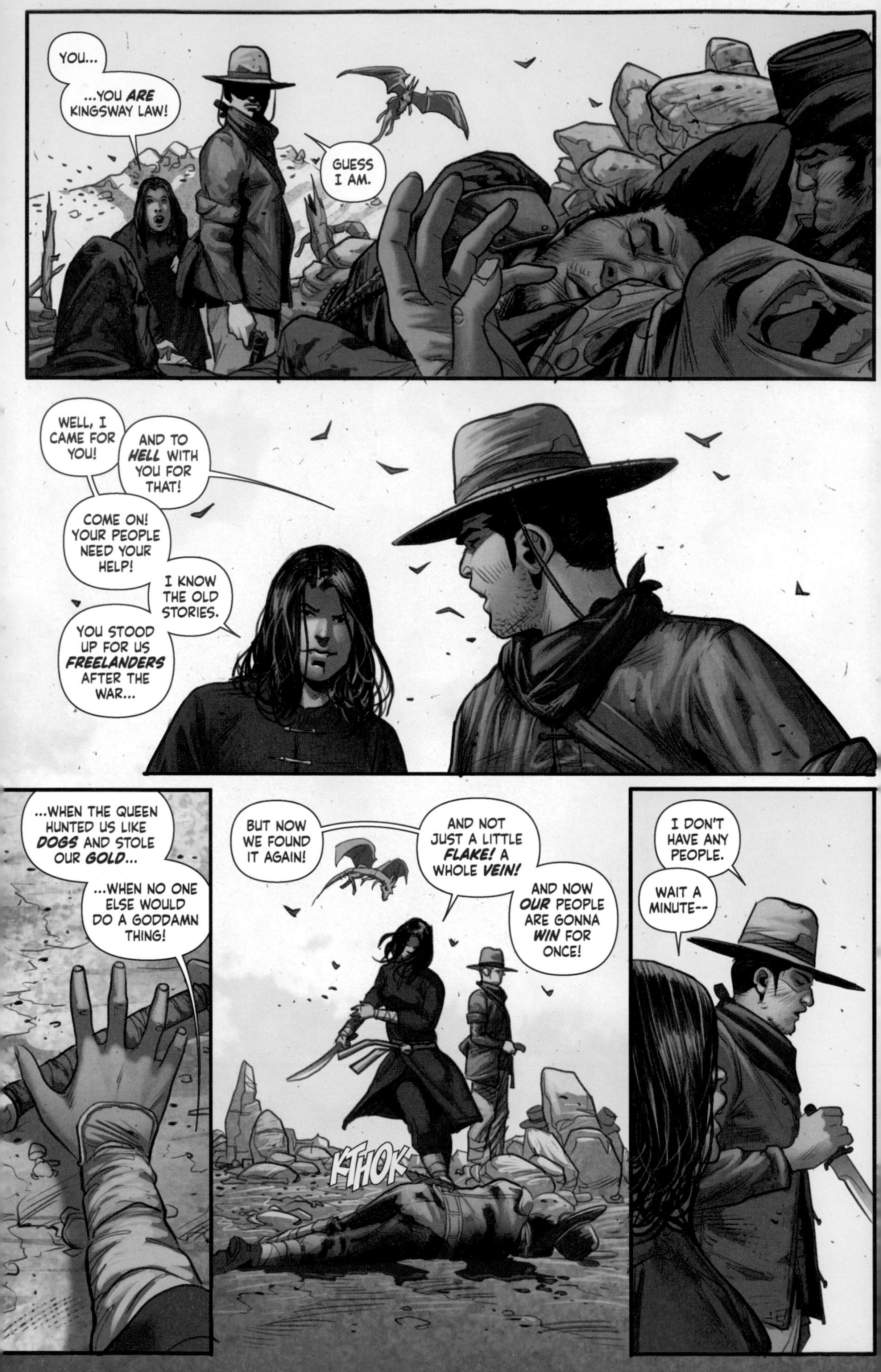
YOU...
...YOU ARE KINGSWAY LAW!
GUESS I AM.
WELL, I CAME FOR YOU!
AND TO HELL WITH YOU FOR THAT!
COME ON! YOUR PEOPLE NEED YOUR HELP!
I KNOW THE OLD STORIES.
YOU STOOD UP FOR US FREELANDERS AFTER THE WAR...
...WHEN THE QUEEN HUNTED US LIKE DOGS AND STOLE OUR GOLD...
...WHEN NO ONE ELSE WOULD DO A GODDAMN THING!
BUT NOW WE FOUND IT AGAIN!
AND NOT JUST A LITTLE FLAKE! A WHOLE VEIN!
AND NOW OUR PEOPLE ARE GONNA WIN FOR ONCE!
KTHOK
I DON'T HAVE ANY PEOPLE.
WAIT A MINUTE--

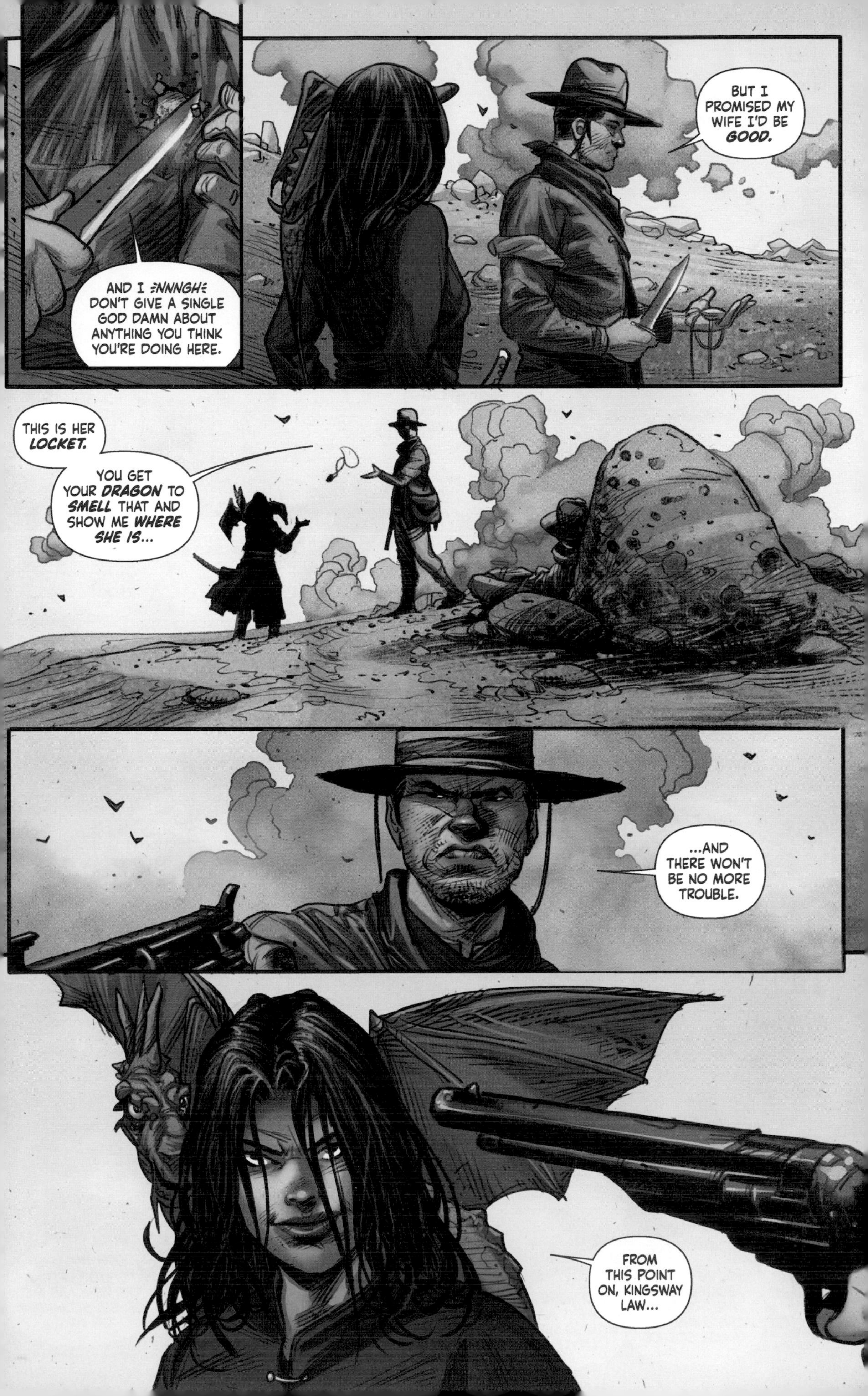

AND I ≈NNNGH≈ DON'T GIVE A SINGLE GOD DAMN ABOUT ANYTHING YOU THINK YOU'RE DOING HERE.
BUT I PROMISED MY WIFE I'D BE **GOOD.**
THIS IS HER **LOCKET.**
YOU GET YOUR **DRAGON** TO **SMELL** THAT AND SHOW ME **WHERE SHE IS...**
...AND THERE WON'T BE NO MORE TROUBLE.
FROM THIS POINT ON, KINGSWAY LAW...

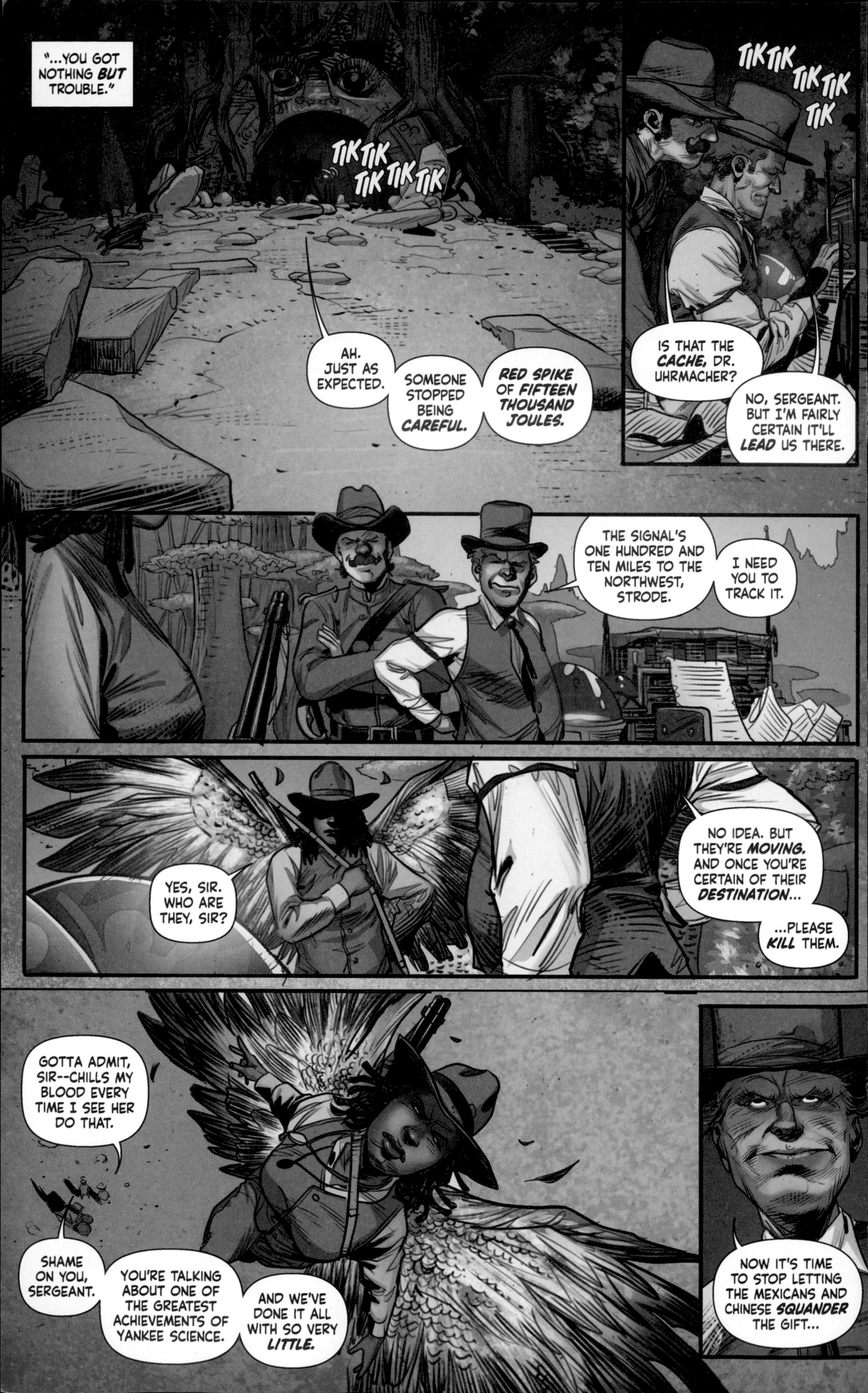

"...YOU GOT NOTHING BUT TROUBLE."
TIK TIK TIK TIK TIK
AH. JUST AS EXPECTED.
SOMEONE STOPPED BEING CAREFUL.
RED SPIKE OF FIFTEEN THOUSAND JOULES.
TIK TIK TIK TIK TIK
IS THAT THE CACHE, DR. UHRMACHER?
NO, SERGEANT. BUT I'M FAIRLY CERTAIN IT'LL LEAD US THERE.
THE SIGNAL'S ONE HUNDRED AND TEN MILES TO THE NORTHWEST, STRODE.
I NEED YOU TO TRACK IT.
YES, SIR. WHO ARE THEY, SIR?
NO IDEA. BUT THEY'RE MOVING. AND ONCE YOU'RE CERTAIN OF THEIR DESTINATION...
...PLEASE KILL THEM.
GOTTA ADMIT, SIR--CHILLS MY BLOOD EVERY TIME I SEE HER DO THAT.
SHAME ON YOU, SERGEANT.
YOU'RE TALKING ABOUT ONE OF THE GREATEST ACHIEVEMENTS OF YANKEE SCIENCE.
AND WE'VE DONE IT ALL WITH SO VERY LITTLE.
NOW IT'S TIME TO STOP LETTING THE MEXICANS AND CHINESE SQUANDER THE GIFT...

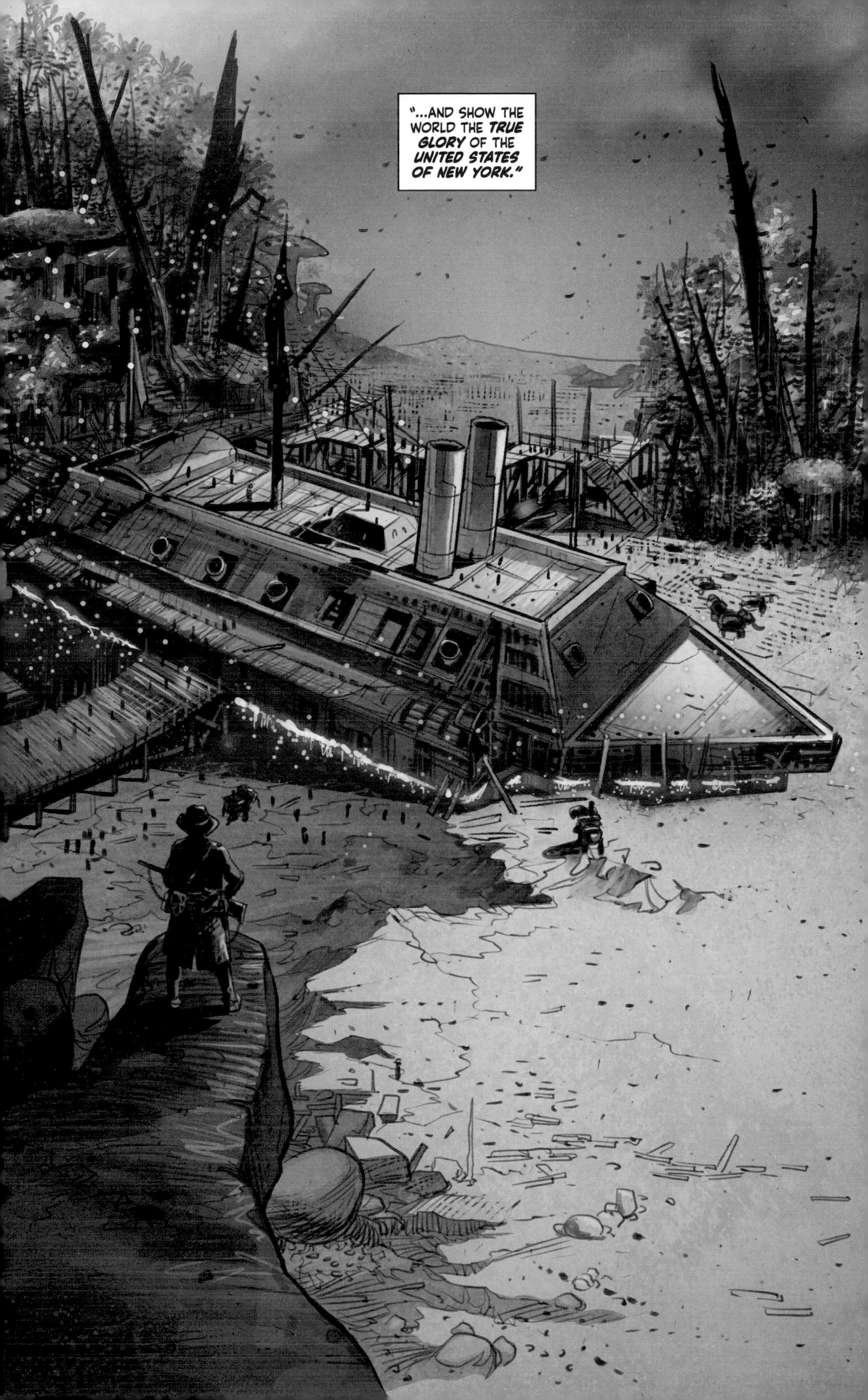
"...AND SHOW THE WORLD THE *TRUE GLORY* OF THE *UNITED STATES OF NEW YORK.*"

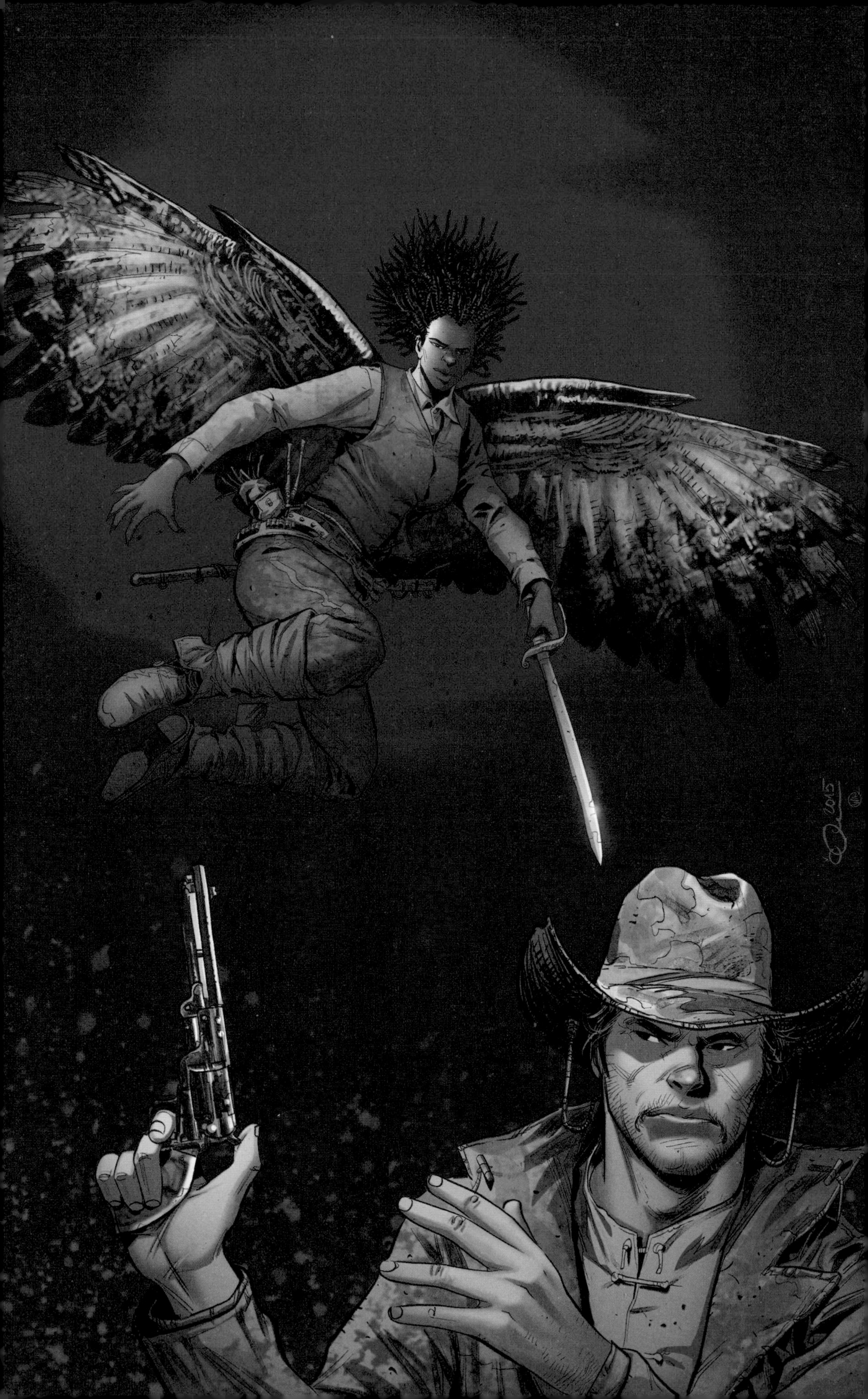

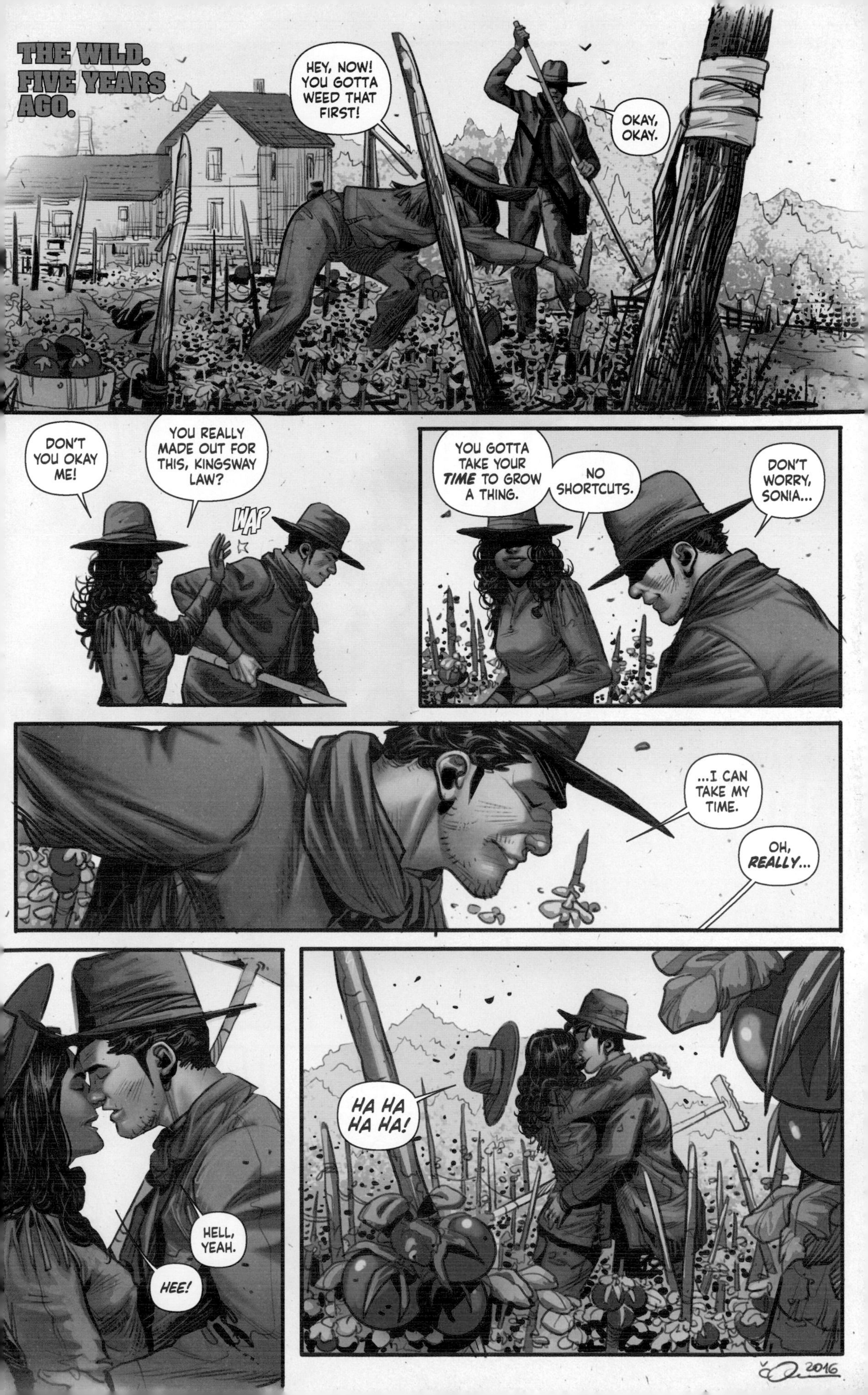
THE WILD. FIVE YEARS AGO.
HEY, NOW! YOU GOTTA WEED THAT FIRST!
OKAY, OKAY.
DON'T YOU OKAY ME!
YOU REALLY MADE OUT FOR THIS, KINGSWAY LAW?
WAP
YOU GOTTA TAKE YOUR TIME TO GROW A THING.
NO SHORTCUTS.
DON'T WORRY, SONIA...
...I CAN TAKE MY TIME.
OH, REALLY...
HELL, YEAH.
HEE!
HA HA HA HA!
2016

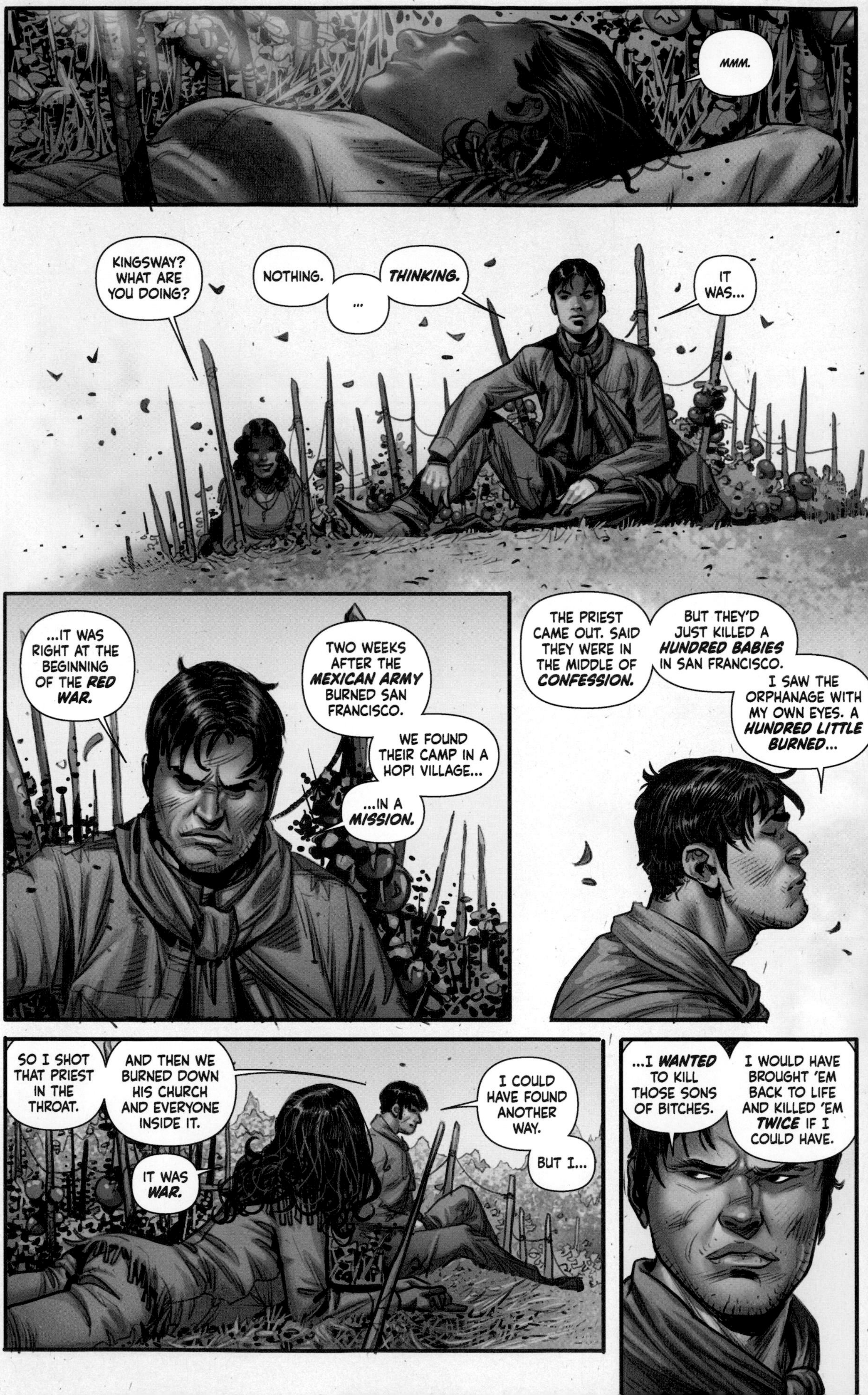
MMM.
KINGSWAY? WHAT ARE YOU DOING?
NOTHING.
...
THINKING.
IT WAS...
...IT WAS RIGHT AT THE BEGINNING OF THE RED WAR.
TWO WEEKS AFTER THE MEXICAN ARMY BURNED SAN FRANCISCO.
WE FOUND THEIR CAMP IN A HOPI VILLAGE...
...IN A MISSION.
THE PRIEST CAME OUT. SAID THEY WERE IN THE MIDDLE OF CONFESSION.
BUT THEY'D JUST KILLED A HUNDRED BABIES IN SAN FRANCISCO.
I SAW THE ORPHANAGE WITH MY OWN EYES. A HUNDRED LITTLE BURNED...
SO I SHOT THAT PRIEST IN THE THROAT.
AND THEN WE BURNED DOWN HIS CHURCH AND EVERYONE INSIDE IT.
IT WAS WAR.
I COULD HAVE FOUND ANOTHER WAY.
BUT I...
...I WANTED TO KILL THOSE SONS OF BITCHES.
I WOULD HAVE BROUGHT 'EM BACK TO LIFE AND KILLED 'EM TWICE IF I COULD HAVE.

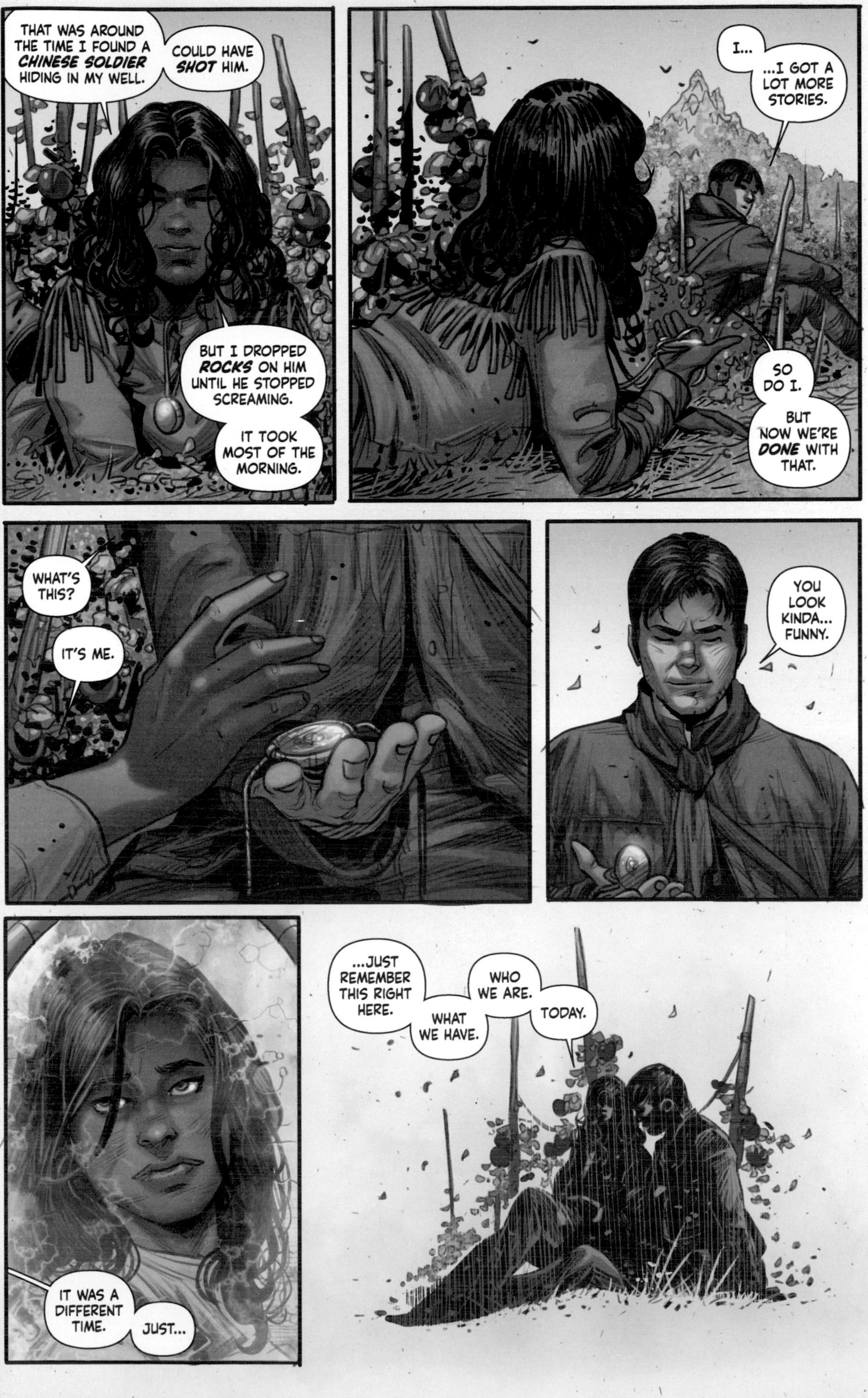
THAT WAS AROUND THE TIME I FOUND A CHINESE SOLDIER HIDING IN MY WELL.
COULD HAVE SHOT HIM.
BUT I DROPPED ROCKS ON HIM UNTIL HE STOPPED SCREAMING.
IT TOOK MOST OF THE MORNING.
I...
...I GOT A LOT MORE STORIES.
SO DO I.
BUT NOW WE'RE DONE WITH THAT.
WHAT'S THIS?
IT'S ME.
YOU LOOK KINDA... FUNNY.
IT WAS A DIFFERENT TIME.
JUST...
...JUST REMEMBER THIS RIGHT HERE.
WHAT WE HAVE.
WHO WE ARE.
TODAY.

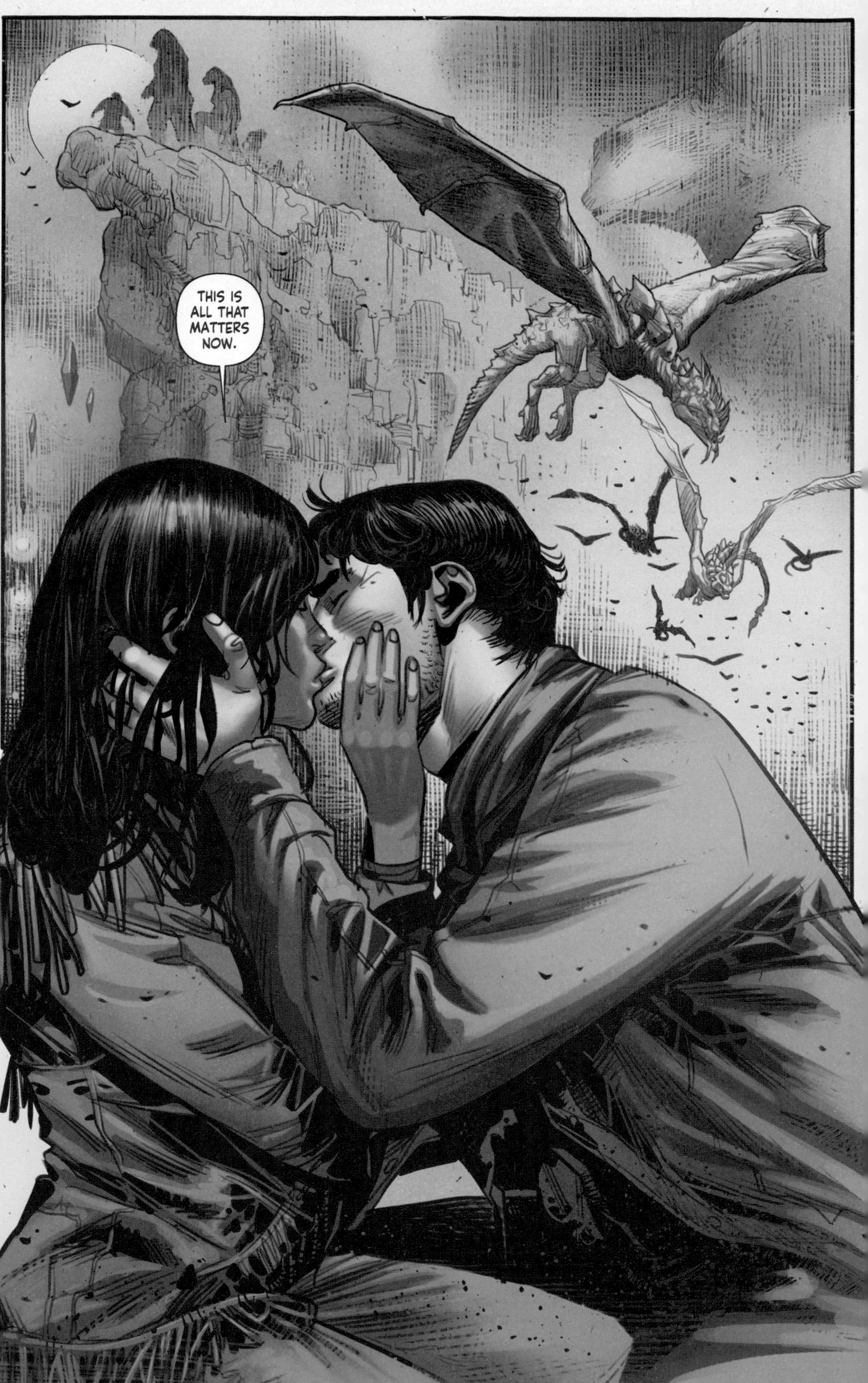
THIS IS ALL THAT MATTERS NOW.

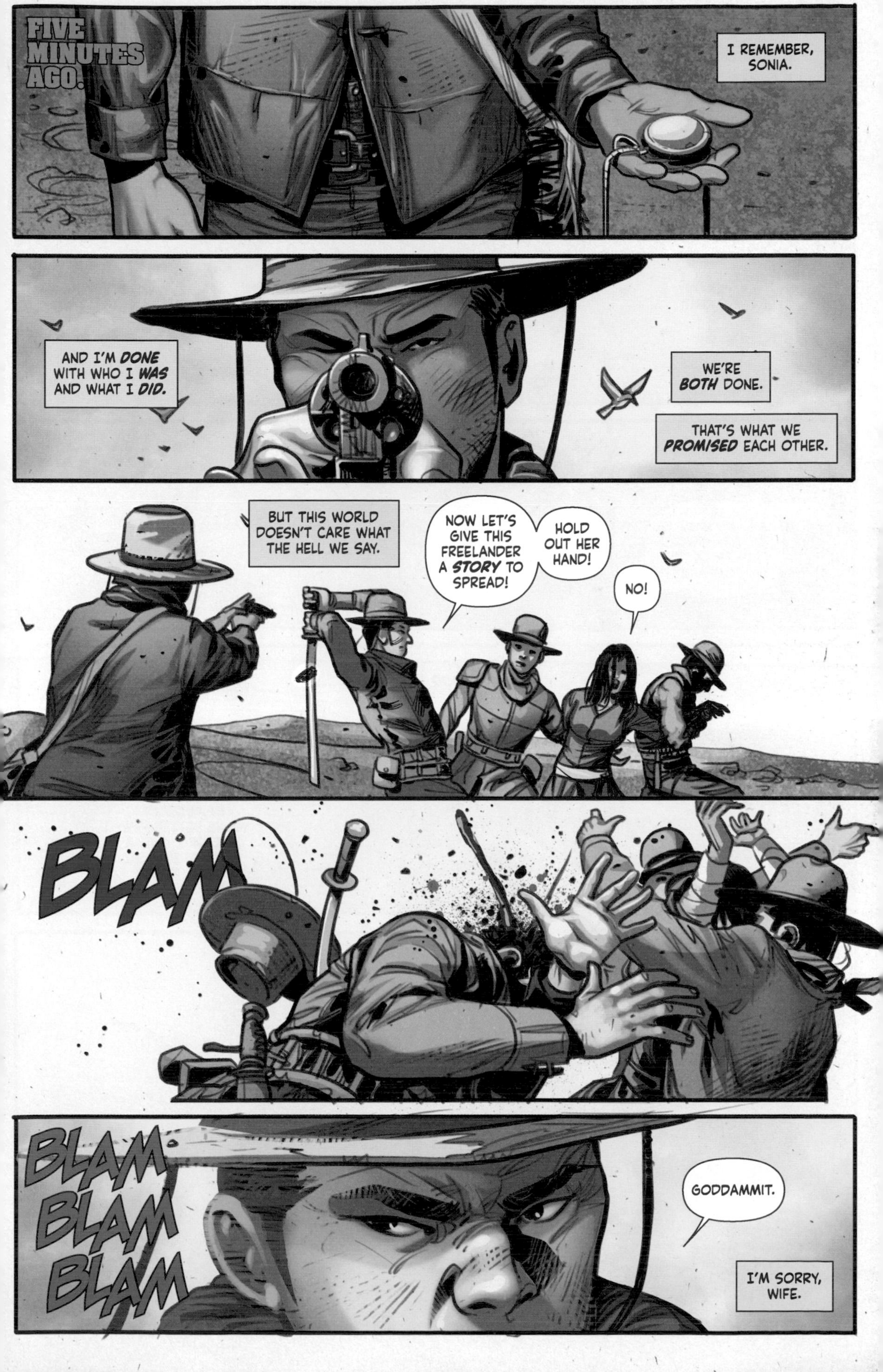
FIVE MINUTES AGO.
I REMEMBER, SONIA.
AND I'M DONE WITH WHO I WAS AND WHAT I DID.
WE'RE BOTH DONE.
THAT'S WHAT WE PROMISED EACH OTHER.
BUT THIS WORLD DOESN'T CARE WHAT THE HELL WE SAY.
NOW LET'S GIVE THIS FREELANDER A STORY TO SPREAD!
HOLD OUT HER HAND!
NO!
BLAM
BLAM BLAM BLAM
GODDAMMIT.
I'M SORRY, WIFE.

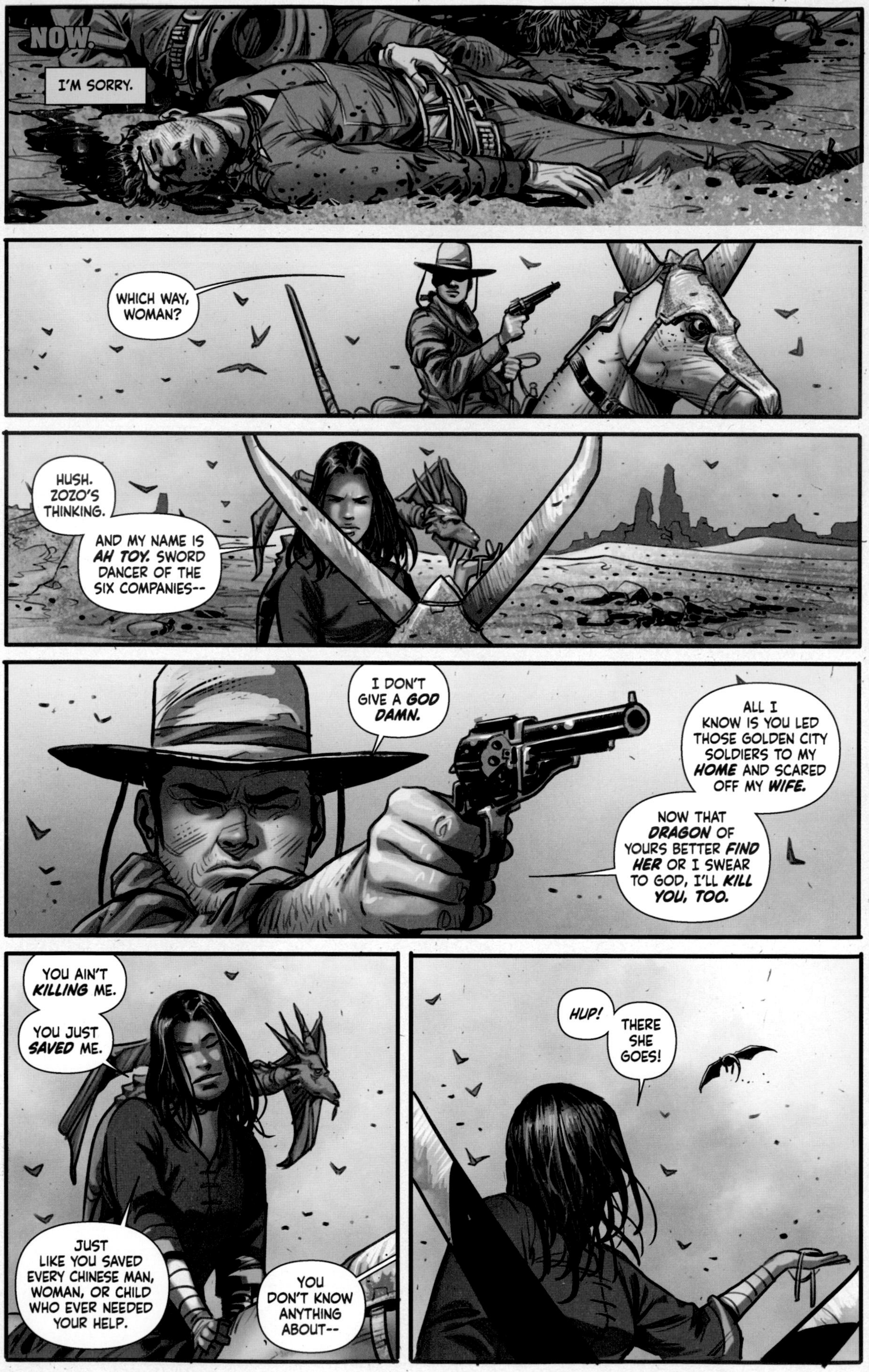
NOW.
I'M SORRY.
WHICH WAY, WOMAN?
HUSH. ZOZO'S THINKING.
AND MY NAME IS AH TOY. SWORD DANCER OF THE SIX COMPANIES--
I DON'T GIVE A GOD DAMN.
ALL I KNOW IS YOU LED THOSE GOLDEN CITY SOLDIERS TO MY HOME AND SCARED OFF MY WIFE.
NOW THAT DRAGON OF YOURS BETTER FIND HER OR I SWEAR TO GOD, I'LL KILL YOU, TOO.
YOU AIN'T KILLING ME.
YOU JUST SAVED ME.
JUST LIKE YOU SAVED EVERY CHINESE MAN, WOMAN, OR CHILD WHO EVER NEEDED YOUR HELP.
YOU DON'T KNOW ANYTHING ABOUT--
HUP!
THERE SHE GOES!

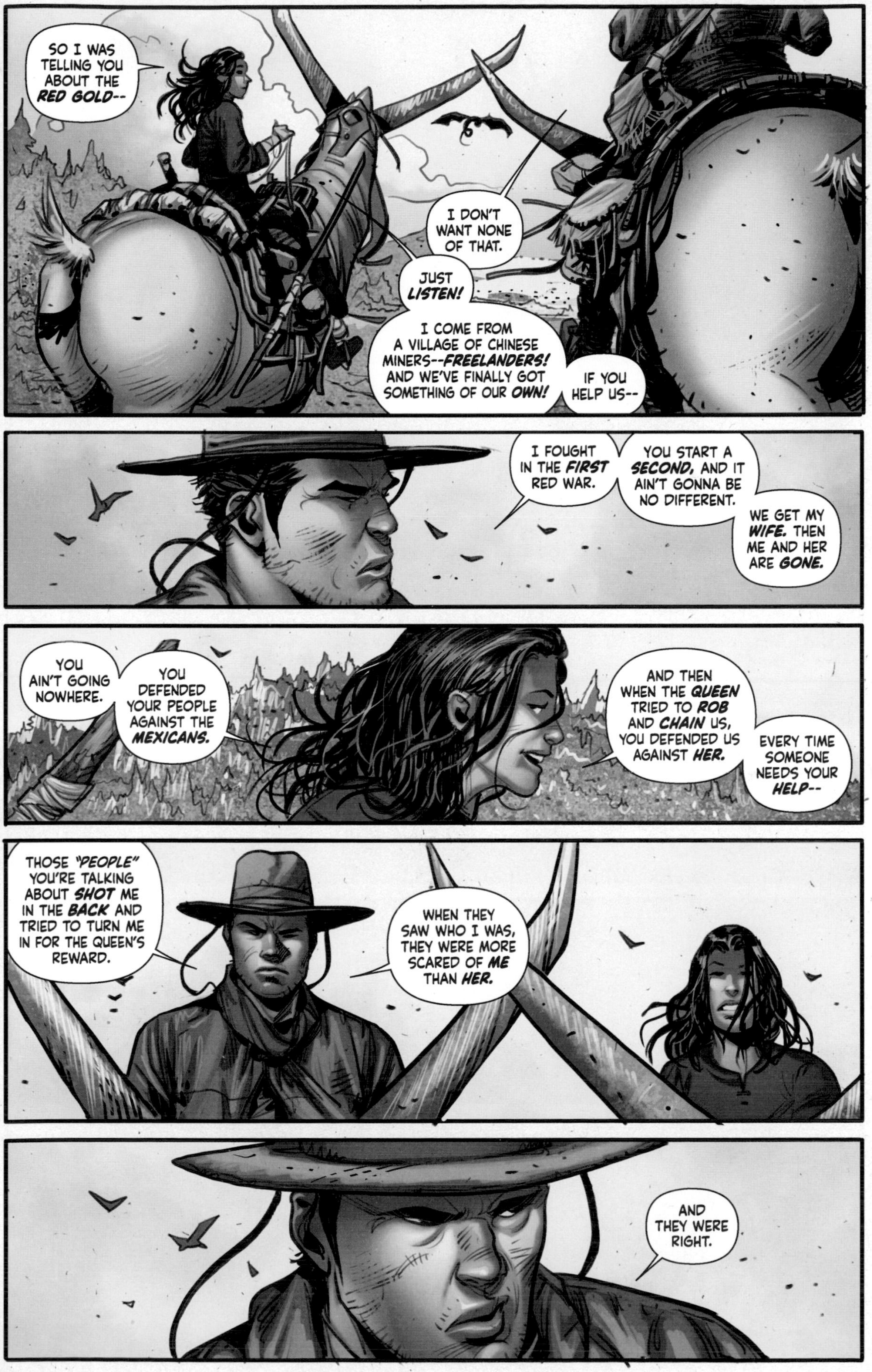
SO I WAS TELLING YOU ABOUT THE RED GOLD--
I DON'T WANT NONE OF THAT.
JUST LISTEN!
I COME FROM A VILLAGE OF CHINESE MINERS--FREELANDERS! AND WE'VE FINALLY GOT SOMETHING OF OUR OWN!
IF YOU HELP US--
I FOUGHT IN THE FIRST RED WAR.
YOU START A SECOND, AND IT AIN'T GONNA BE NO DIFFERENT.
WE GET MY WIFE. THEN ME AND HER ARE GONE.
YOU AIN'T GOING NOWHERE.
YOU DEFENDED YOUR PEOPLE AGAINST THE MEXICANS.
AND THEN WHEN THE QUEEN TRIED TO ROB AND CHAIN US, YOU DEFENDED US AGAINST HER.
EVERY TIME SOMEONE NEEDS YOUR HELP--
THOSE "PEOPLE" YOU'RE TALKING ABOUT SHOT ME IN THE BACK AND TRIED TO TURN ME IN FOR THE QUEEN'S REWARD.
WHEN THEY SAW WHO I WAS, THEY WERE MORE SCARED OF ME THAN HER.
AND THEY WERE RIGHT.

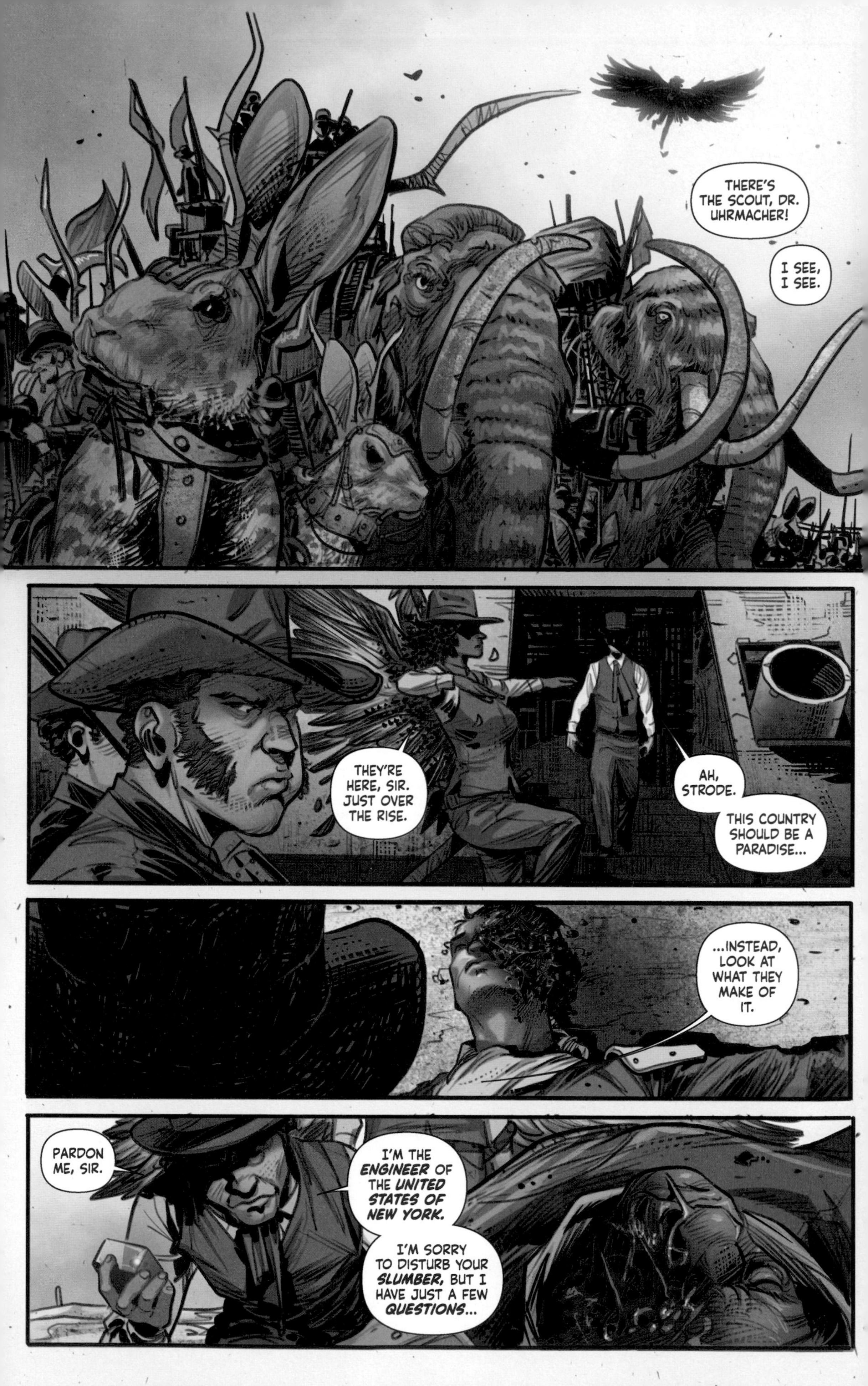
THERE'S THE SCOUT, DR. UHRMACHER!
I SEE, I SEE.
THEY'RE HERE, SIR. JUST OVER THE RISE.
AH, STRODE.
THIS COUNTRY SHOULD BE A PARADISE...
...INSTEAD, LOOK AT WHAT THEY MAKE OF IT.
PARDON ME, SIR.
I'M THE ENGINEER OF THE UNITED STATES OF NEW YORK.
I'M SORRY TO DISTURB YOUR SLUMBER, BUT I HAVE JUST A FEW QUESTIONS...

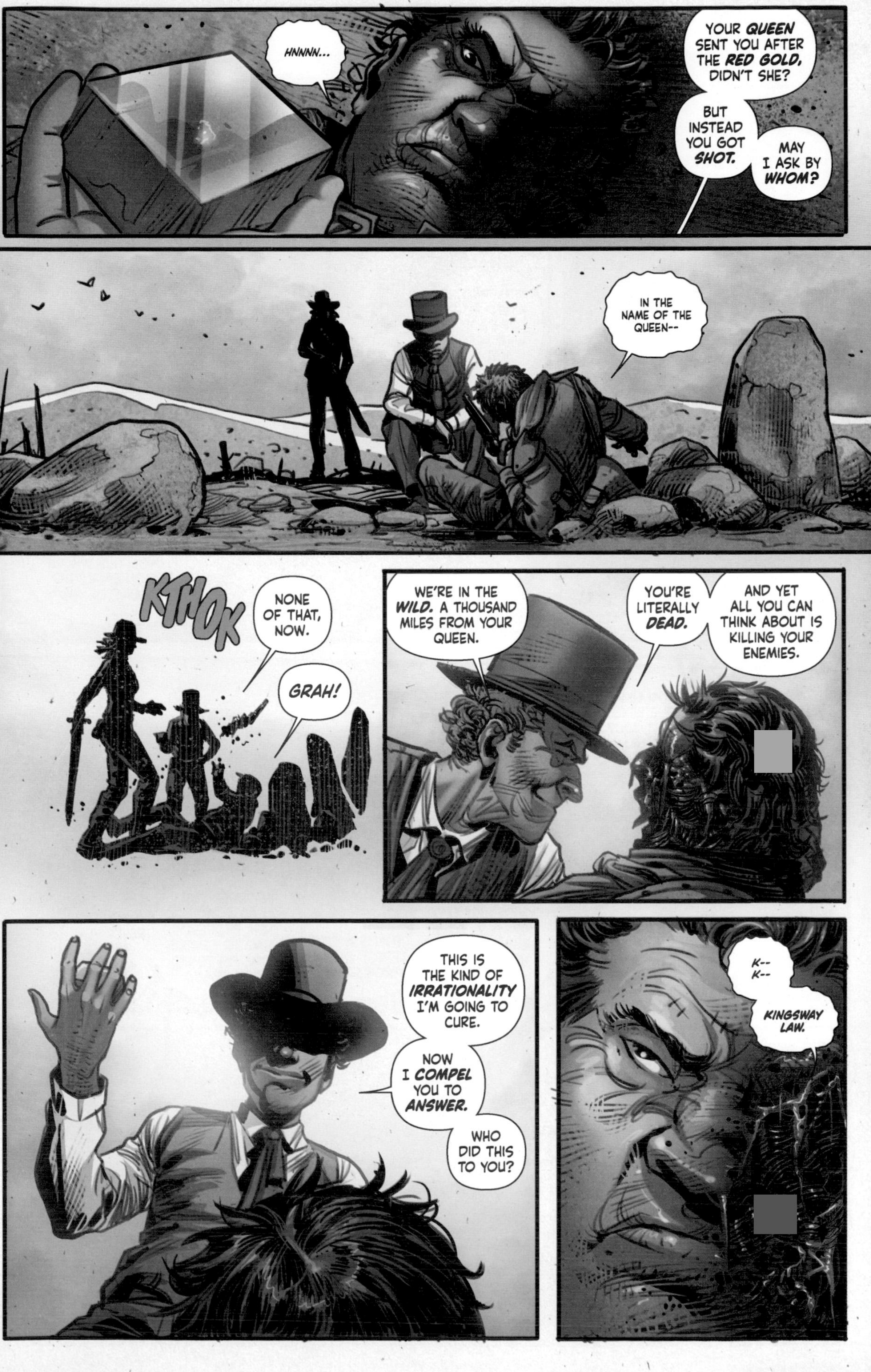
HNNNN...
YOUR QUEEN SENT YOU AFTER THE RED GOLD, DIDN'T SHE?
BUT INSTEAD YOU GOT SHOT.
MAY I ASK BY WHOM?
IN THE NAME OF THE QUEEN--
KTHOK
NONE OF THAT, NOW.
GRAH!
WE'RE IN THE WILD. A THOUSAND MILES FROM YOUR QUEEN.
YOU'RE LITERALLY DEAD.
AND YET ALL YOU CAN THINK ABOUT IS KILLING YOUR ENEMIES.
THIS IS THE KIND OF IRRATIONALITY I'M GOING TO CURE.
NOW I COMPEL YOU TO ANSWER.
WHO DID THIS TO YOU?
K-- K--
KINGSWAY LAW.

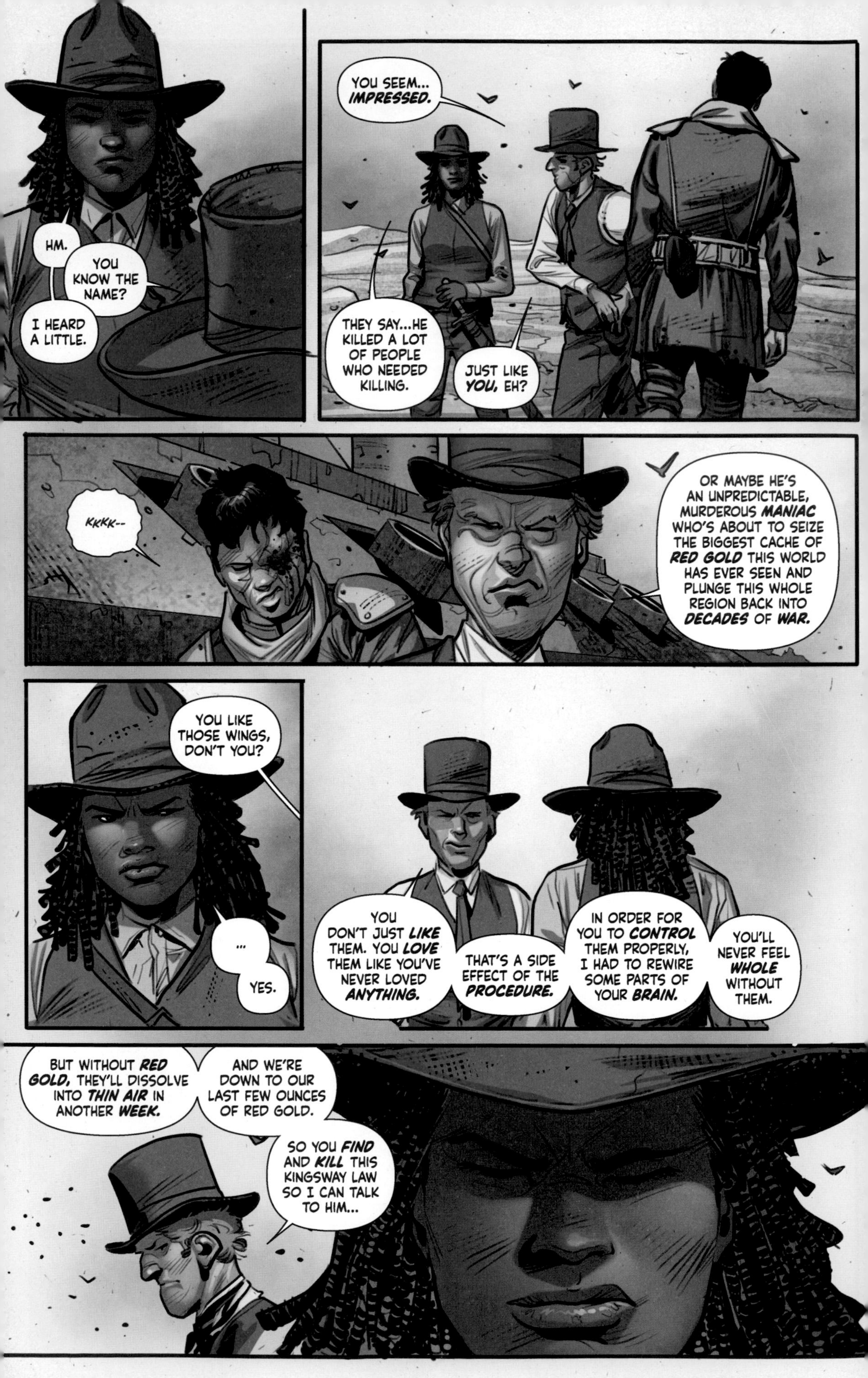
HM.
YOU KNOW THE NAME?
I HEARD A LITTLE.
YOU SEEM... IMPRESSED.
THEY SAY...HE KILLED A LOT OF PEOPLE WHO NEEDED KILLING.
JUST LIKE YOU, EH?
KKKK--
OR MAYBE HE'S AN UNPREDICTABLE, MURDEROUS MANIAC WHO'S ABOUT TO SEIZE THE BIGGEST CACHE OF RED GOLD THIS WORLD HAS EVER SEEN AND PLUNGE THIS WHOLE REGION BACK INTO DECADES OF WAR.
YOU LIKE THOSE WINGS, DON'T YOU?
...
YES.
YOU DON'T JUST LIKE THEM. YOU LOVE THEM LIKE YOU'VE NEVER LOVED ANYTHING.
THAT'S A SIDE EFFECT OF THE PROCEDURE.
IN ORDER FOR YOU TO CONTROL THEM PROPERLY, I HAD TO REWIRE SOME PARTS OF YOUR BRAIN.
YOU'LL NEVER FEEL WHOLE WITHOUT THEM.
BUT WITHOUT RED GOLD, THEY'LL DISSOLVE INTO THIN AIR IN ANOTHER WEEK.
AND WE'RE DOWN TO OUR LAST FEW OUNCES OF RED GOLD.
SO YOU FIND AND KILL THIS KINGSWAY LAW SO I CAN TALK TO HIM...

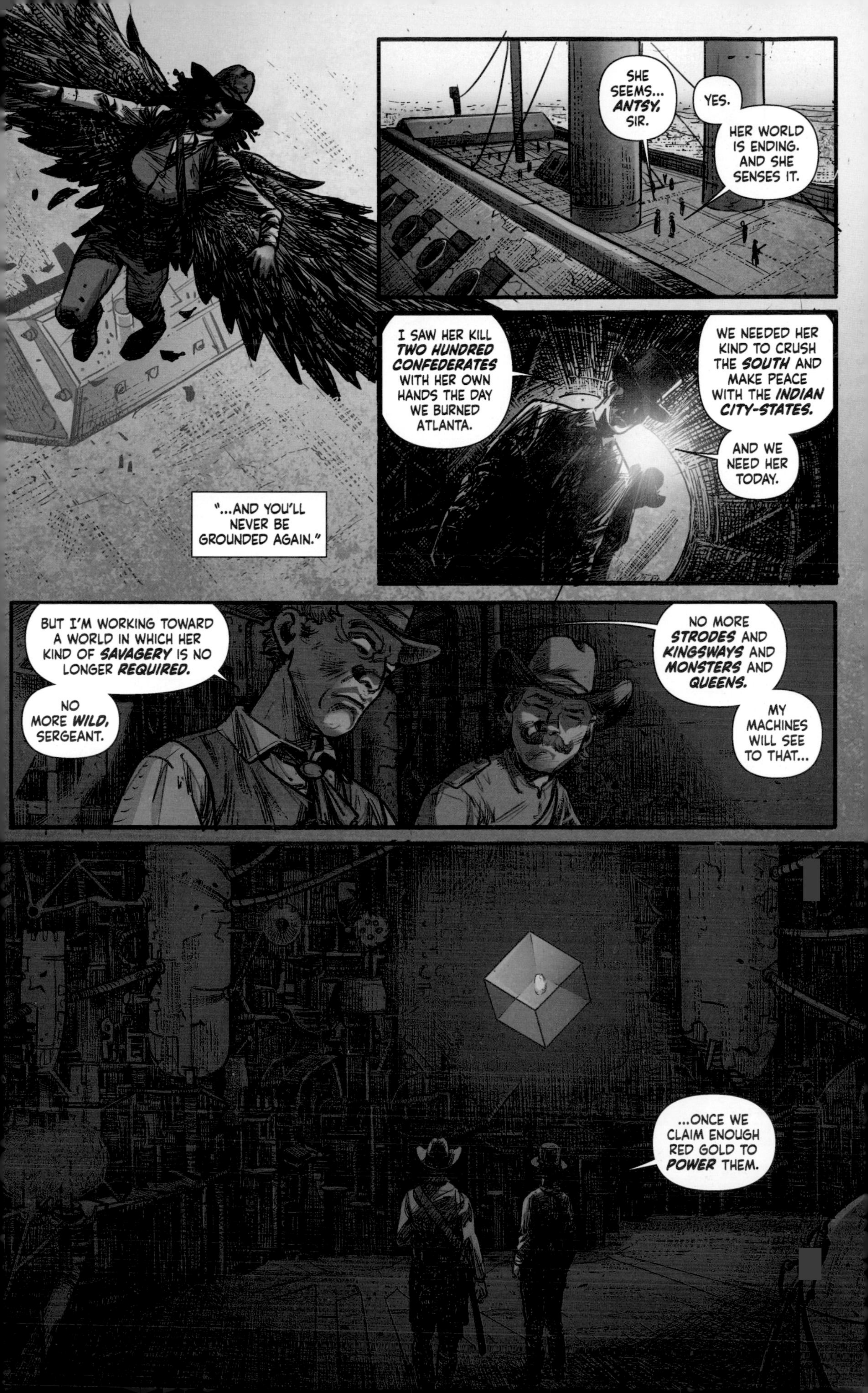
SHE SEEMS... ANTSY, SIR.
YES.
HER WORLD IS ENDING. AND SHE SENSES IT.
"...AND YOU'LL NEVER BE GROUNDED AGAIN."
I SAW HER KILL TWO HUNDRED CONFEDERATES WITH HER OWN HANDS THE DAY WE BURNED ATLANTA.
WE NEEDED HER KIND TO CRUSH THE SOUTH AND MAKE PEACE WITH THE INDIAN CITY-STATES.
AND WE NEED HER TODAY.
BUT I'M WORKING TOWARD A WORLD IN WHICH HER KIND OF SAVAGERY IS NO LONGER REQUIRED.
NO MORE WILD, SERGEANT.
NO MORE STRODES AND KINGSWAYS AND MONSTERS AND QUEENS.
MY MACHINES WILL SEE TO THAT...
...ONCE WE CLAIM ENOUGH RED GOLD TO POWER THEM.

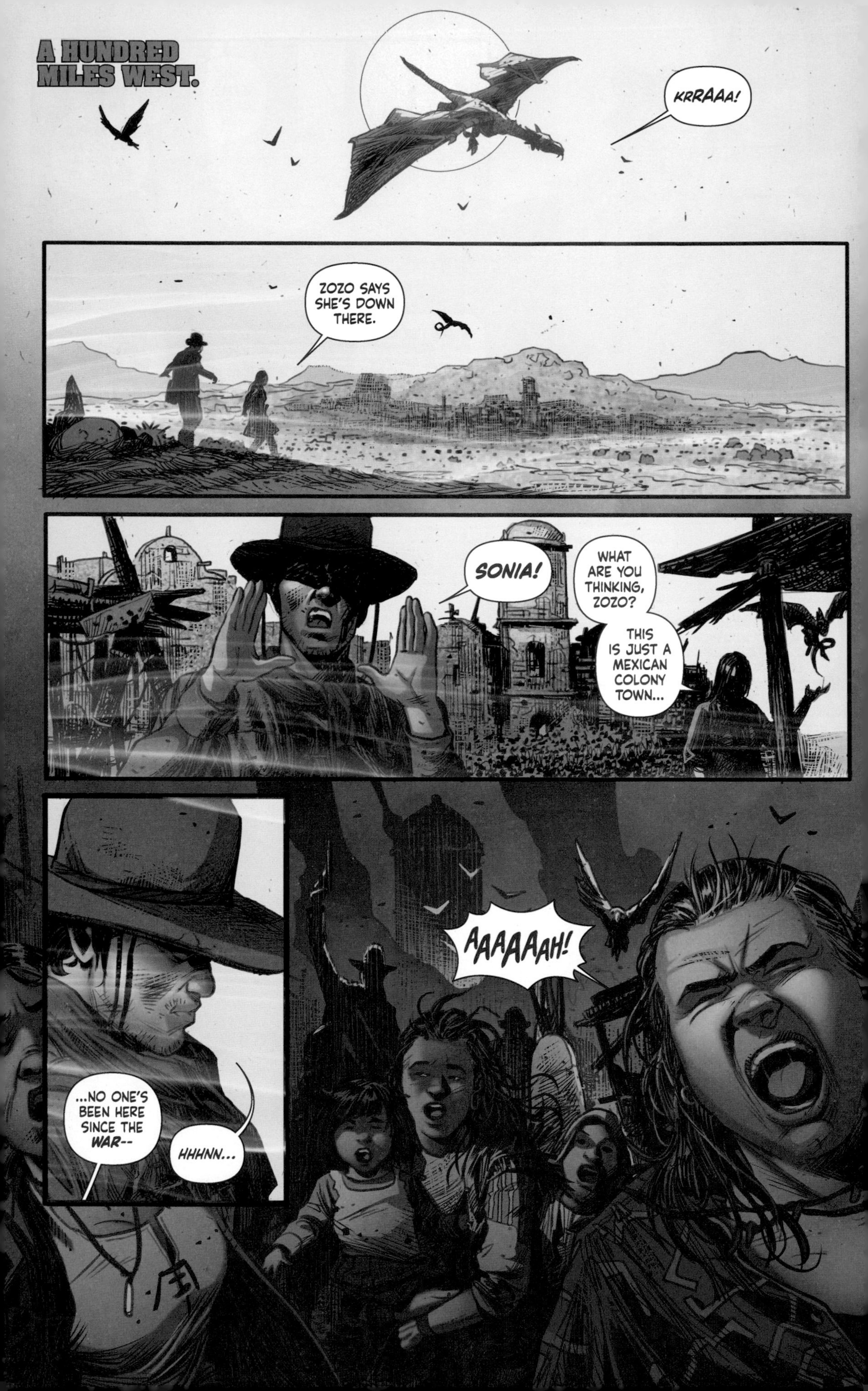
A HUNDRED MILES WEST.
KRRAAA!
ZOZO SAYS SHE'S DOWN THERE.
SONIA!
WHAT ARE YOU THINKING, ZOZO?
THIS IS JUST A MEXICAN COLONY TOWN...
...NO ONE'S BEEN HERE SINCE THE WAR--
HHHNN...
AAAAAAH!

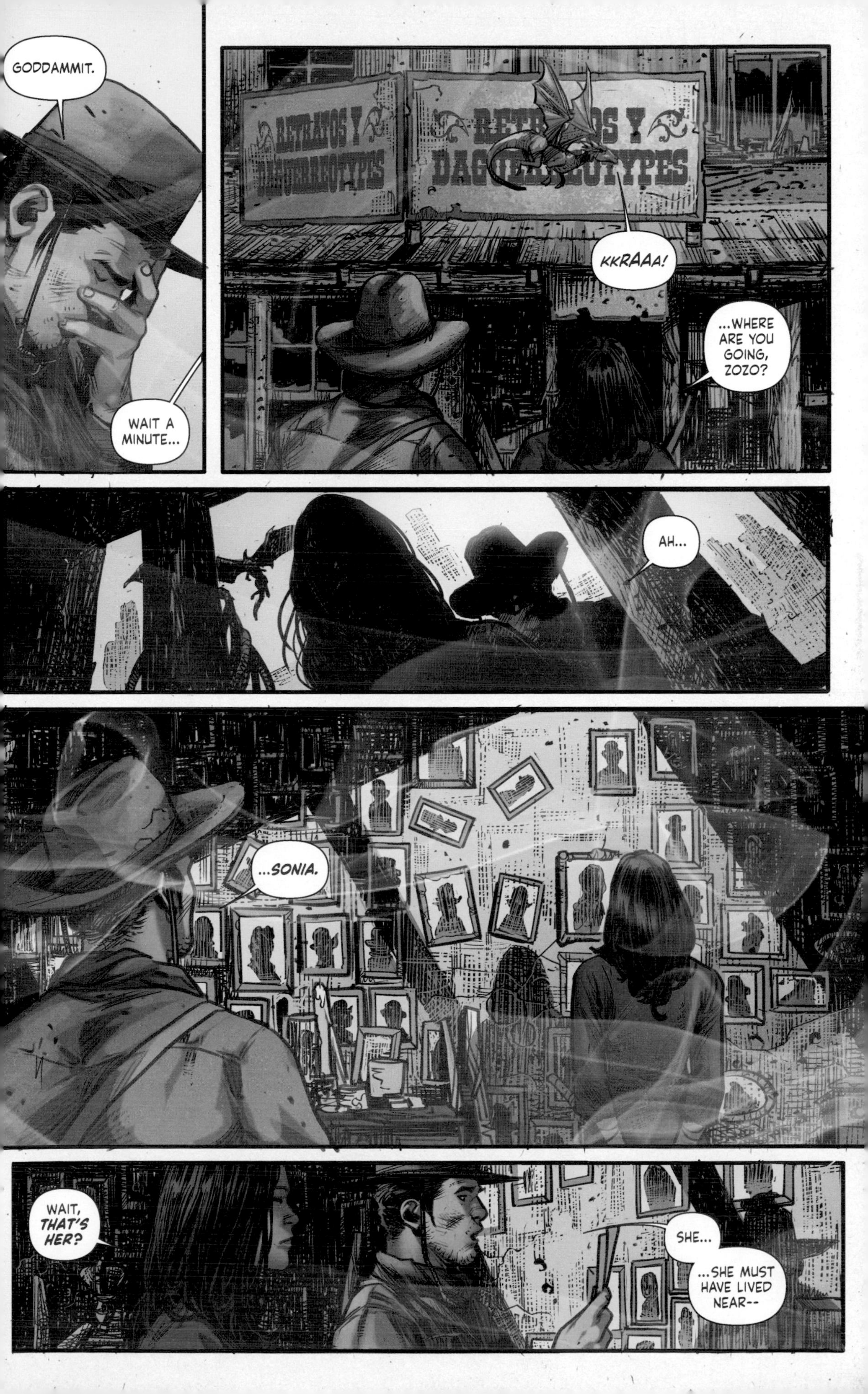
GODDAMMIT.
WAIT A MINUTE...
RETRATOS Y DAGUERREOTYPES
RETRATOS Y DAGUERREOTYPES
KKRAAA!
...WHERE ARE YOU GOING, ZOZO?
AH...
...SONIA.
WAIT, THAT'S HER?
SHE...
...SHE MUST HAVE LIVED NEAR--

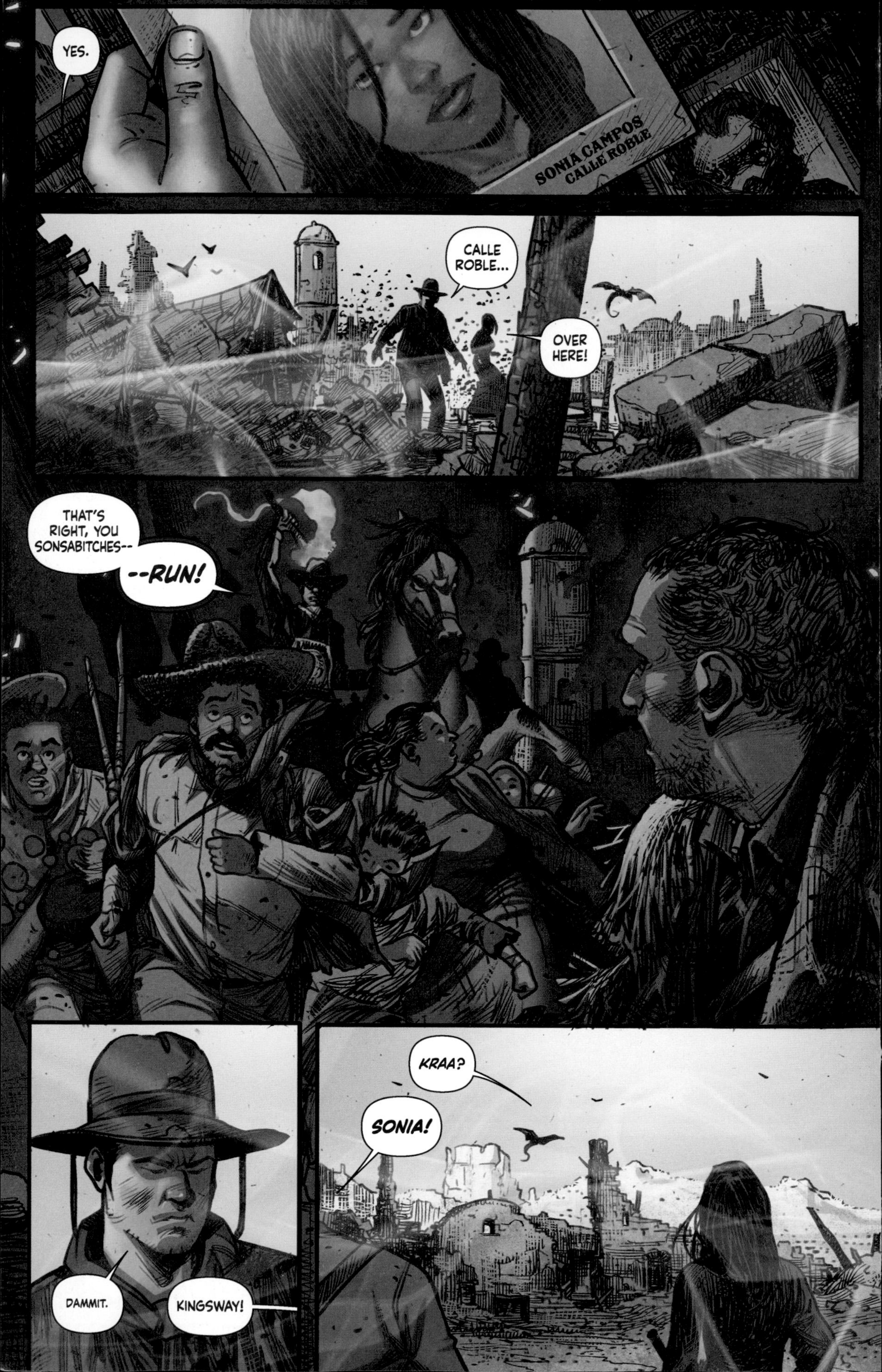
YES.
SONIA CAMPOS
CALLE ROBLE
CALLE ROBLE...
OVER HERE!
THAT'S RIGHT, YOU SONSABITCHES--
--RUN!
DAMMIT.
KINGSWAY!
KRAA?
SONIA!

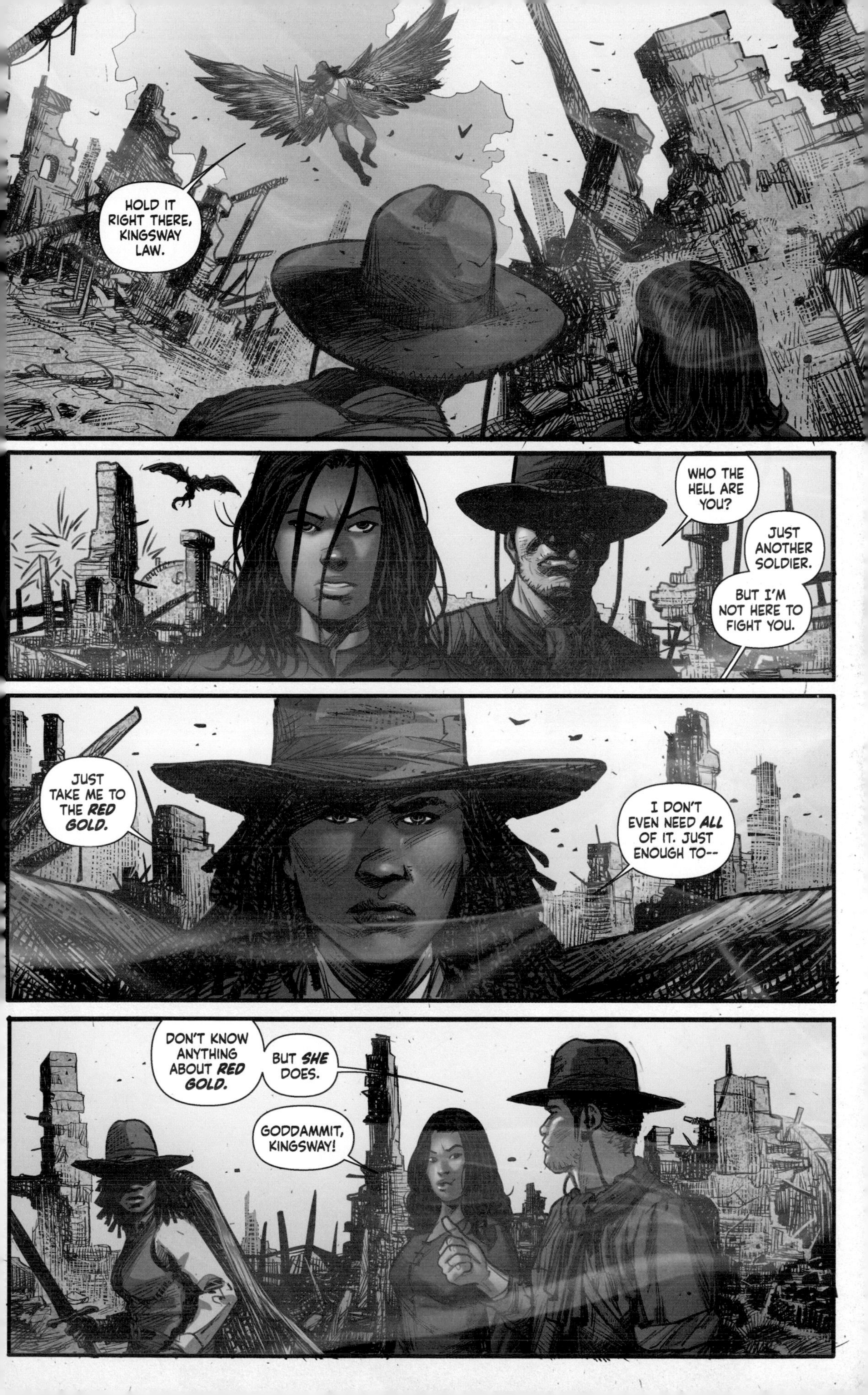
HOLD IT RIGHT THERE, KINGSWAY LAW.
WHO THE HELL ARE YOU?
JUST ANOTHER SOLDIER.
BUT I'M NOT HERE TO FIGHT YOU.
JUST TAKE ME TO THE *RED GOLD.*
I DON'T EVEN NEED *ALL* OF IT. JUST ENOUGH TO--
DON'T KNOW ANYTHING ABOUT *RED GOLD.*
BUT *SHE* DOES.
GODDAMMIT, KINGSWAY!

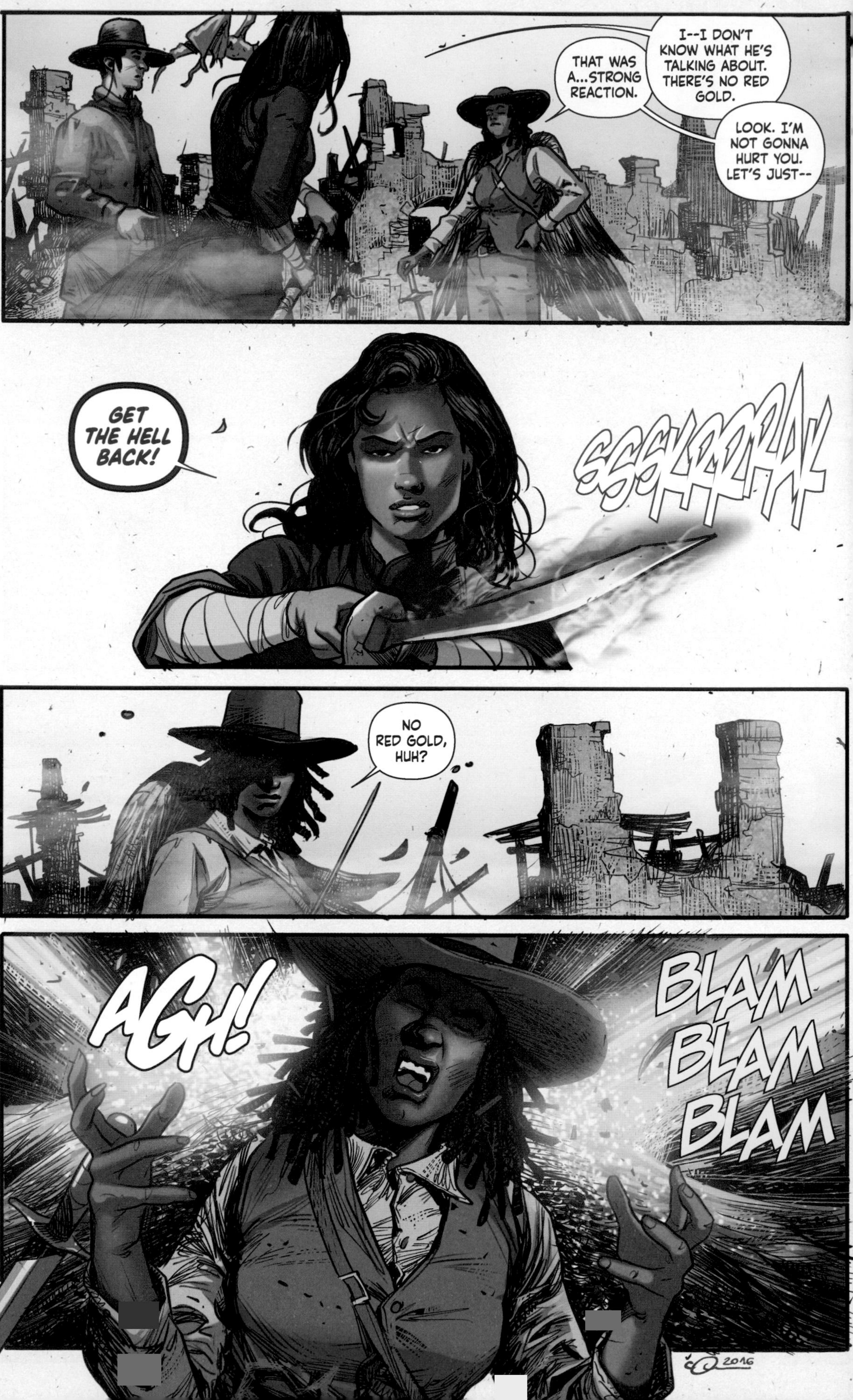
THAT WAS A...STRONG REACTION.
I--I DON'T KNOW WHAT HE'S TALKING ABOUT. THERE'S NO RED GOLD.
LOOK. I'M NOT GONNA HURT YOU. LET'S JUST--
GET THE HELL BACK!
SSSKRRRAK
NO RED GOLD, HUH?
AGH!
BLAM BLAM BLAM

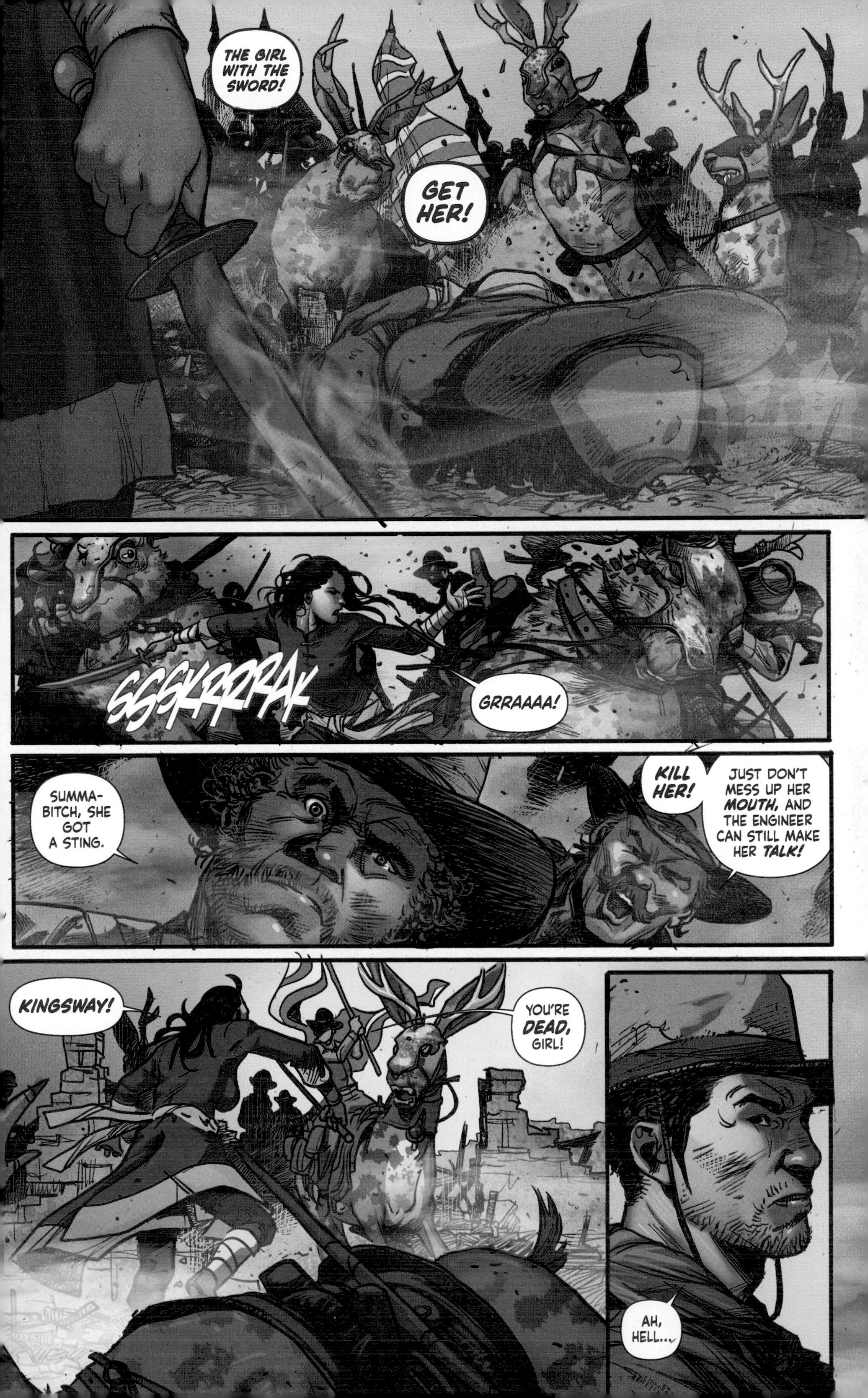
THE GIRL WITH THE SWORD!
GET HER!
SSSKRRRAK
GRRAAAA!
SUMMA-BITCH, SHE GOT A STING.
KILL HER!
JUST DON'T MESS UP HER MOUTH, AND THE ENGINEER CAN STILL MAKE HER TALK!
KINGSWAY!
YOU'RE DEAD, GIRL!
AH, HELL...

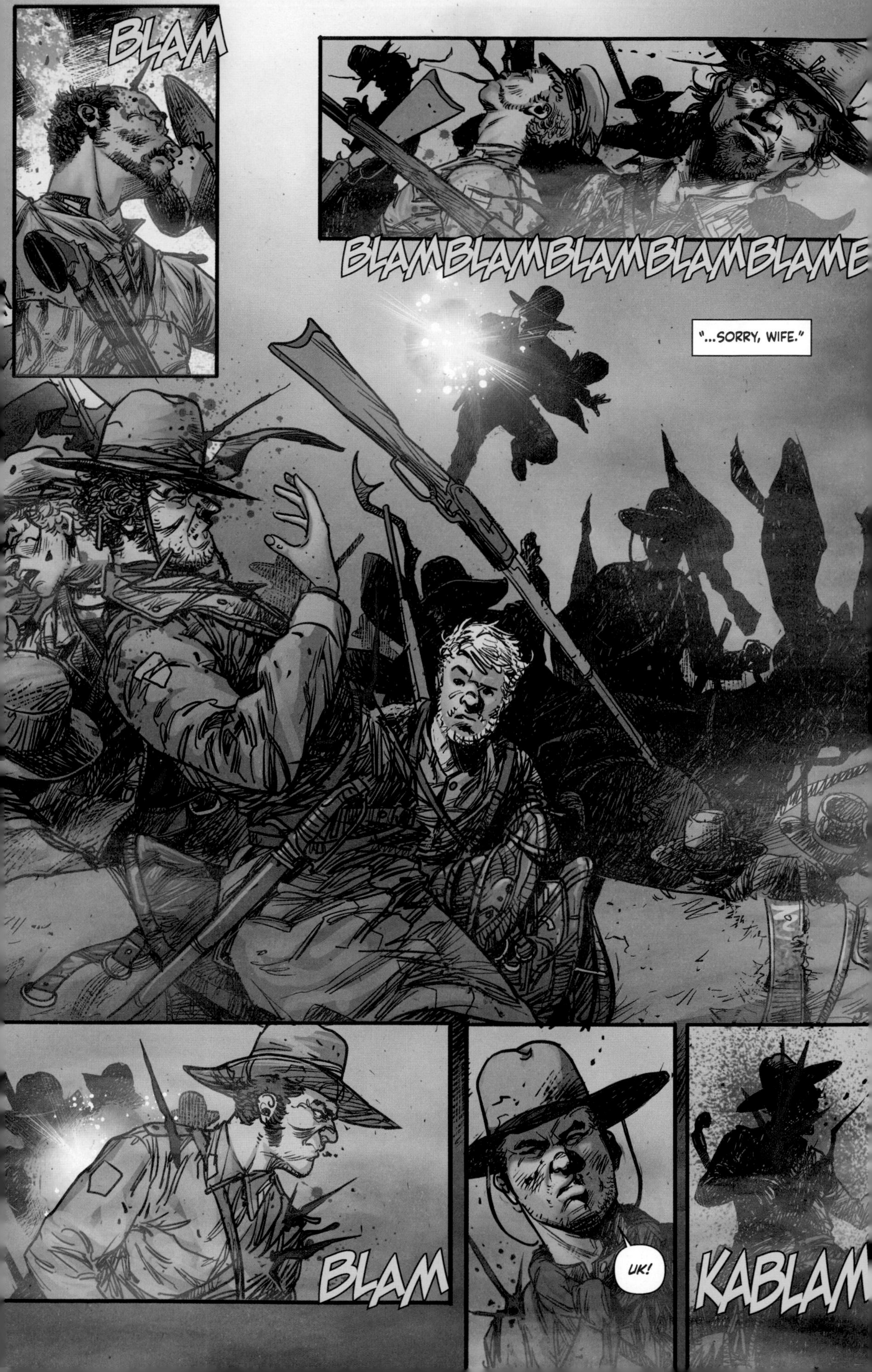
BLAM
BLAMBLAMBLAMBLAMBLAMB
"...SORRY, WIFE."
BLAM
UK!
KABLAM

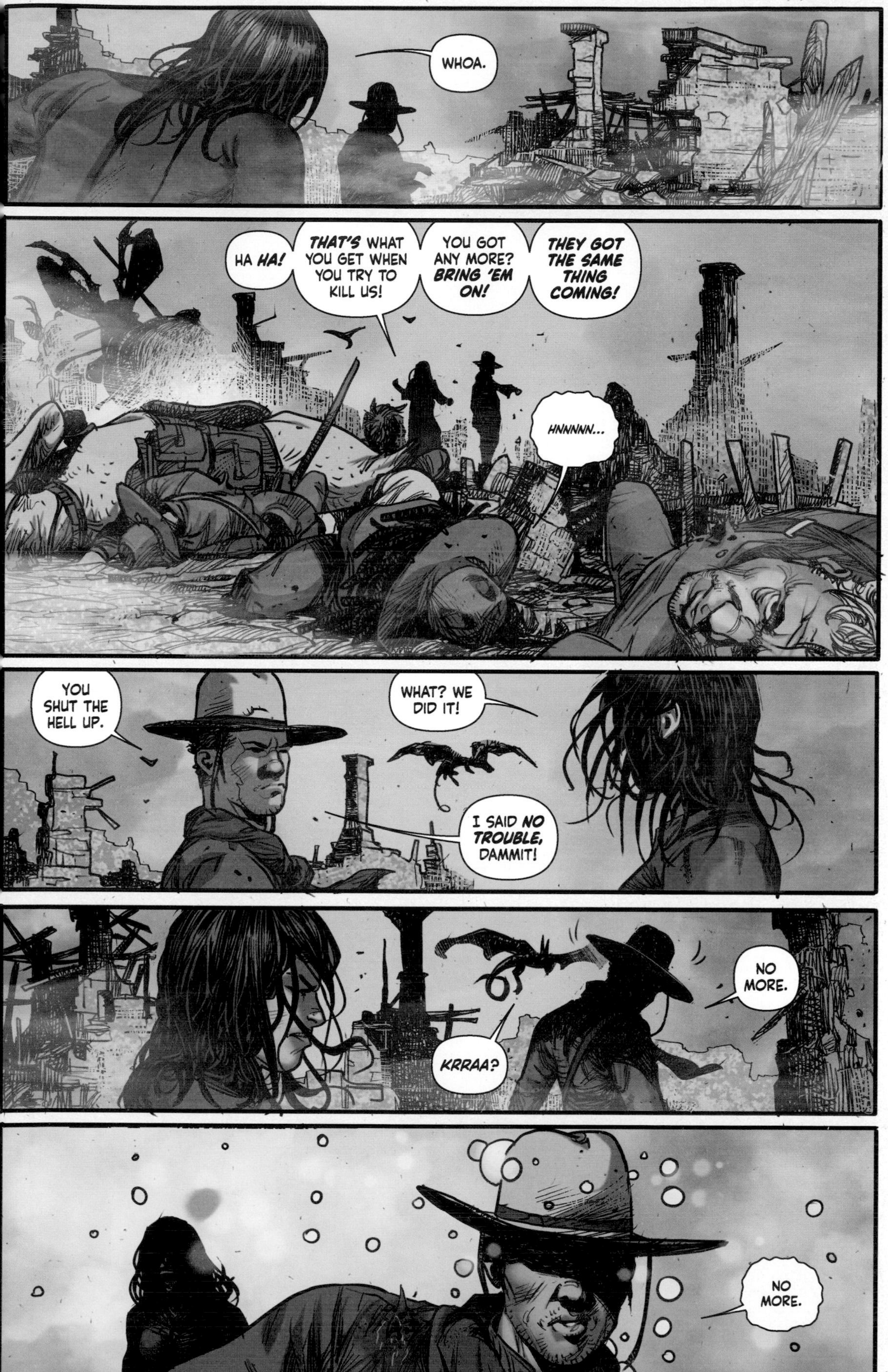
WHOA.
HA *HA!*
THAT'S WHAT YOU GET WHEN YOU TRY TO KILL US!
YOU GOT ANY MORE? *BRING 'EM ON!*
THEY GOT THE SAME THING COMING!
HNNNNN...
YOU SHUT THE HELL UP.
WHAT? WE DID IT!
I SAID *NO TROUBLE,* DAMMIT!
NO MORE.
KRRAA?
NO MORE.

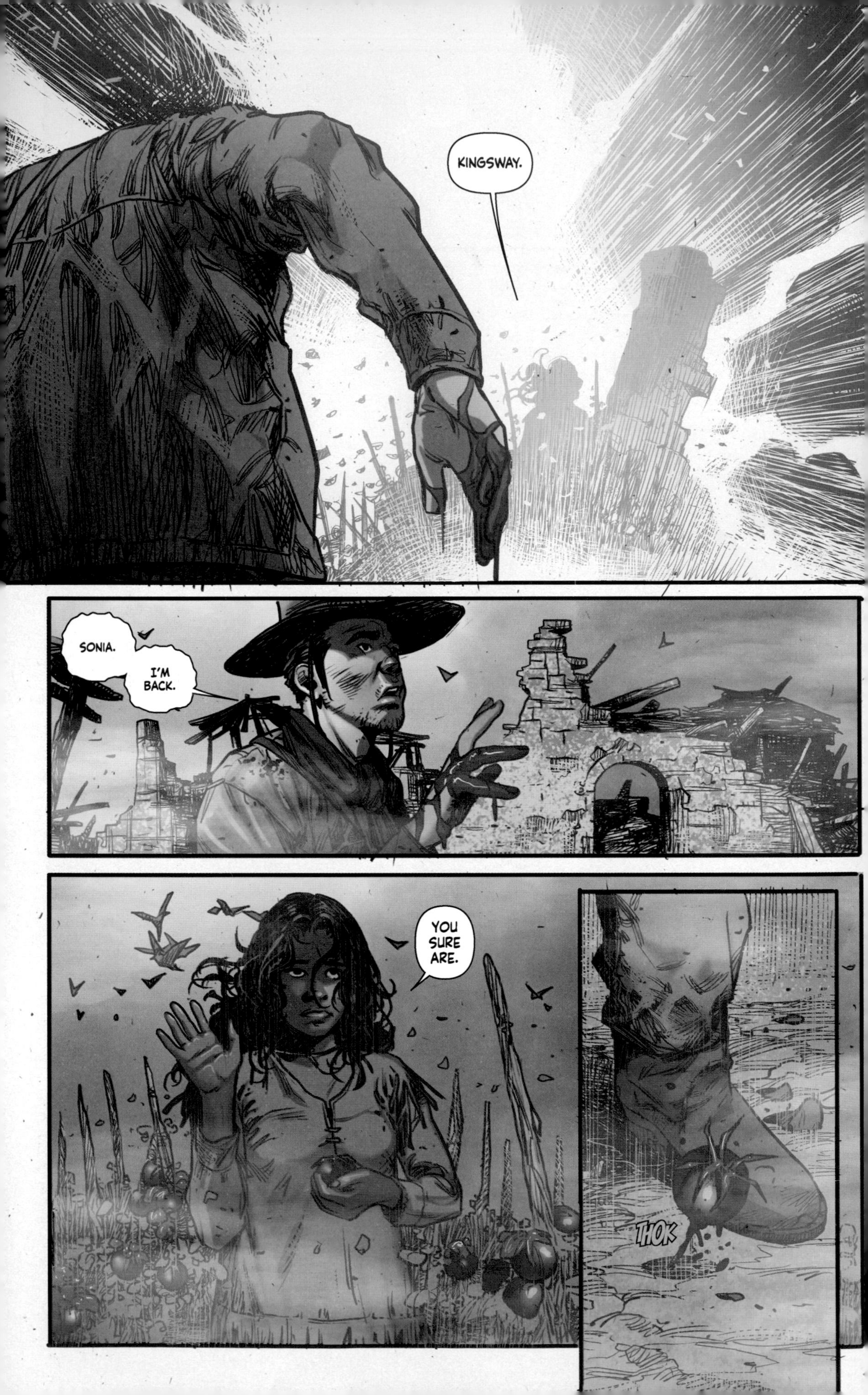
KINGSWAY.
SONIA.
I'M BACK.
YOU SURE ARE.
THOK

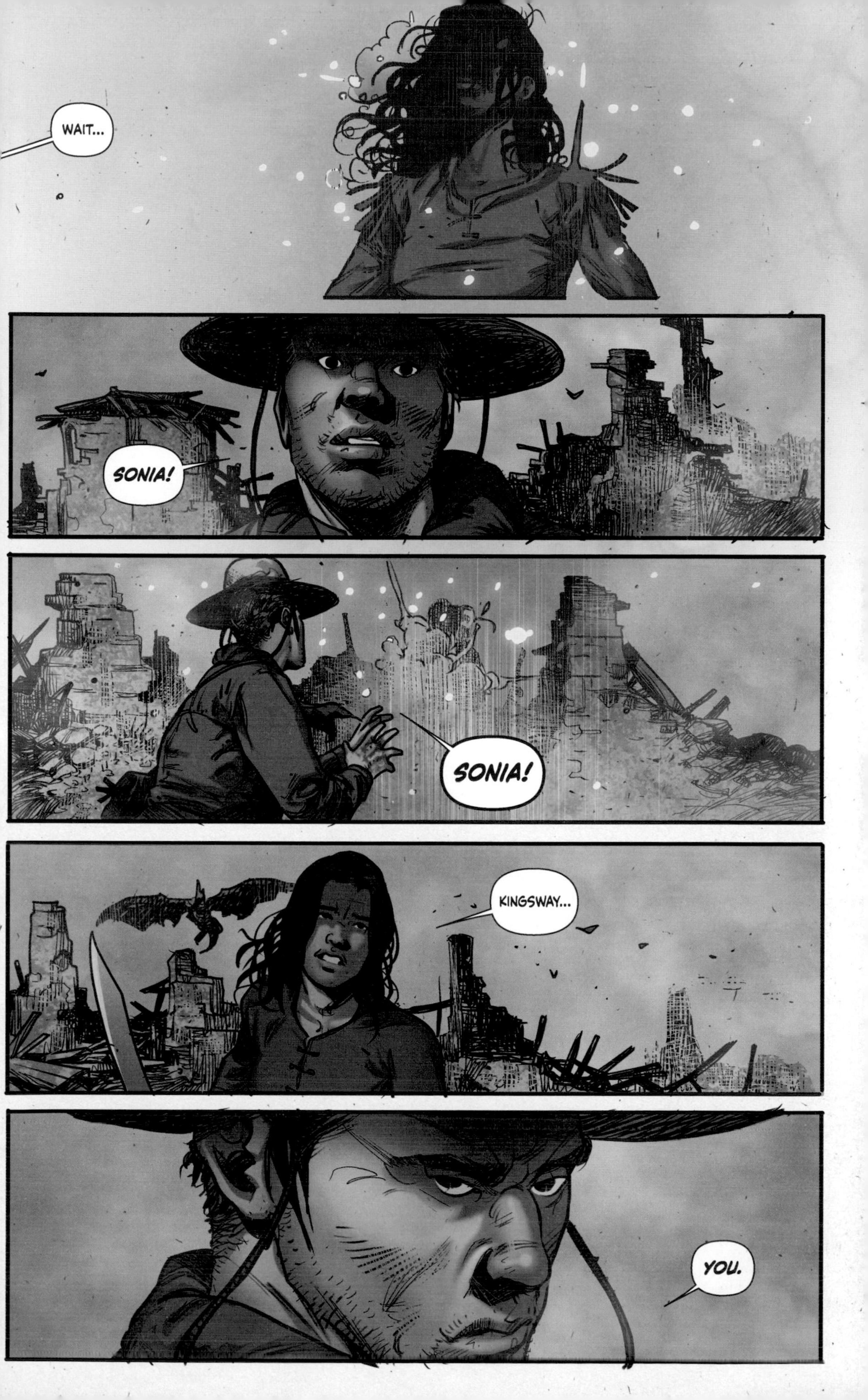
WAIT...
SONIA!
SONIA!
KINGSWAY...
YOU.

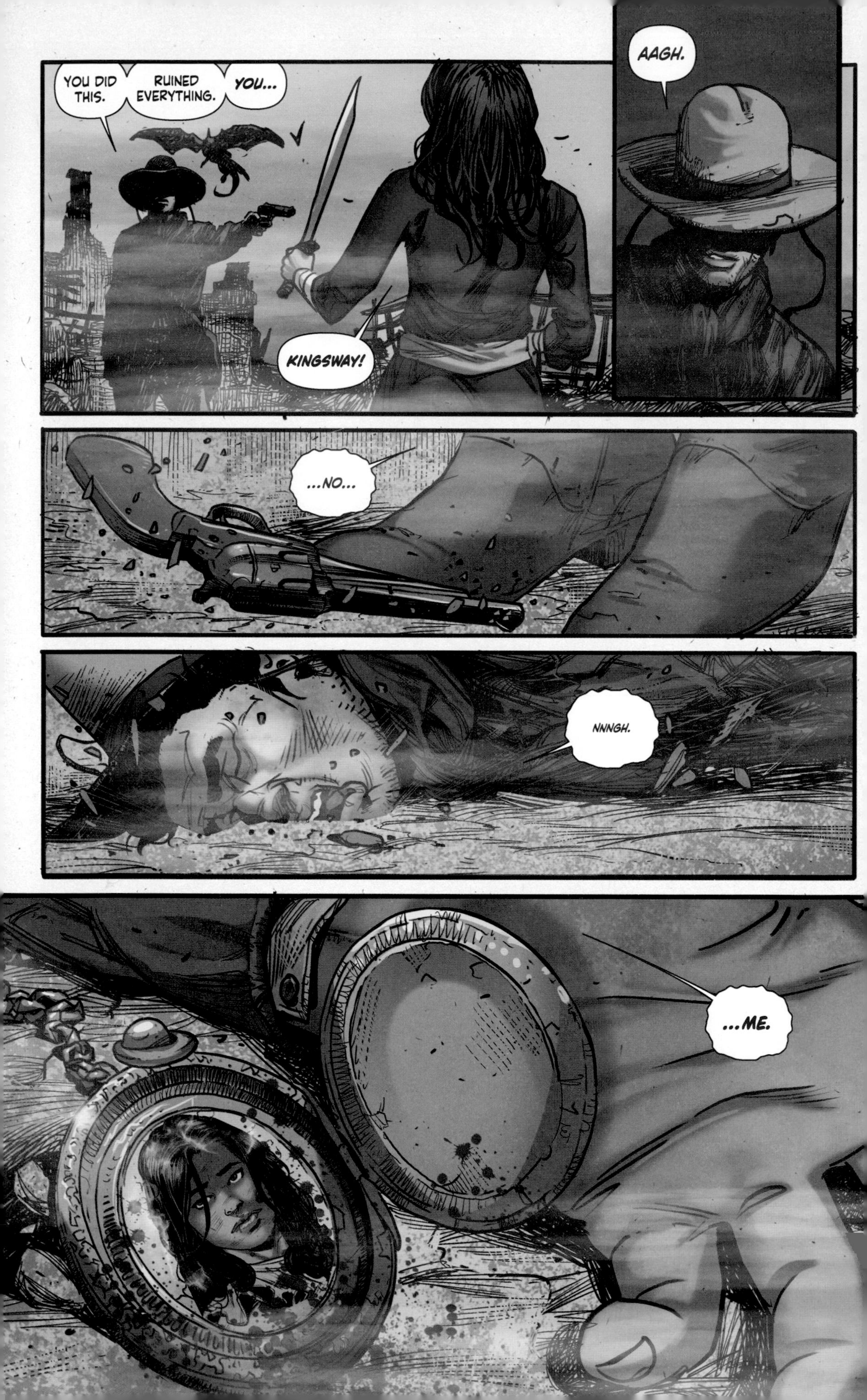
YOU DID THIS.
RUINED EVERYTHING.
YOU...
KINGSWAY!
AAGH.
...NO...
NNNGH.
...ME.

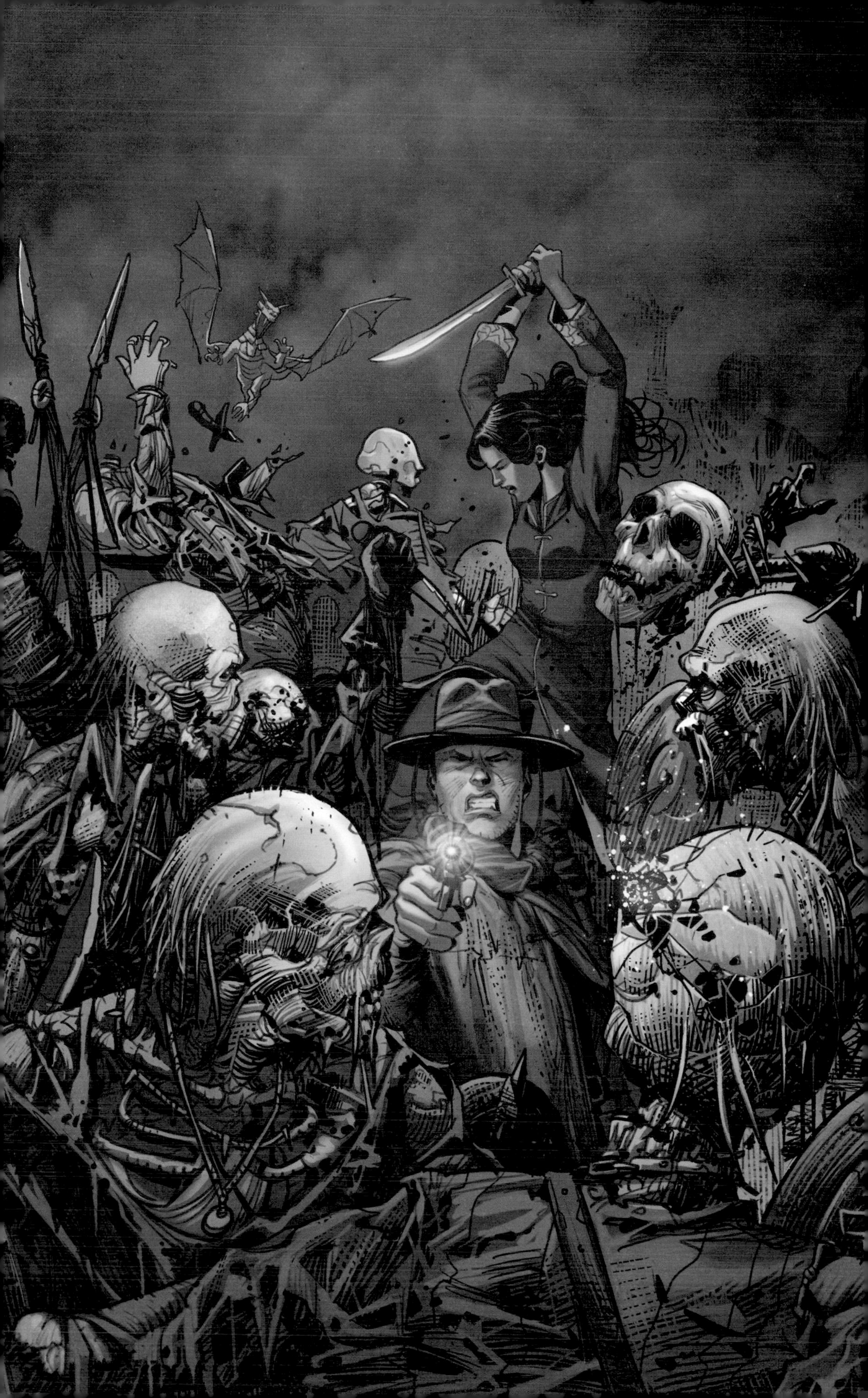

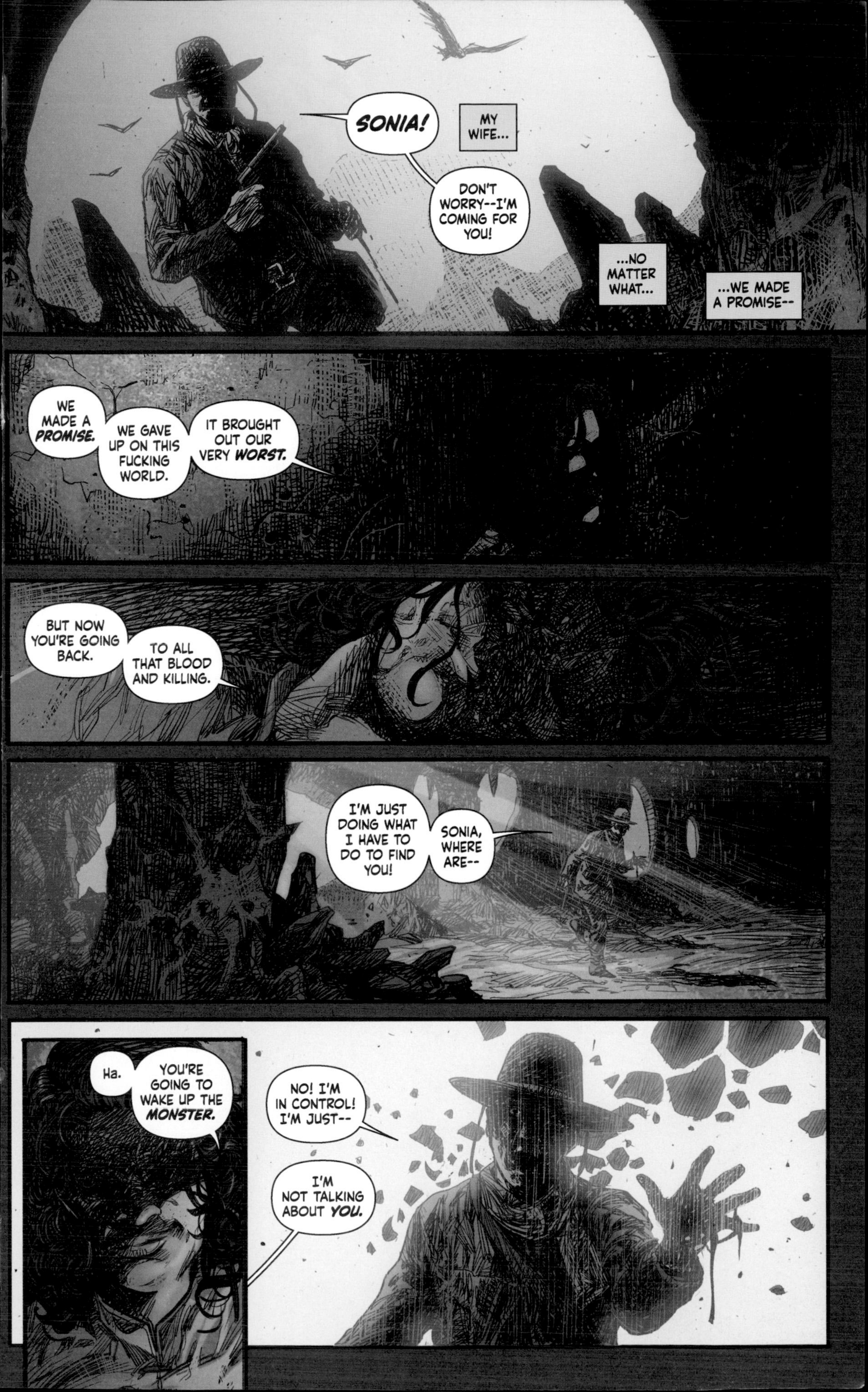
SONIA!
MY WIFE...
DON'T WORRY--I'M COMING FOR YOU!
...NO MATTER WHAT...
...WE MADE A PROMISE--
WE MADE A PROMISE.
WE GAVE UP ON THIS FUCKING WORLD.
IT BROUGHT OUT OUR VERY WORST.
BUT NOW YOU'RE GOING BACK.
TO ALL THAT BLOOD AND KILLING.
I'M JUST DOING WHAT I HAVE TO DO TO FIND YOU!
SONIA, WHERE ARE--
Ha.
YOU'RE GOING TO WAKE UP THE MONSTER.
NO! I'M IN CONTROL! I'M JUST--
I'M NOT TALKING ABOUT YOU.

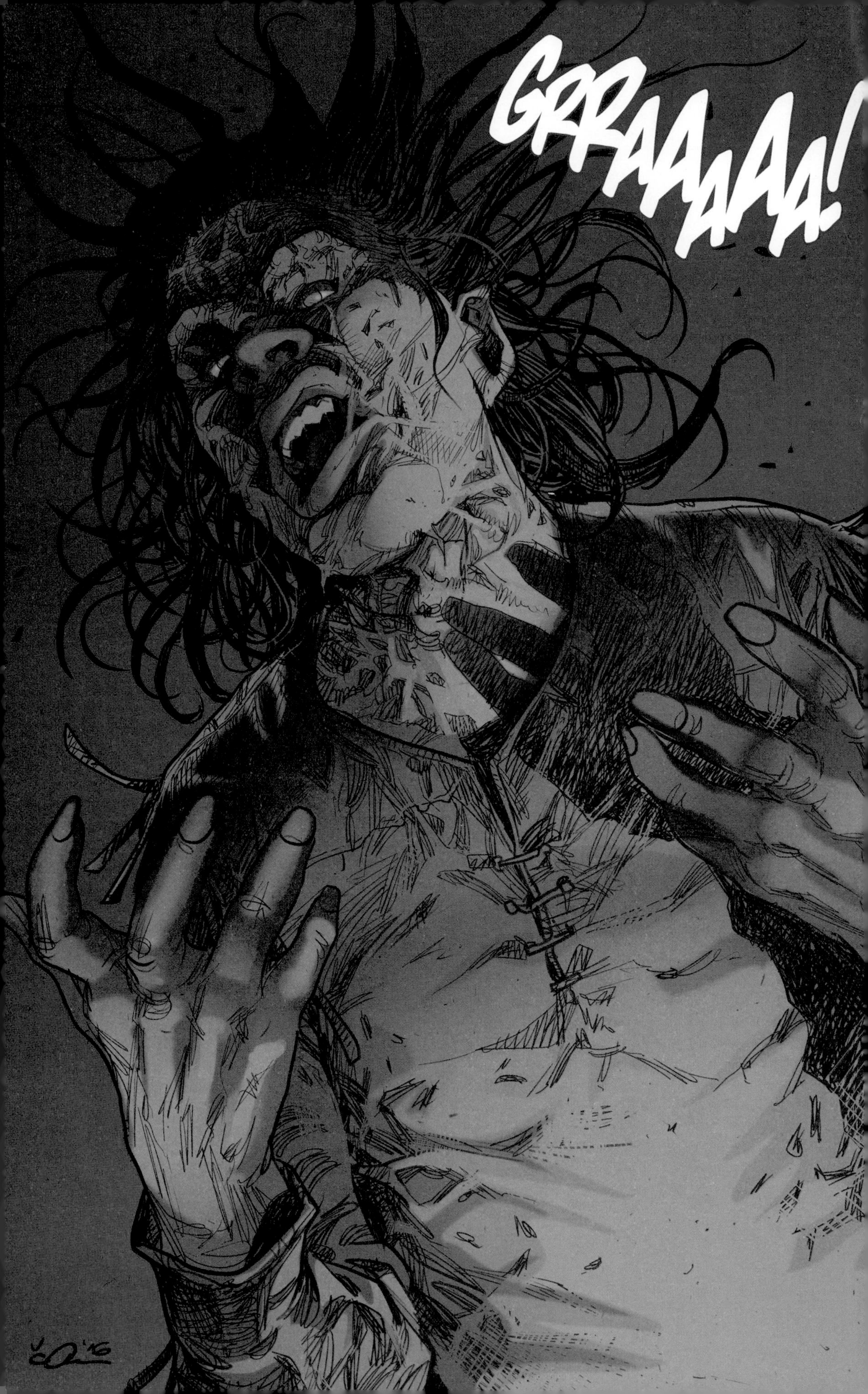
GRRAAAAAA!

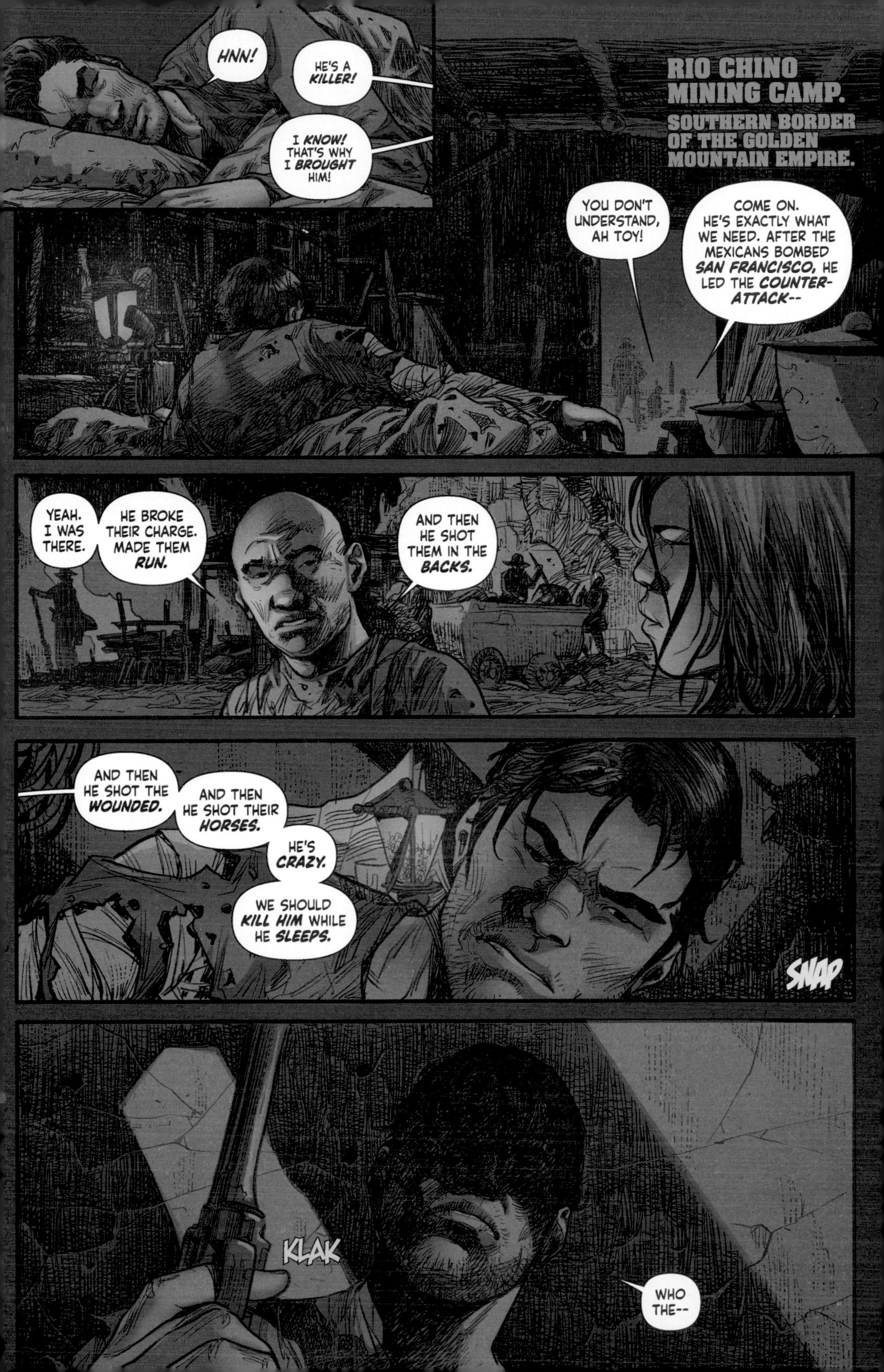
HNN!
HE'S A KILLER!
I KNOW! THAT'S WHY I BROUGHT HIM!
RIO CHINO MINING CAMP.
SOUTHERN BORDER OF THE GOLDEN MOUNTAIN EMPIRE.
YOU DON'T UNDERSTAND, AH TOY!
COME ON. HE'S EXACTLY WHAT WE NEED. AFTER THE MEXICANS BOMBED SAN FRANCISCO, HE LED THE COUNTER-ATTACK--
YEAH. I WAS THERE.
HE BROKE THEIR CHARGE. MADE THEM RUN.
AND THEN HE SHOT THEM IN THE BACKS.
AND THEN HE SHOT THE WOUNDED.
AND THEN HE SHOT THEIR HORSES.
HE'S CRAZY.
WE SHOULD KILL HIM WHILE HE SLEEPS.
SNAP
KLAK
WHO THE--

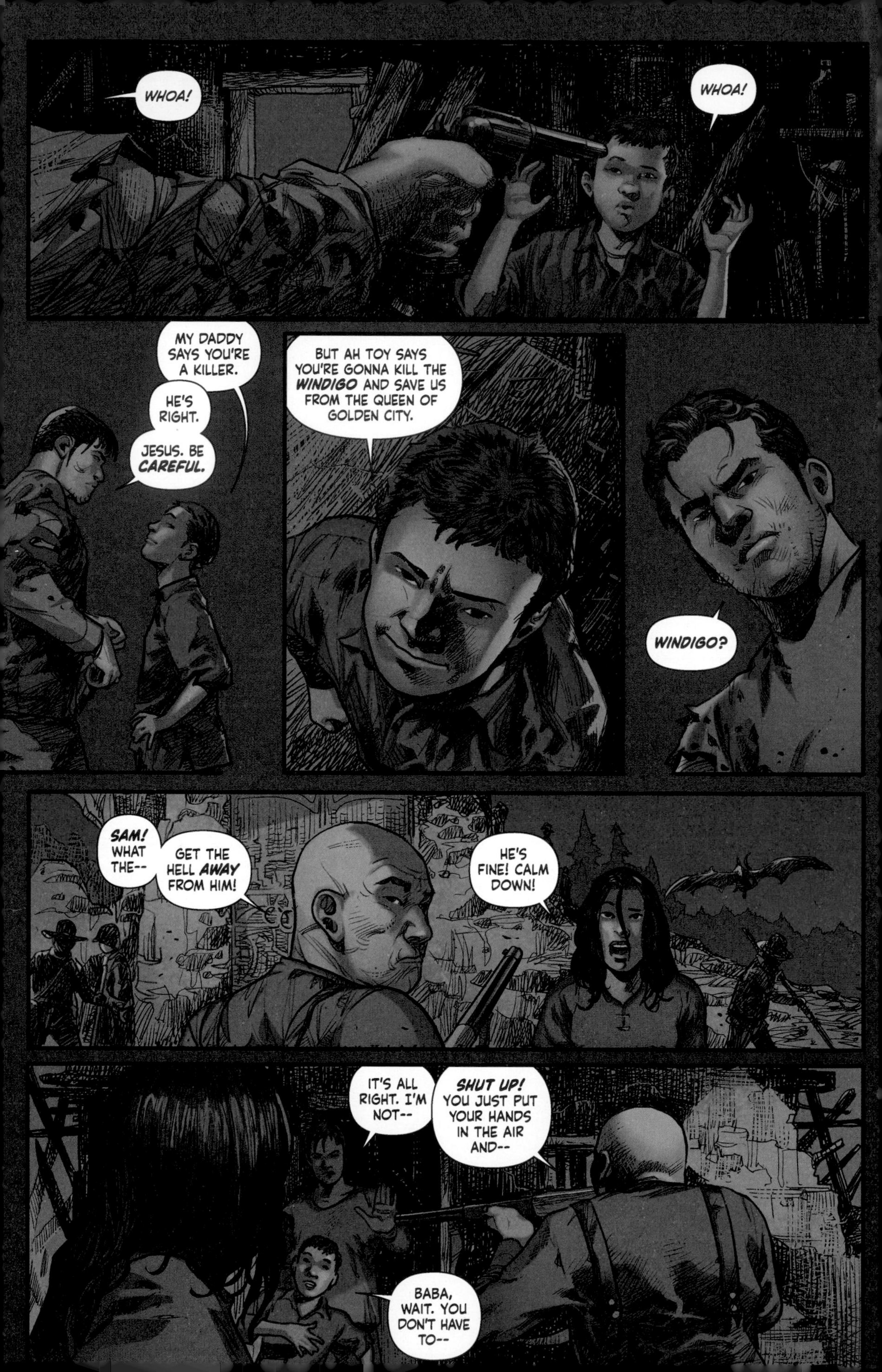

WHOA!
WHOA!
MY DADDY SAYS YOU'RE A KILLER.
HE'S RIGHT.
JESUS. BE *CAREFUL.*
BUT AH TOY SAYS YOU'RE GONNA KILL THE *WINDIGO* AND SAVE US FROM THE QUEEN OF GOLDEN CITY.
WINDIGO?
SAM! WHAT THE--
GET THE HELL *AWAY* FROM HIM!
HE'S FINE! CALM DOWN!
IT'S ALL RIGHT. I'M NOT--
SHUT UP! YOU JUST PUT YOUR HANDS IN THE AIR AND--
BABA, WAIT. YOU DON'T HAVE TO--

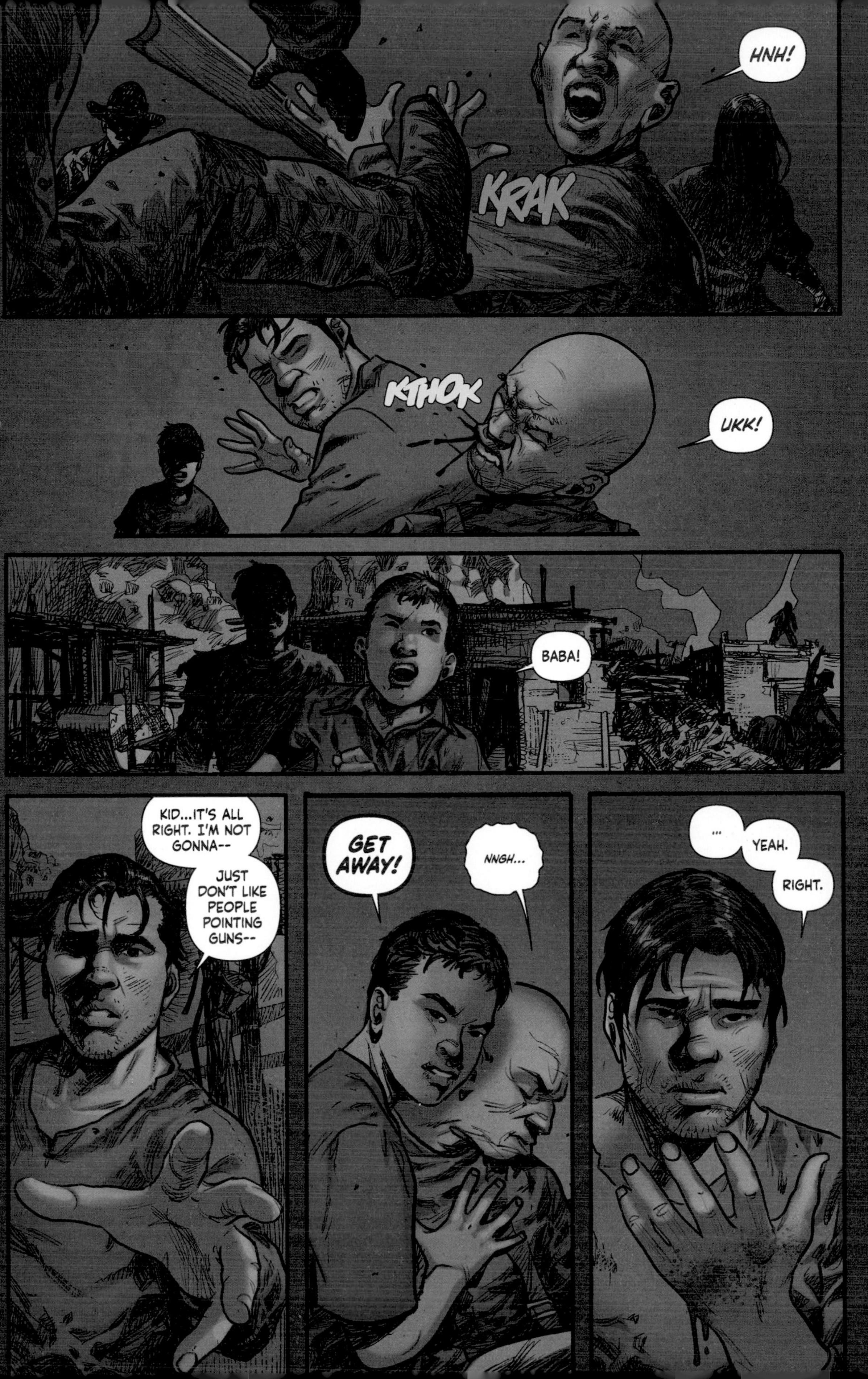
HNH!
KRAK
KTHOK
UKK!
BABA!
KID...IT'S ALL RIGHT. I'M NOT GONNA--
JUST DON'T LIKE PEOPLE POINTING GUNS--
GET AWAY!
NNGH...
...
YEAH.
RIGHT.

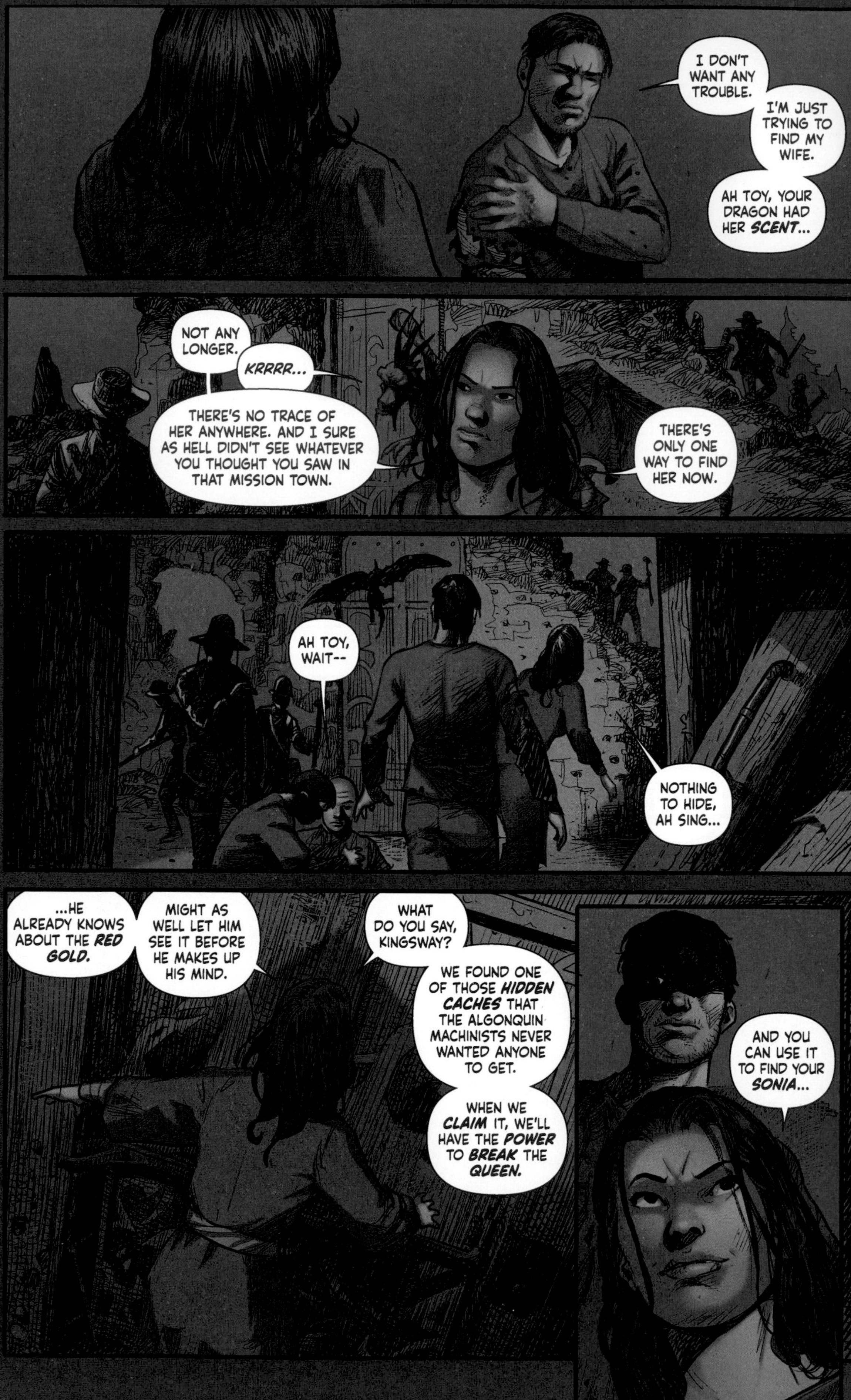
I DON'T WANT ANY TROUBLE.
I'M JUST TRYING TO FIND MY WIFE.
AH TOY, YOUR DRAGON HAD HER SCENT...
NOT ANY LONGER.
KRRRR...
THERE'S NO TRACE OF HER ANYWHERE. AND I SURE AS HELL DIDN'T SEE WHATEVER YOU THOUGHT YOU SAW IN THAT MISSION TOWN.
THERE'S ONLY ONE WAY TO FIND HER NOW.
AH TOY, WAIT--
NOTHING TO HIDE, AH SING...
...HE ALREADY KNOWS ABOUT THE RED GOLD.
MIGHT AS WELL LET HIM SEE IT BEFORE HE MAKES UP HIS MIND.
WHAT DO YOU SAY, KINGSWAY?
WE FOUND ONE OF THOSE HIDDEN CACHES THAT THE ALGONQUIN MACHINISTS NEVER WANTED ANYONE TO GET.
WHEN WE CLAIM IT, WE'LL HAVE THE POWER TO BREAK THE QUEEN.
AND YOU CAN USE IT TO FIND YOUR SONIA...

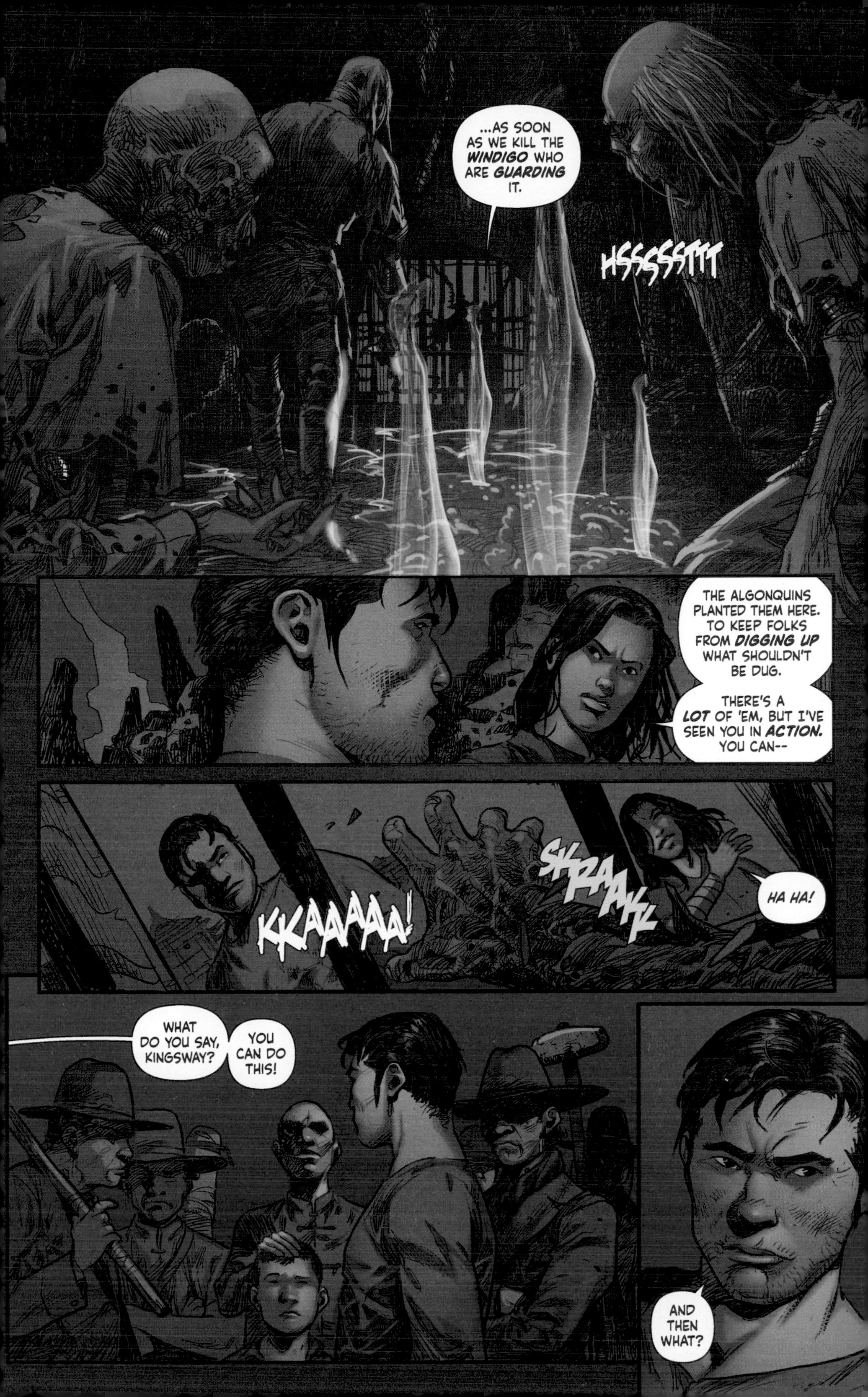
...AS SOON AS WE KILL THE WINDIGO WHO ARE GUARDING IT.
HSSSSSTTT
THE ALGONQUINS PLANTED THEM HERE. TO KEEP FOLKS FROM DIGGING UP WHAT SHOULDN'T BE DUG.
THERE'S A LOT OF 'EM, BUT I'VE SEEN YOU IN ACTION. YOU CAN--
KKAAAAA!
SKRAAKK
HA HA!
WHAT DO YOU SAY, KINGSWAY?
YOU CAN DO THIS!
AND THEN WHAT?

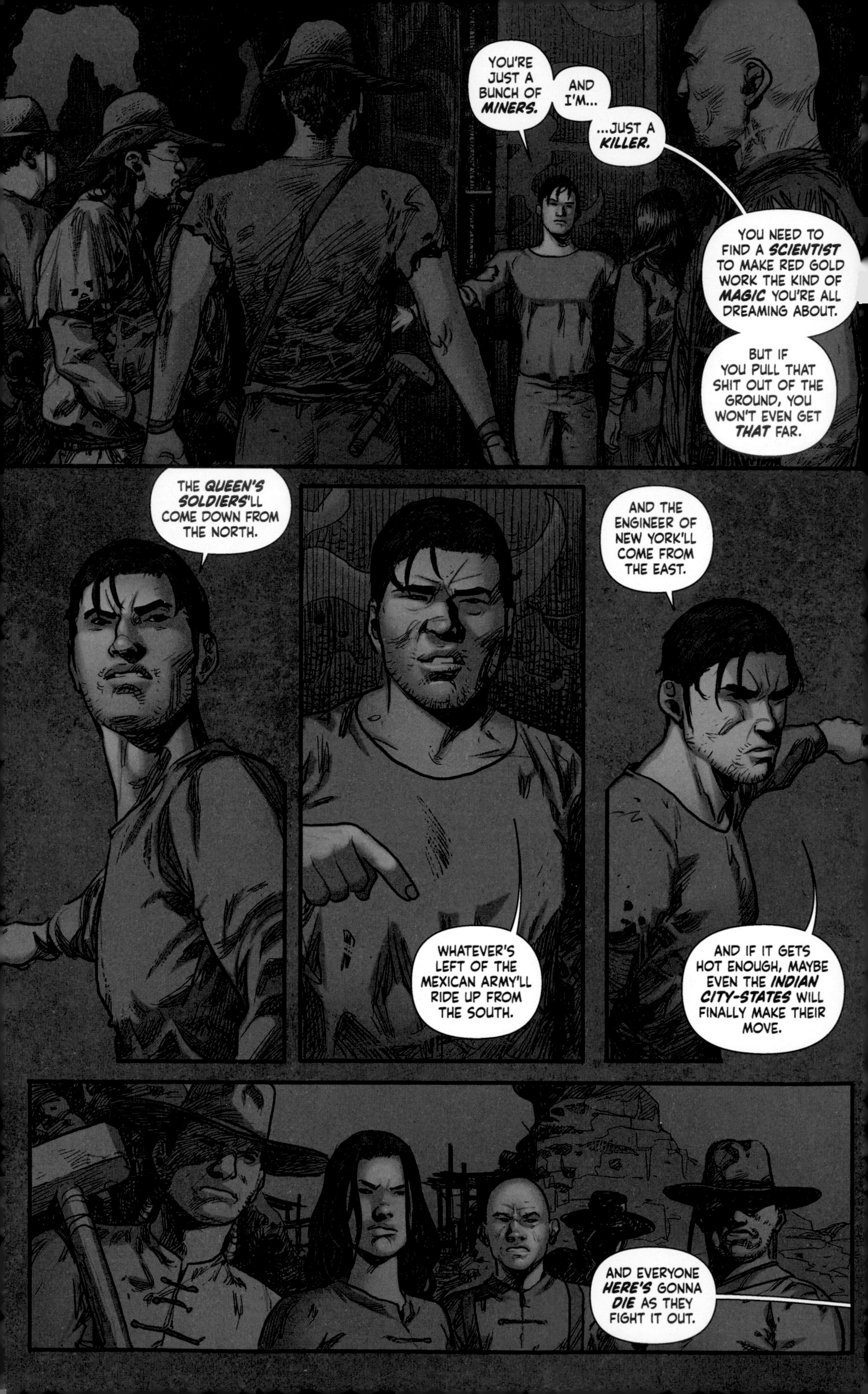
YOU'RE JUST A BUNCH OF MINERS.
AND I'M...
...JUST A KILLER.
YOU NEED TO FIND A SCIENTIST TO MAKE RED GOLD WORK THE KIND OF MAGIC YOU'RE ALL DREAMING ABOUT.
BUT IF YOU PULL THAT SHIT OUT OF THE GROUND, YOU WON'T EVEN GET THAT FAR.
THE QUEEN'S SOLDIERS'LL COME DOWN FROM THE NORTH.
WHATEVER'S LEFT OF THE MEXICAN ARMY'LL RIDE UP FROM THE SOUTH.
AND THE ENGINEER OF NEW YORK'LL COME FROM THE EAST.
AND IF IT GETS HOT ENOUGH, MAYBE EVEN THE INDIAN CITY-STATES WILL FINALLY MAKE THEIR MOVE.
AND EVERYONE HERE'S GONNA DIE AS THEY FIGHT IT OUT.

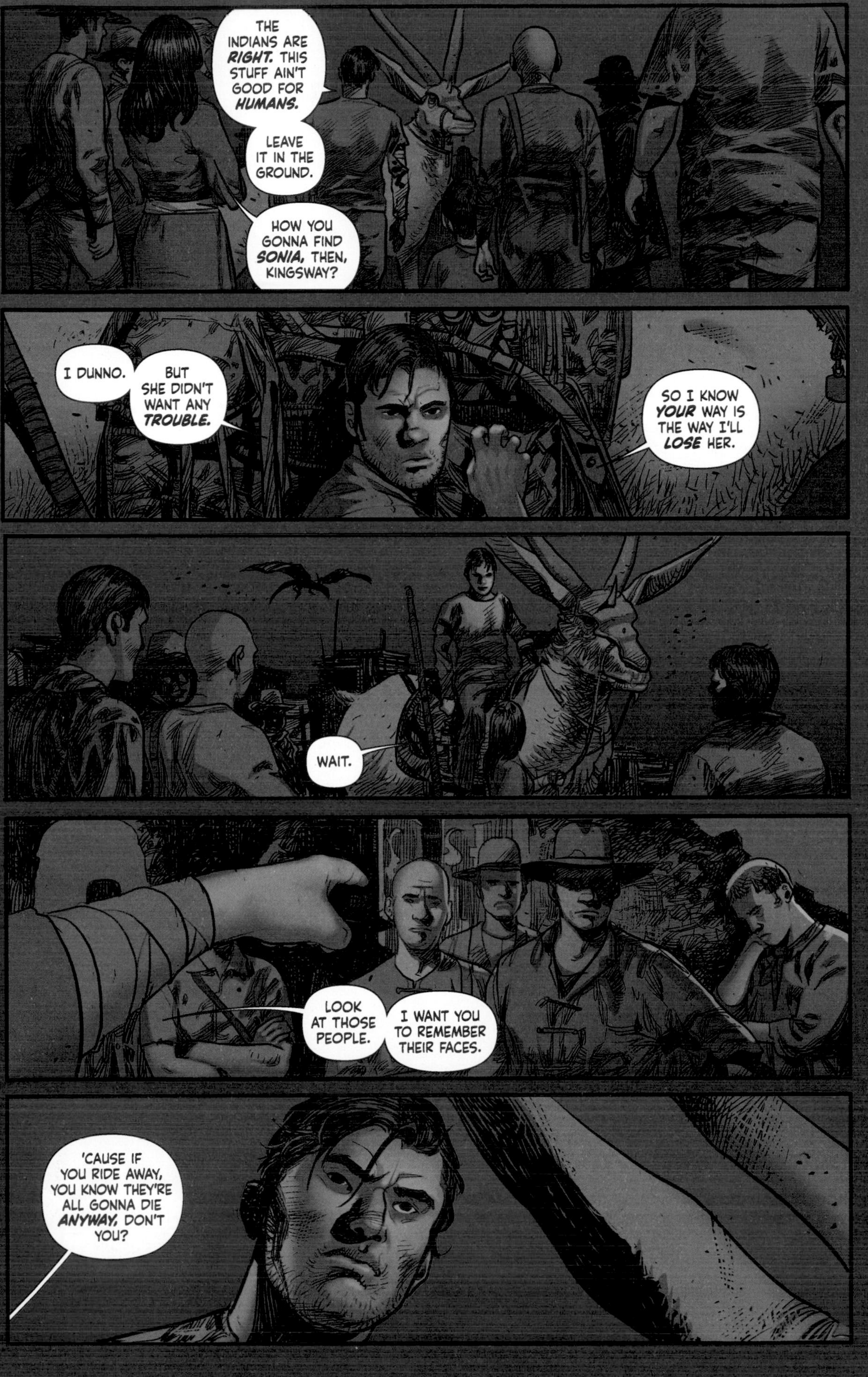
THE INDIANS ARE RIGHT. THIS STUFF AIN'T GOOD FOR HUMANS.
LEAVE IT IN THE GROUND.
HOW YOU GONNA FIND SONIA, THEN, KINGSWAY?
I DUNNO.
BUT SHE DIDN'T WANT ANY TROUBLE.
SO I KNOW YOUR WAY IS THE WAY I'LL LOSE HER.
WAIT.
LOOK AT THOSE PEOPLE.
I WANT YOU TO REMEMBER THEIR FACES.
'CAUSE IF YOU RIDE AWAY, YOU KNOW THEY'RE ALL GONNA DIE ANYWAY, DON'T YOU?

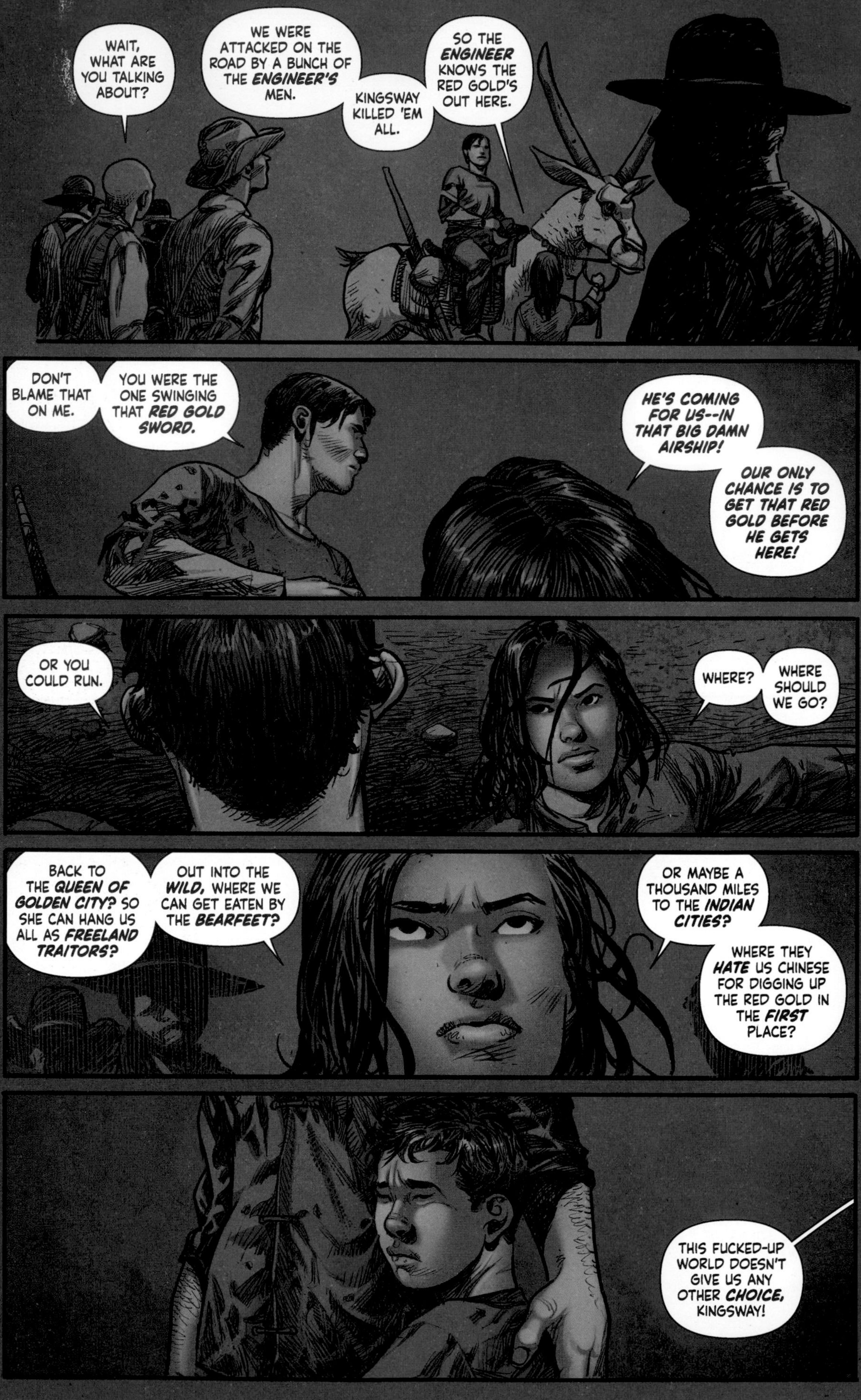
WAIT, WHAT ARE YOU TALKING ABOUT?
WE WERE ATTACKED ON THE ROAD BY A BUNCH OF THE ENGINEER'S MEN.
KINGSWAY KILLED 'EM ALL.
SO THE ENGINEER KNOWS THE RED GOLD'S OUT HERE.
DON'T BLAME THAT ON ME.
YOU WERE THE ONE SWINGING THAT RED GOLD SWORD.
HE'S COMING FOR US--IN THAT BIG DAMN AIRSHIP!
OUR ONLY CHANCE IS TO GET THAT RED GOLD BEFORE HE GETS HERE!
OR YOU COULD RUN.
WHERE?
WHERE SHOULD WE GO?
BACK TO THE QUEEN OF GOLDEN CITY? SO SHE CAN HANG US ALL AS FREELAND TRAITORS?
OUT INTO THE WILD, WHERE WE CAN GET EATEN BY THE BEARFEET?
OR MAYBE A THOUSAND MILES TO THE INDIAN CITIES?
WHERE THEY HATE US CHINESE FOR DIGGING UP THE RED GOLD IN THE FIRST PLACE?
THIS FUCKED-UP WORLD DOESN'T GIVE US ANY OTHER CHOICE, KINGSWAY!

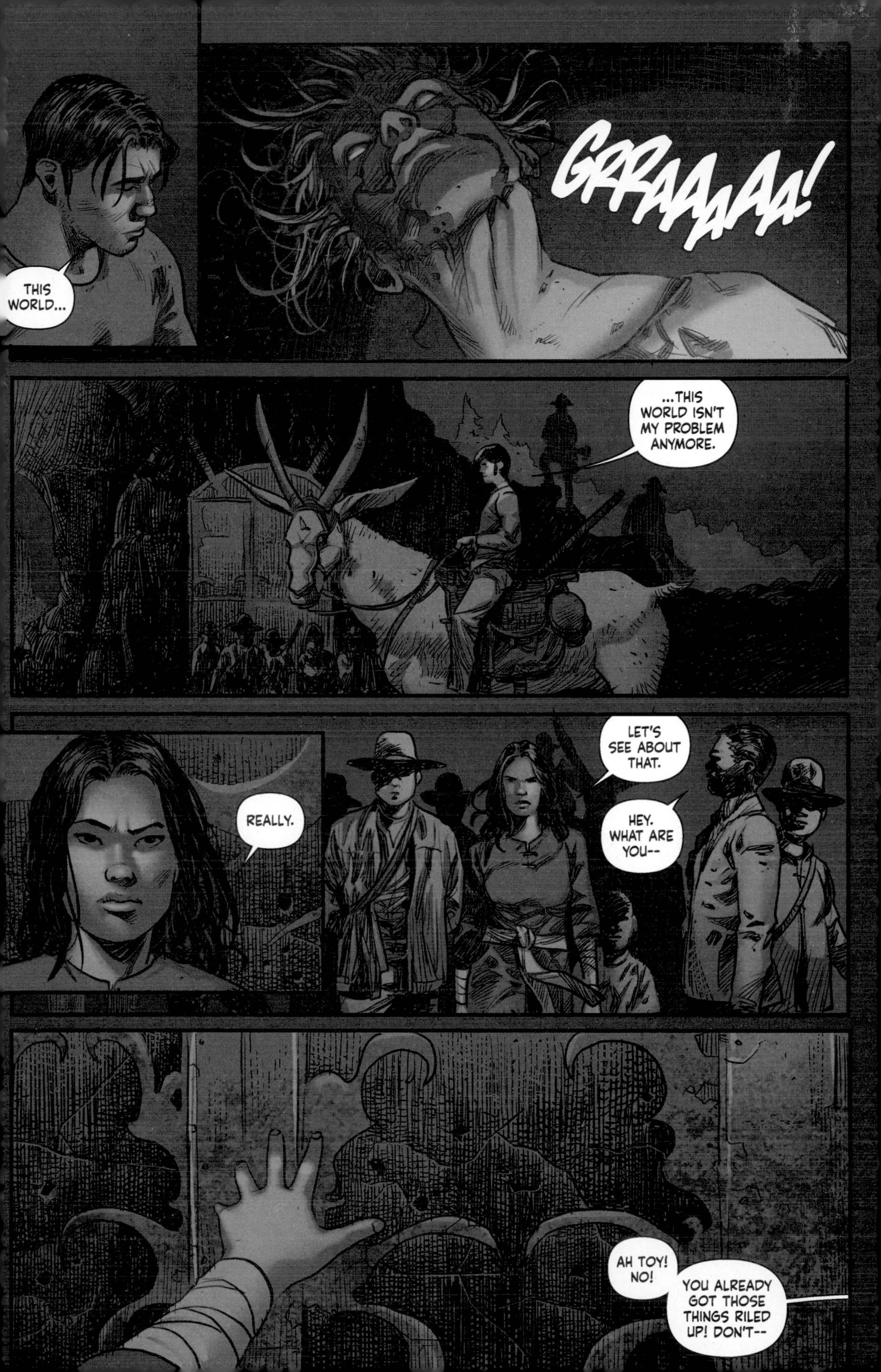
THIS WORLD...
GRRAAAAAA!
...THIS WORLD ISN'T MY PROBLEM ANYMORE.
REALLY.
LET'S SEE ABOUT THAT.
HEY. WHAT ARE YOU--
AH TOY! NO!
YOU ALREADY GOT THOSE THINGS RILED UP! DON'T--

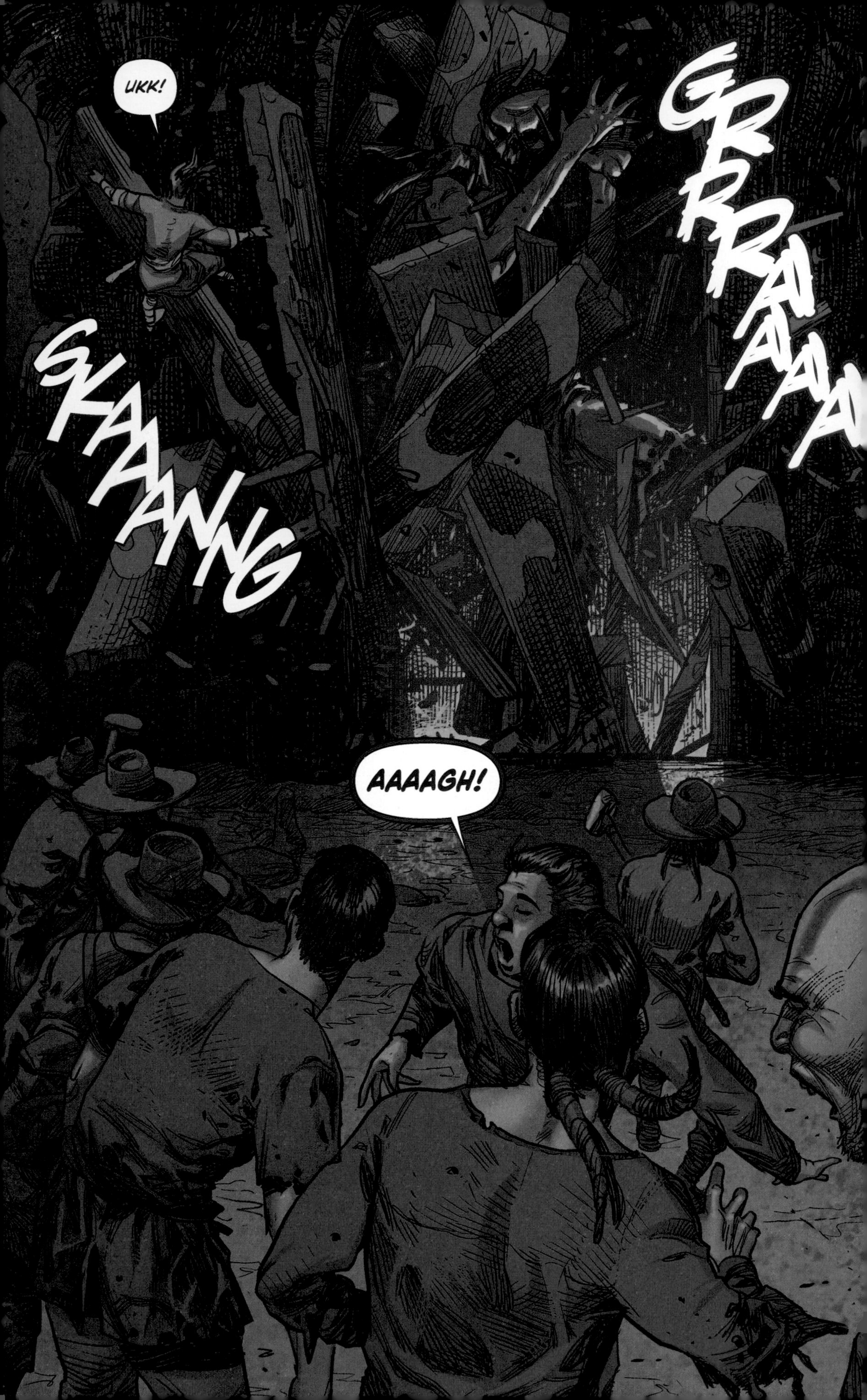
UKK!
GRRAAAAAA
SKAAANNG
AAAAGH!

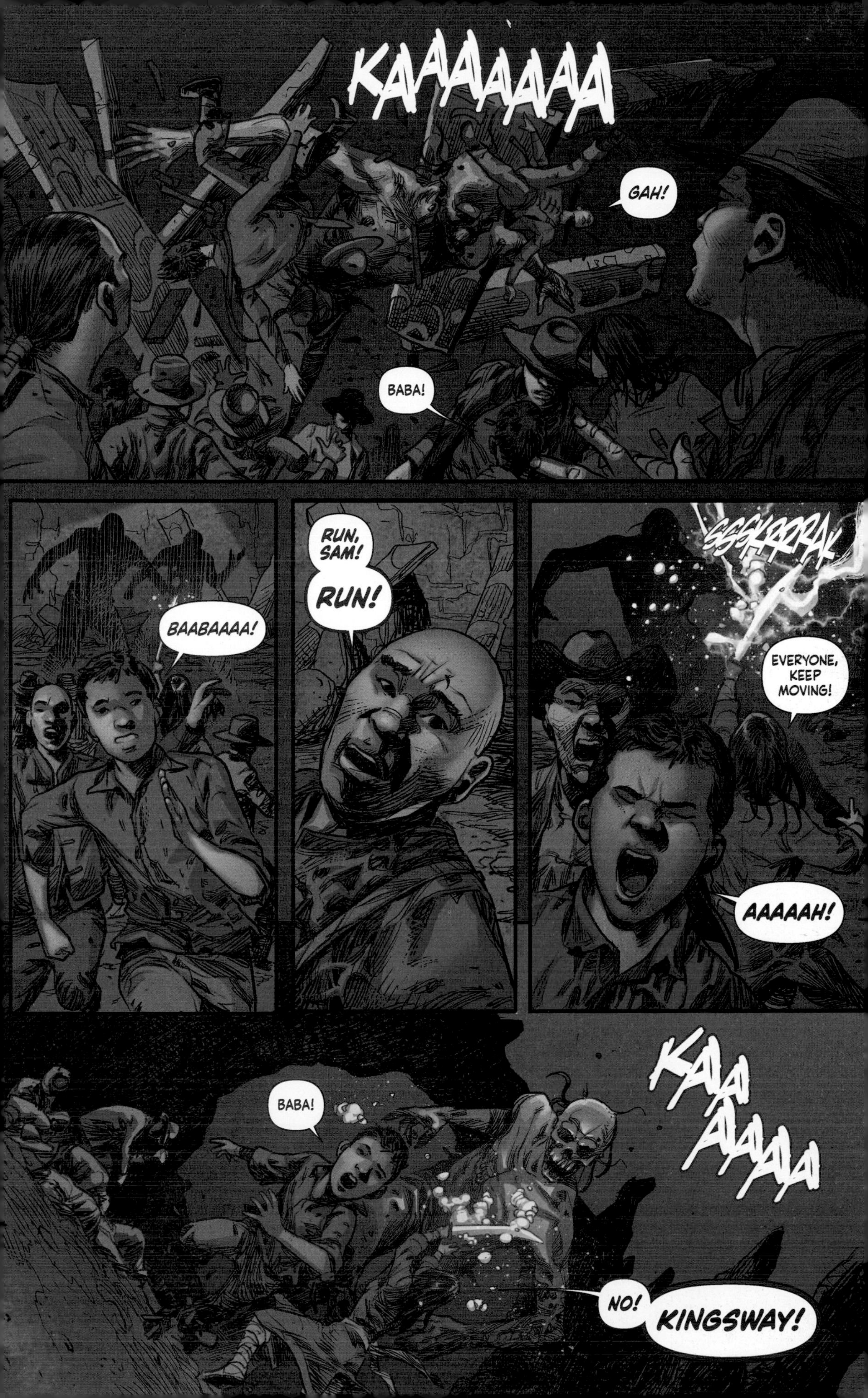
KAAAAAAAA
GAH!
BABA!
BAABAAAA!
RUN, SAM!
RUN!
SSSKRRRAK
EVERYONE, KEEP MOVING!
AAAAAH!
KAAAAAAA
BABA!
NO!
KINGSWAY!

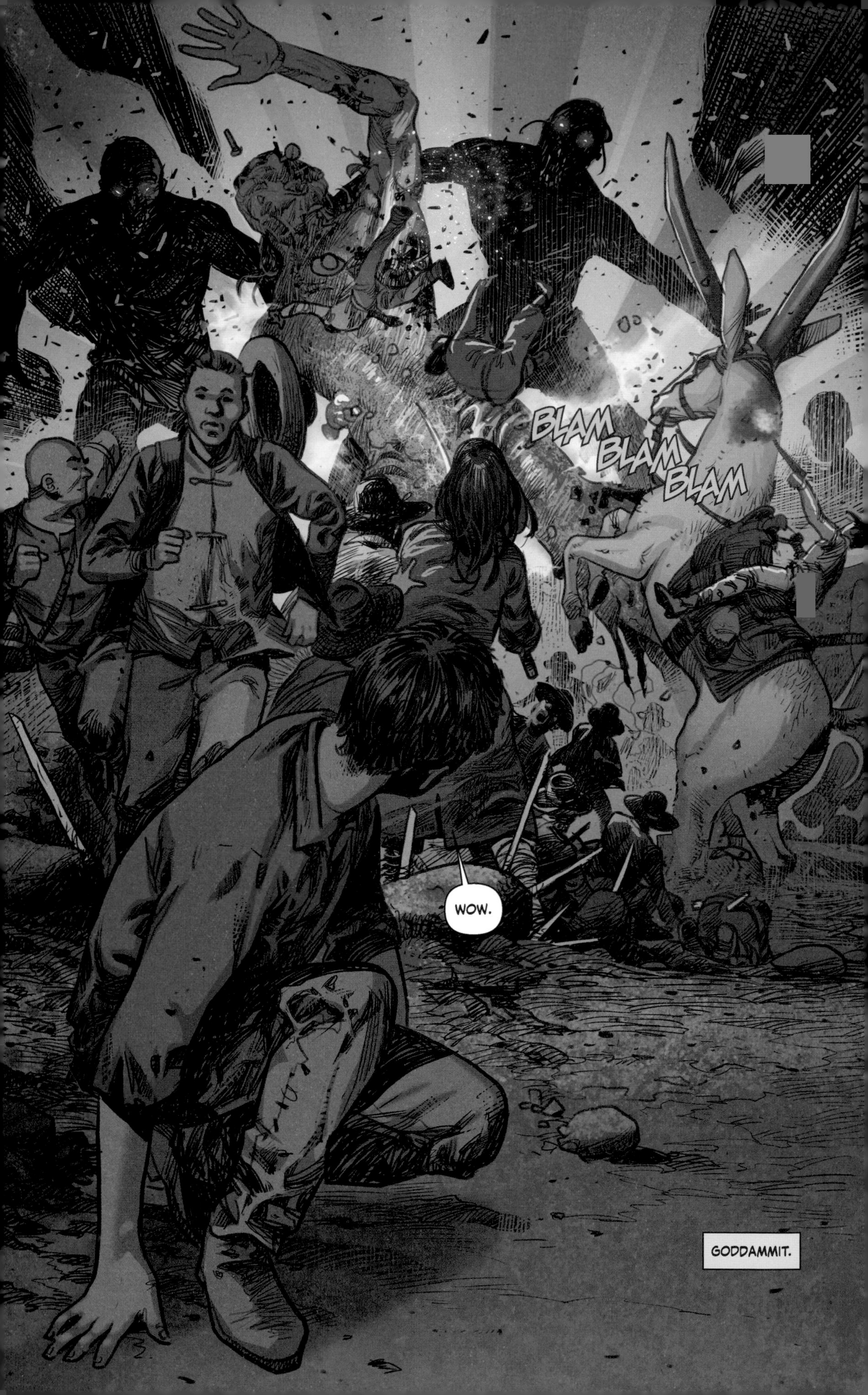
BLAM
BLAM
BLAM
WOW.
GODDAMMIT.

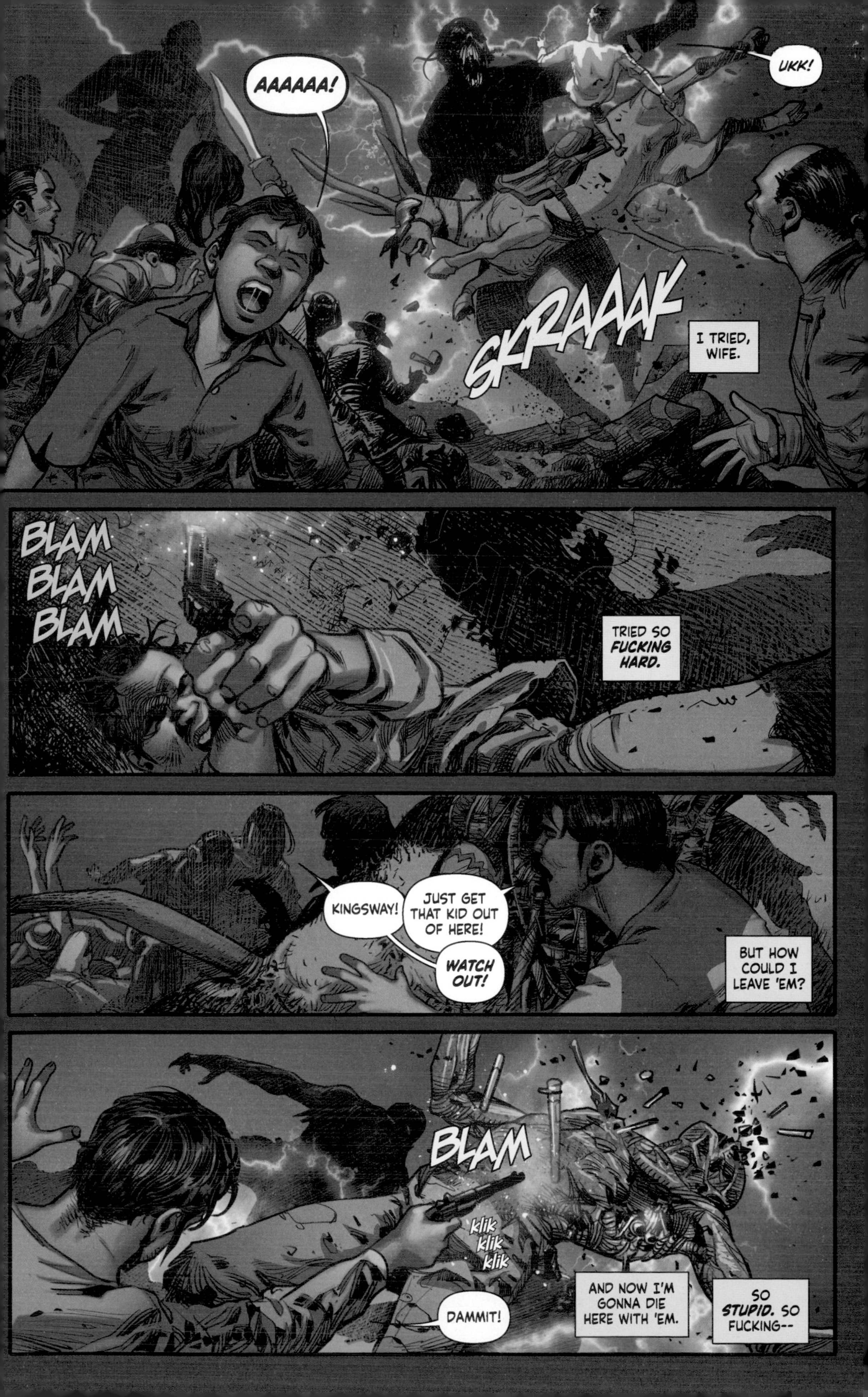
AAAAAA!
UKK!
SKRAAAK
I TRIED, WIFE.
BLAM BLAM BLAM
TRIED SO FUCKING HARD.
KINGSWAY!
JUST GET THAT KID OUT OF HERE!
WATCH OUT!
BUT HOW COULD I LEAVE 'EM?
BLAM
klik klik klik
DAMMIT!
AND NOW I'M GONNA DIE HERE WITH 'EM.
SO STUPID. SO FUCKING--

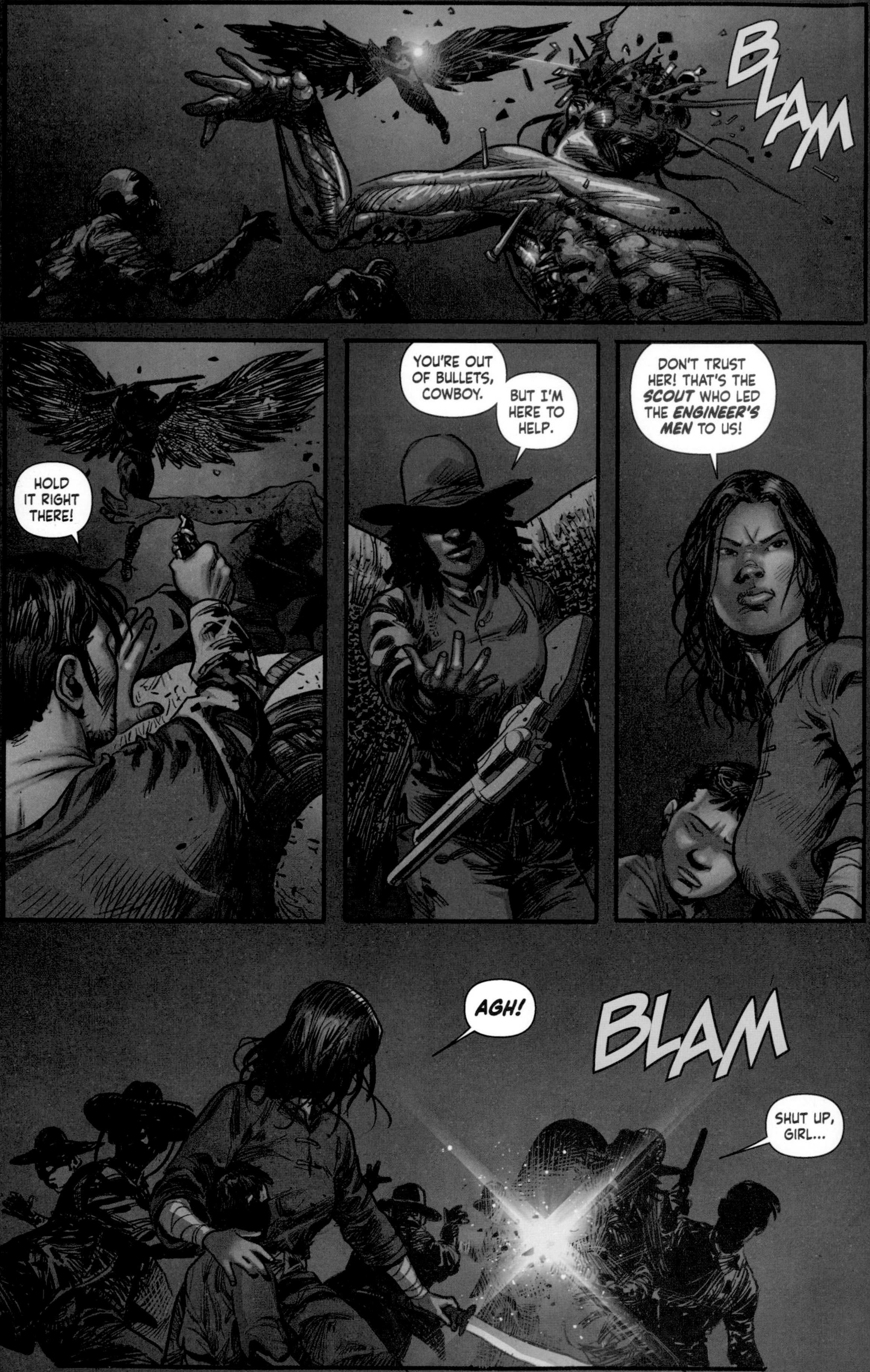
BLAM
HOLD IT RIGHT THERE!
YOU'RE OUT OF BULLETS, COWBOY.
BUT I'M HERE TO HELP.
DON'T TRUST HER! THAT'S THE *SCOUT* WHO LED THE *ENGINEER'S MEN* TO US!
AGH!
BLAM
SHUT UP, GIRL...

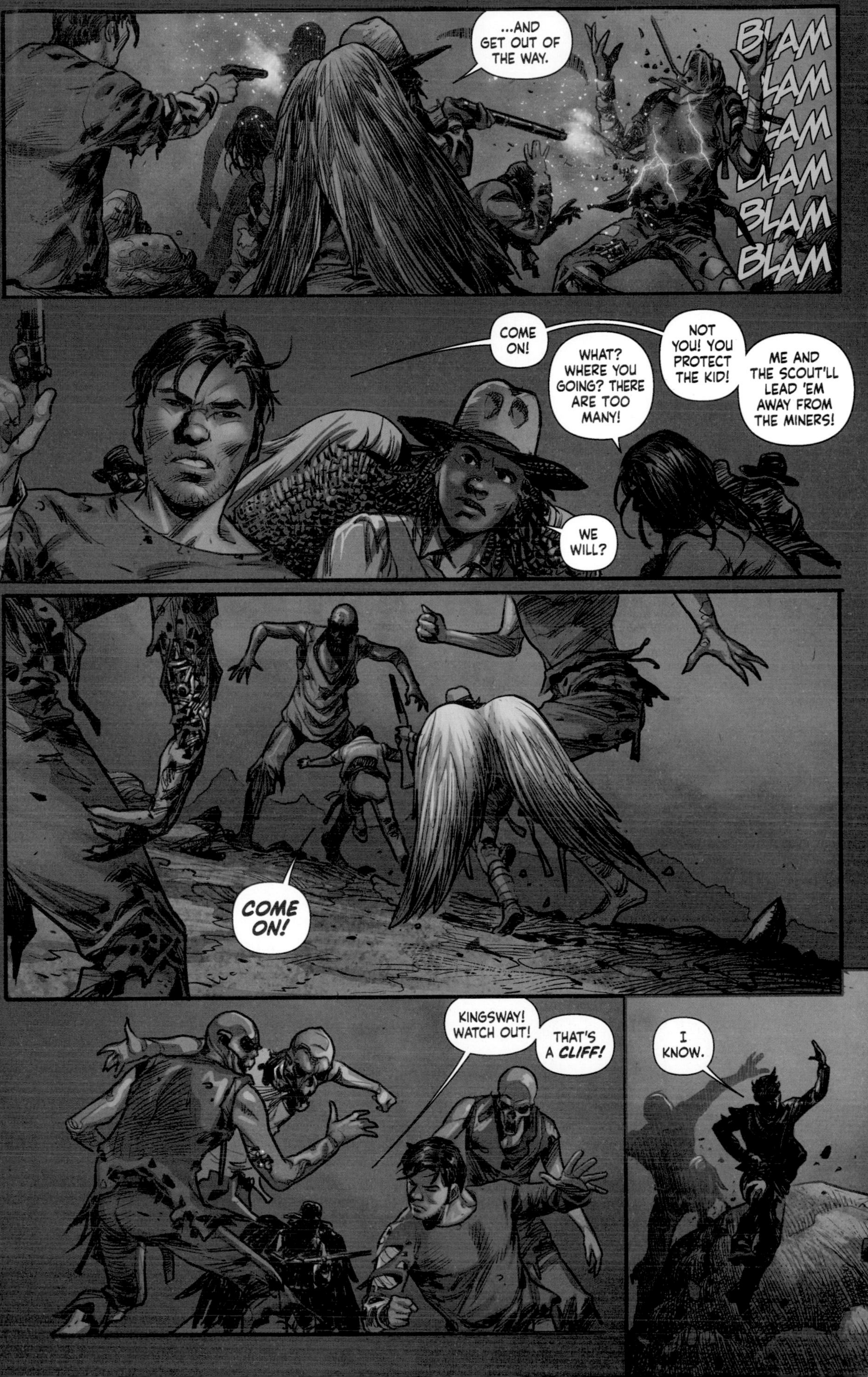
...AND GET OUT OF THE WAY.
BLAM BLAM BLAM BLAM BLAM BLAM
COME ON!
WHAT? WHERE YOU GOING? THERE ARE TOO MANY!
NOT YOU! YOU PROTECT THE KID!
ME AND THE SCOUT'LL LEAD 'EM AWAY FROM THE MINERS!
WE WILL?
COME ON!
KINGSWAY! WATCH OUT!
THAT'S A *CLIFF!*
I KNOW.

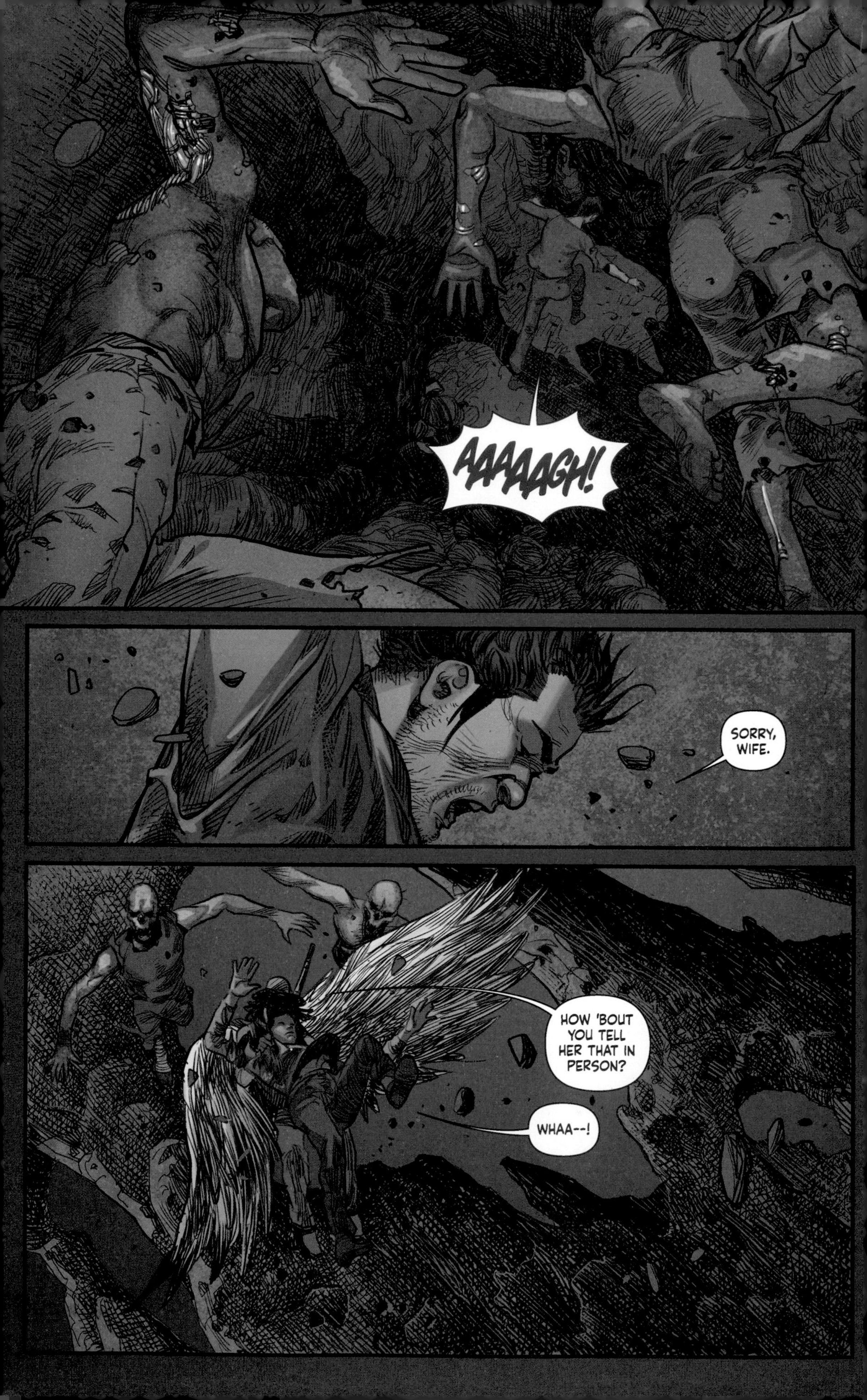
AAAAAAGH!
SORRY, WIFE.
HOW 'BOUT YOU TELL HER THAT IN PERSON?
WHAA--!

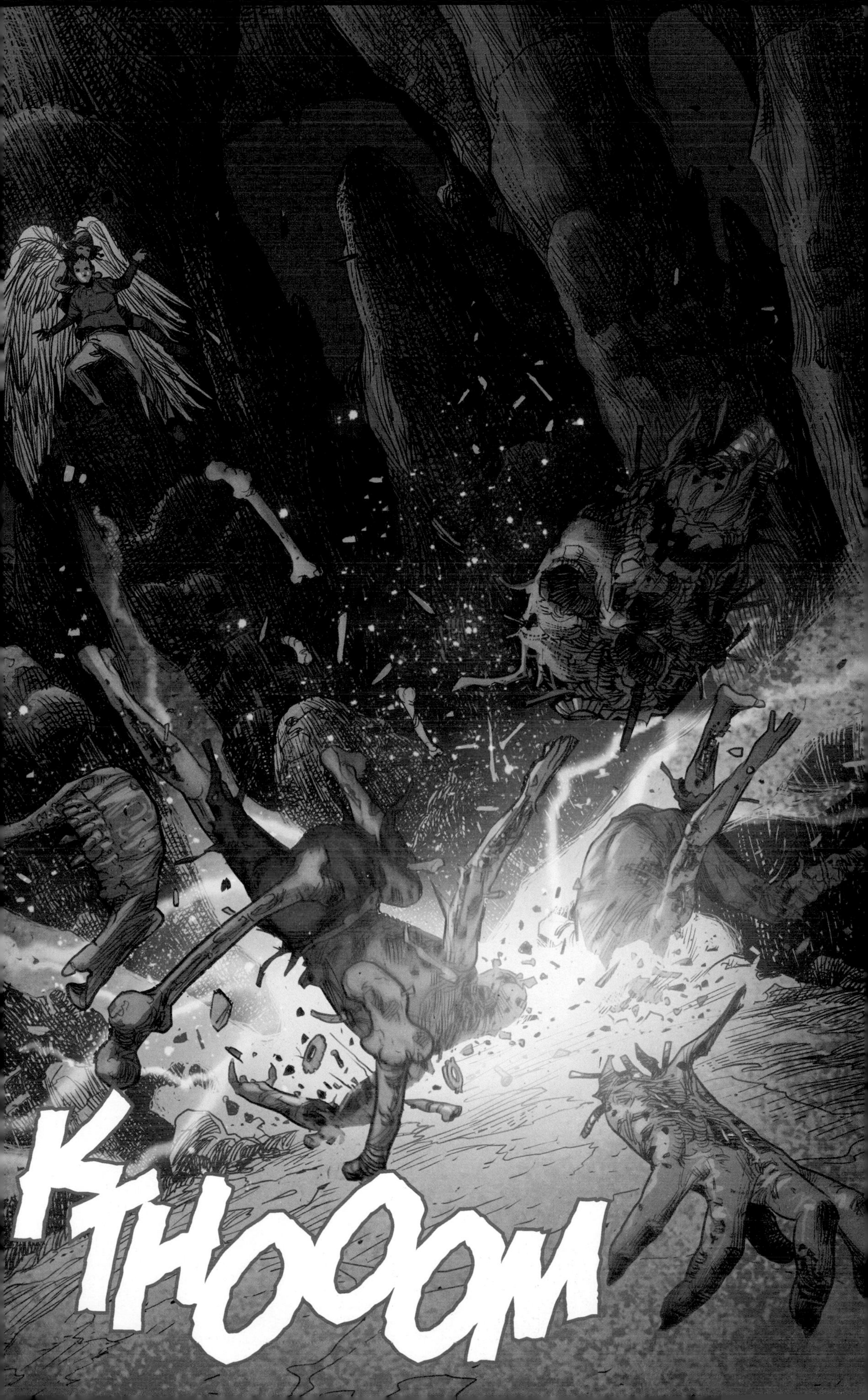
KTHOOOM

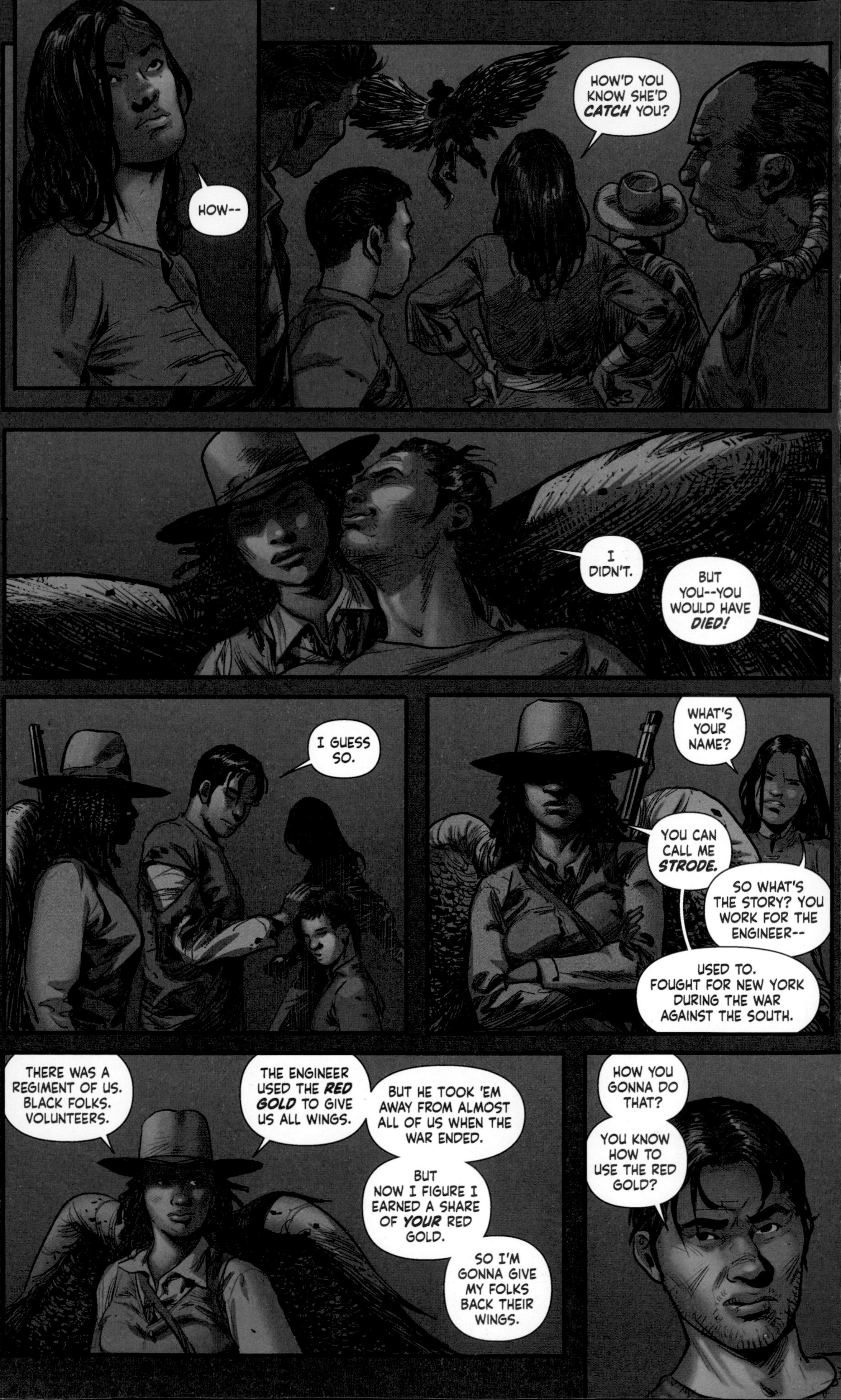

HOW--
HOW'D YOU KNOW SHE'D CATCH YOU?
I DIDN'T.
BUT YOU--YOU WOULD HAVE DIED!
I GUESS SO.
WHAT'S YOUR NAME?
YOU CAN CALL ME STRODE.
SO WHAT'S THE STORY? YOU WORK FOR THE ENGINEER--
USED TO. FOUGHT FOR NEW YORK DURING THE WAR AGAINST THE SOUTH.
THERE WAS A REGIMENT OF US. BLACK FOLKS. VOLUNTEERS.
THE ENGINEER USED THE RED GOLD TO GIVE US ALL WINGS.
BUT HE TOOK 'EM AWAY FROM ALMOST ALL OF US WHEN THE WAR ENDED.
BUT NOW I FIGURE I EARNED A SHARE OF YOUR RED GOLD.
SO I'M GONNA GIVE MY FOLKS BACK THEIR WINGS.
HOW YOU GONNA DO THAT?
YOU KNOW HOW TO USE THE RED GOLD?

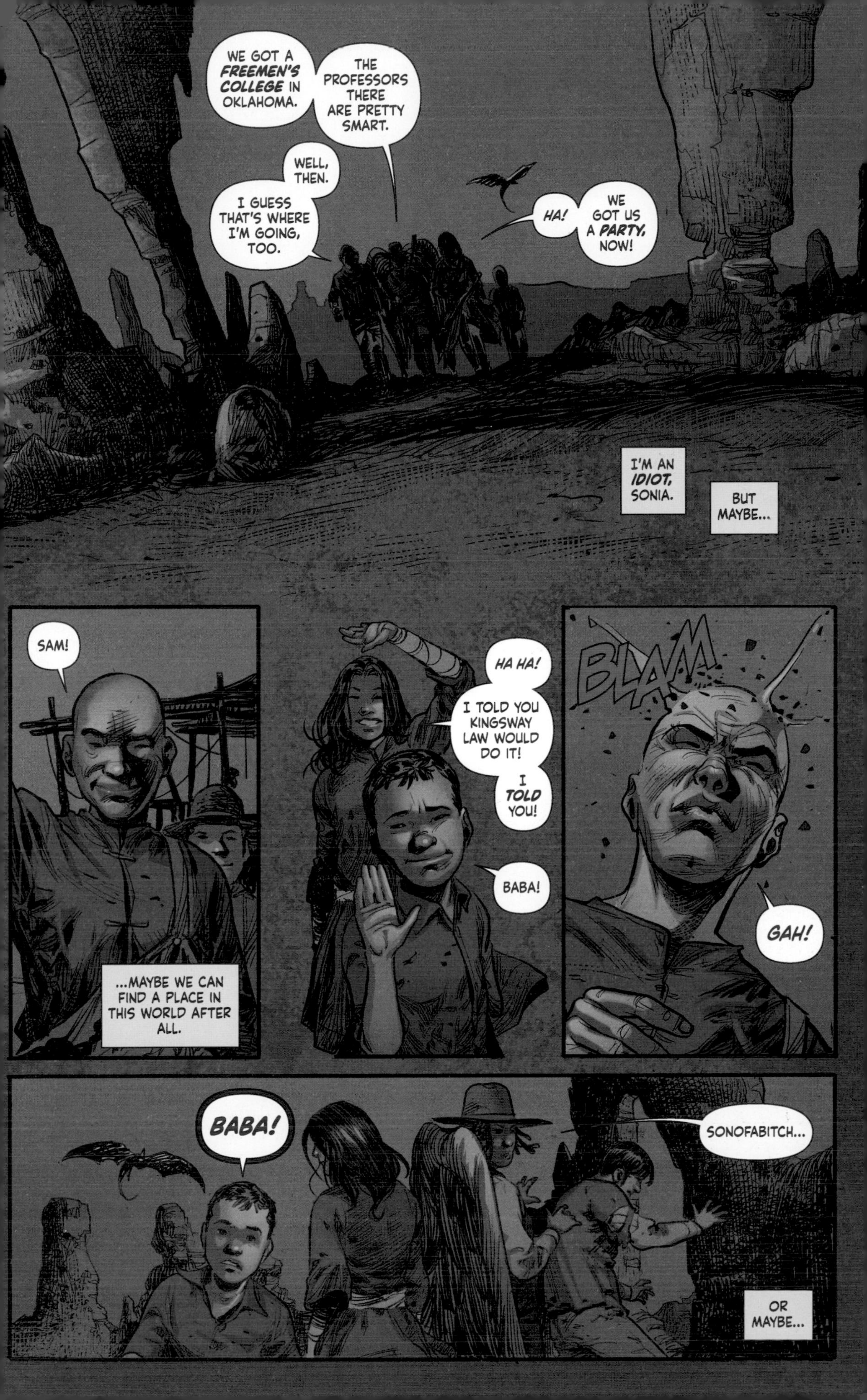
WE GOT A FREEMEN'S COLLEGE IN OKLAHOMA.
THE PROFESSORS THERE ARE PRETTY SMART.
WELL, THEN.
I GUESS THAT'S WHERE I'M GOING, TOO.
HA!
WE GOT US A PARTY, NOW!
I'M AN IDIOT, SONIA.
BUT MAYBE...
SAM!
...MAYBE WE CAN FIND A PLACE IN THIS WORLD AFTER ALL.
HA HA!
I TOLD YOU KINGSWAY LAW WOULD DO IT!
I TOLD YOU!
BABA!
BLAM
GAH!
BABA!
SONOFABITCH...
OR MAYBE...

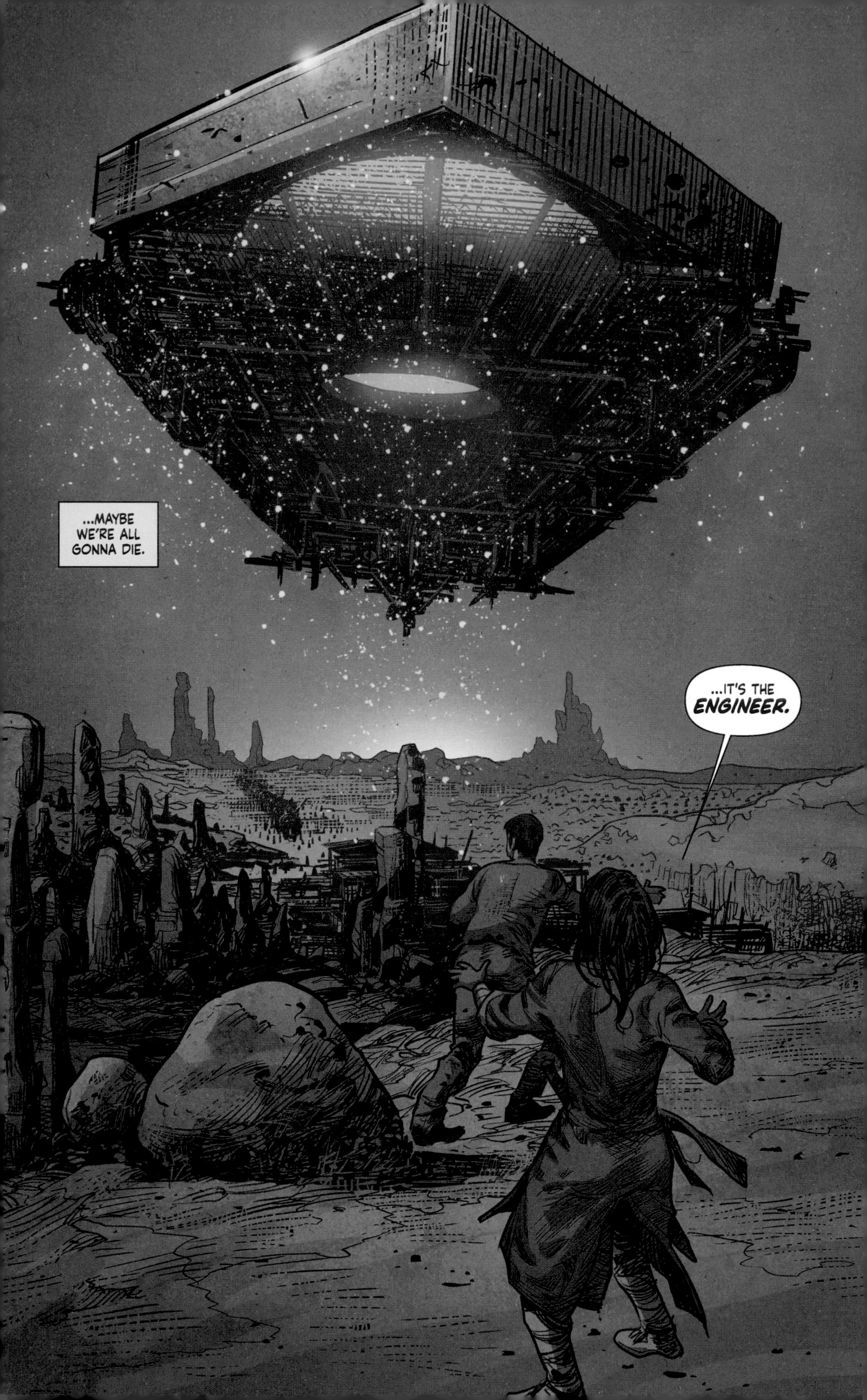
...MAYBE WE'RE ALL GONNA DIE.
...IT'S THE ENGINEER.

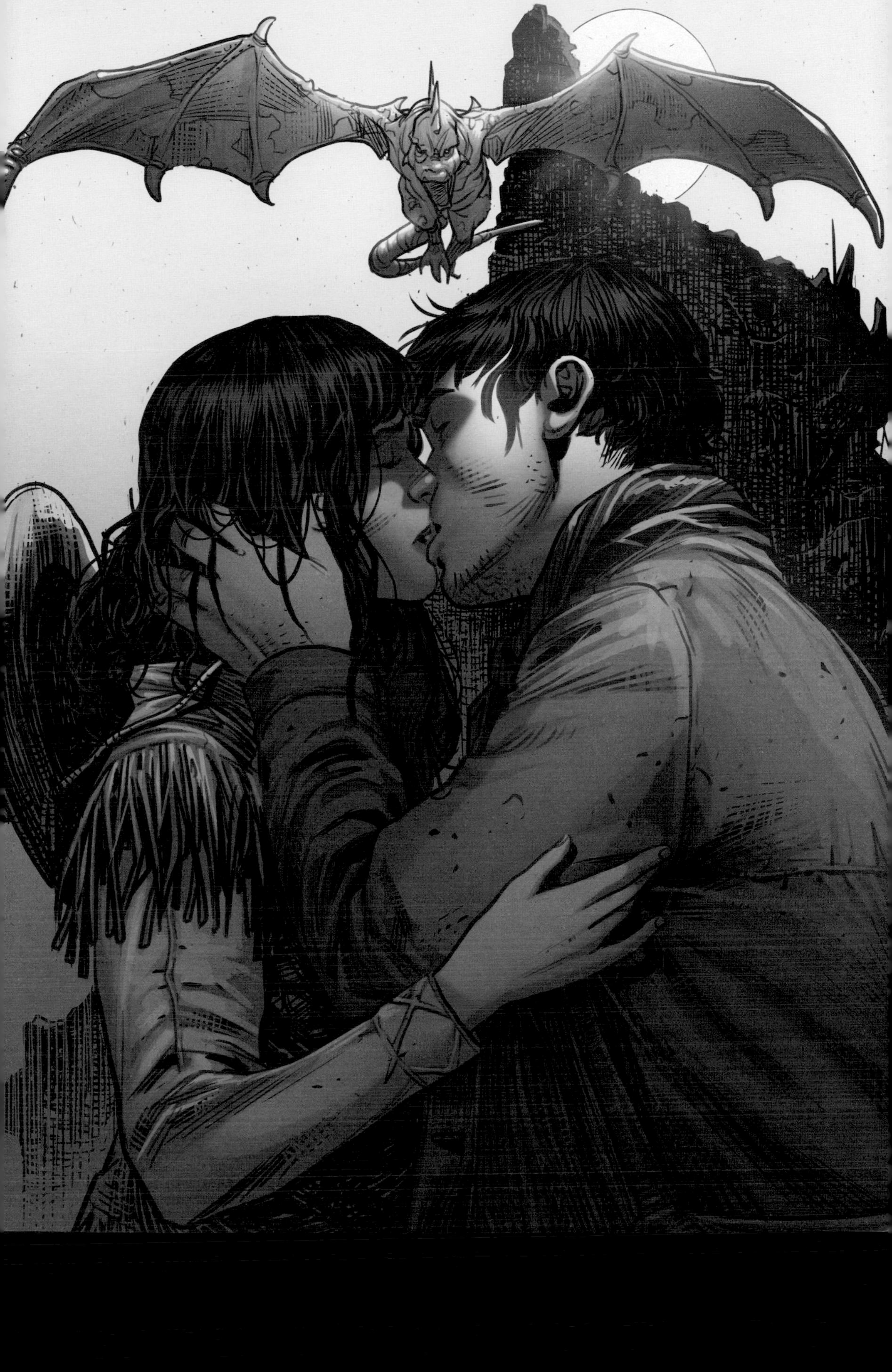

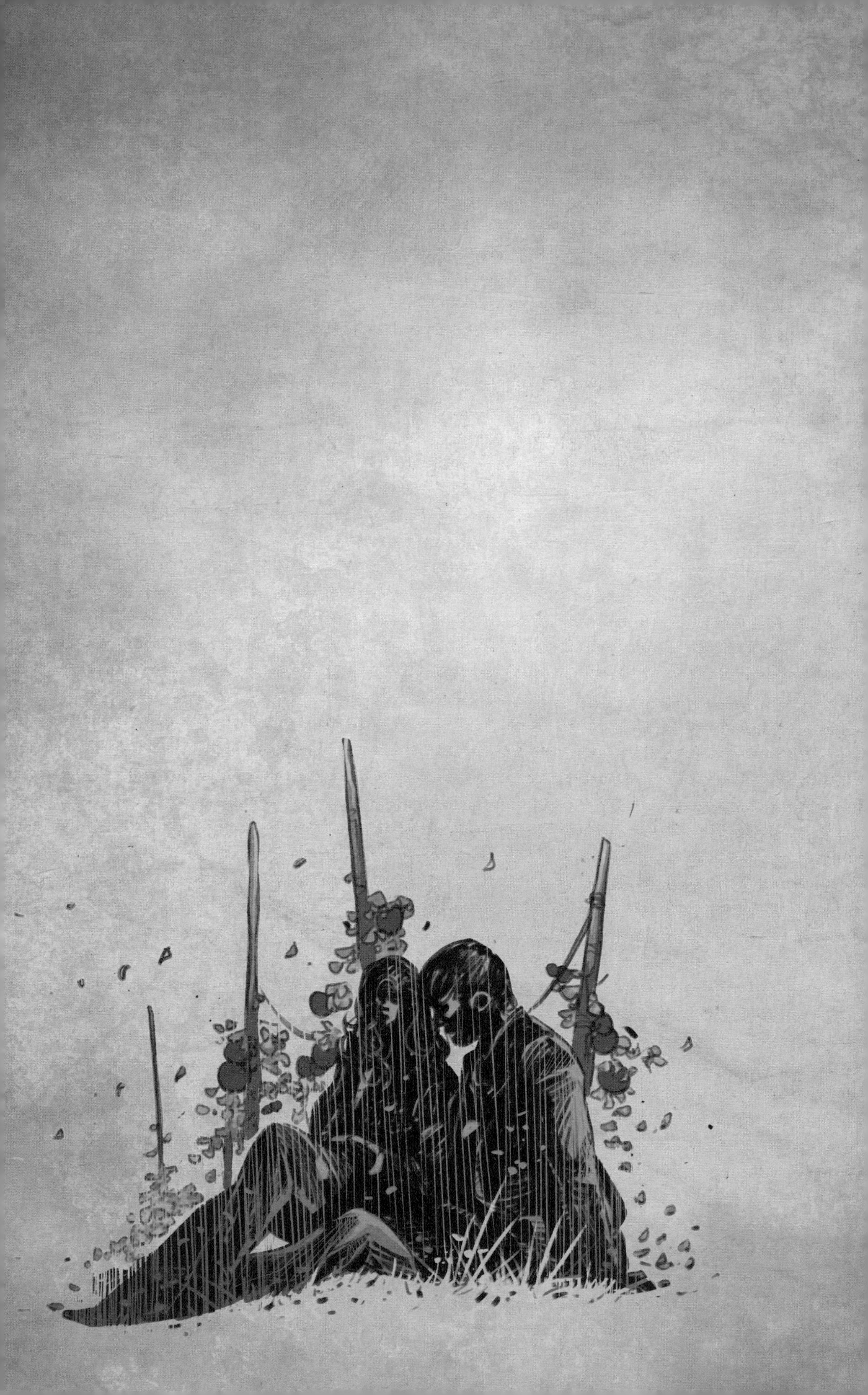

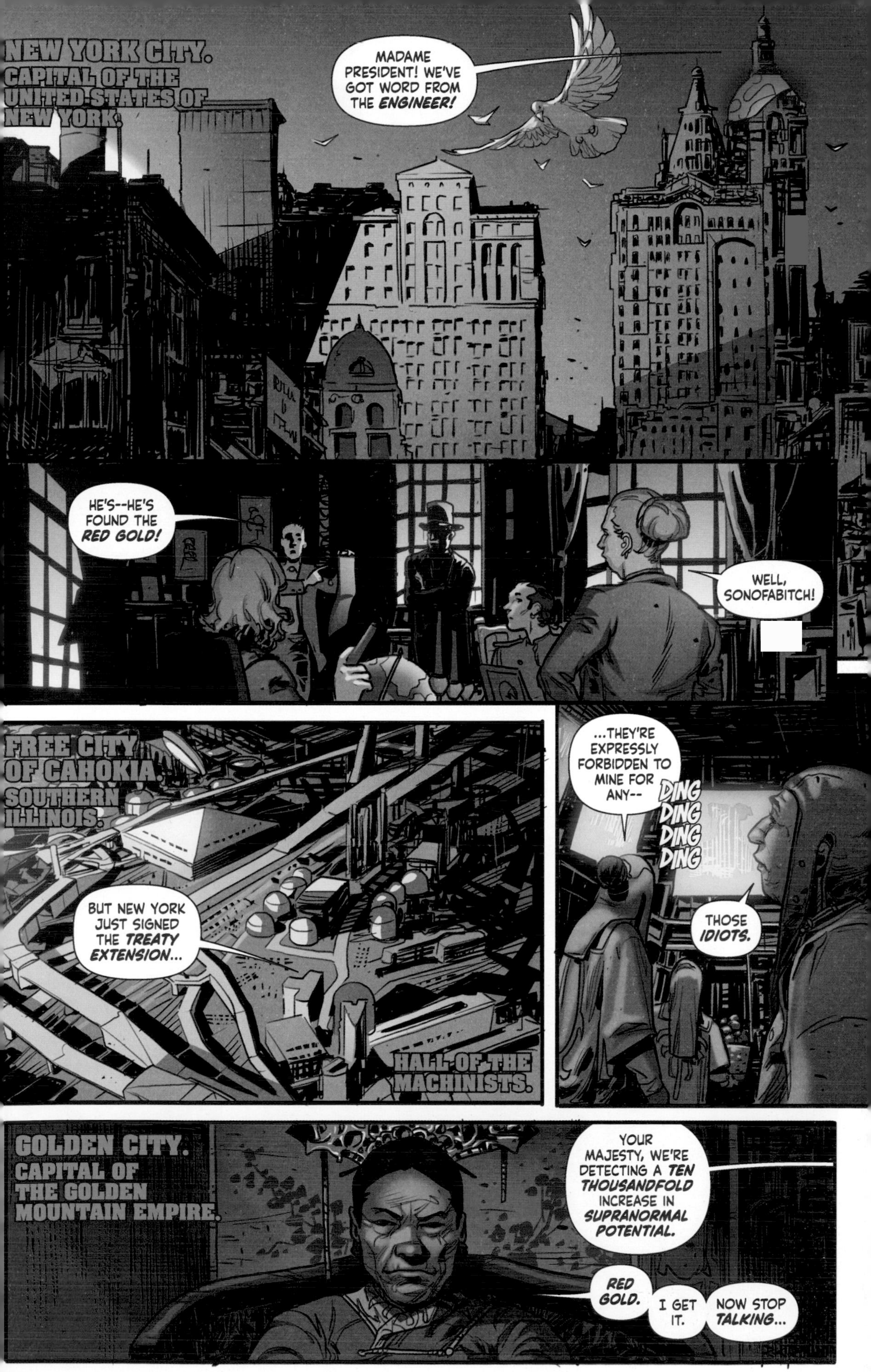
NEW YORK CITY.
CAPITAL OF THE UNITED STATES OF NEW YORK.
MADAME PRESIDENT! WE'VE GOT WORD FROM THE ENGINEER!
HE'S--HE'S FOUND THE RED GOLD!
WELL, SONOFABITCH!
FREE CITY OF CAHOKIA.
SOUTHERN ILLINOIS.
BUT NEW YORK JUST SIGNED THE TREATY EXTENSION...
HALL OF THE MACHINISTS.
...THEY'RE EXPRESSLY FORBIDDEN TO MINE FOR ANY--
DING DING DING DING
THOSE IDIOTS.
GOLDEN CITY.
CAPITAL OF THE GOLDEN MOUNTAIN EMPIRE.
YOUR MAJESTY, WE'RE DETECTING A TEN THOUSANDFOLD INCREASE IN SUPRANORMAL POTENTIAL.
RED GOLD.
I GET IT.
NOW STOP TALKING...

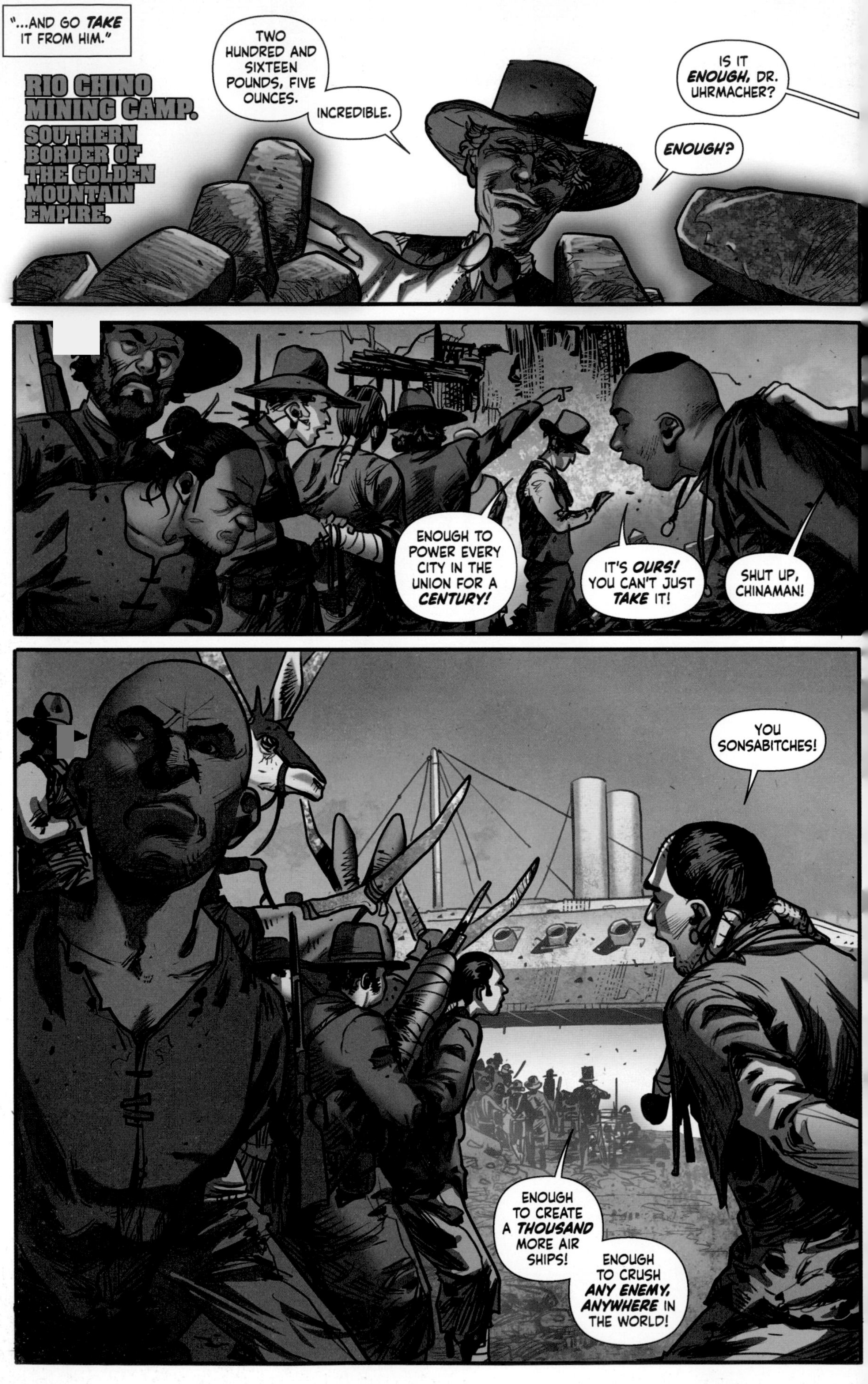
"...AND GO TAKE IT FROM HIM."
RIO CHINO MINING CAMP.
SOUTHERN BORDER OF THE GOLDEN MOUNTAIN EMPIRE.
TWO HUNDRED AND SIXTEEN POUNDS, FIVE OUNCES.
INCREDIBLE.
IS IT ENOUGH, DR. UHRMACHER?
ENOUGH?
ENOUGH TO POWER EVERY CITY IN THE UNION FOR A CENTURY!
IT'S OURS! YOU CAN'T JUST TAKE IT!
SHUT UP, CHINAMAN!
YOU SONSABITCHES!
ENOUGH TO CREATE A THOUSAND MORE AIR SHIPS!
ENOUGH TO CRUSH ANY ENEMY, ANYWHERE IN THE WORLD!

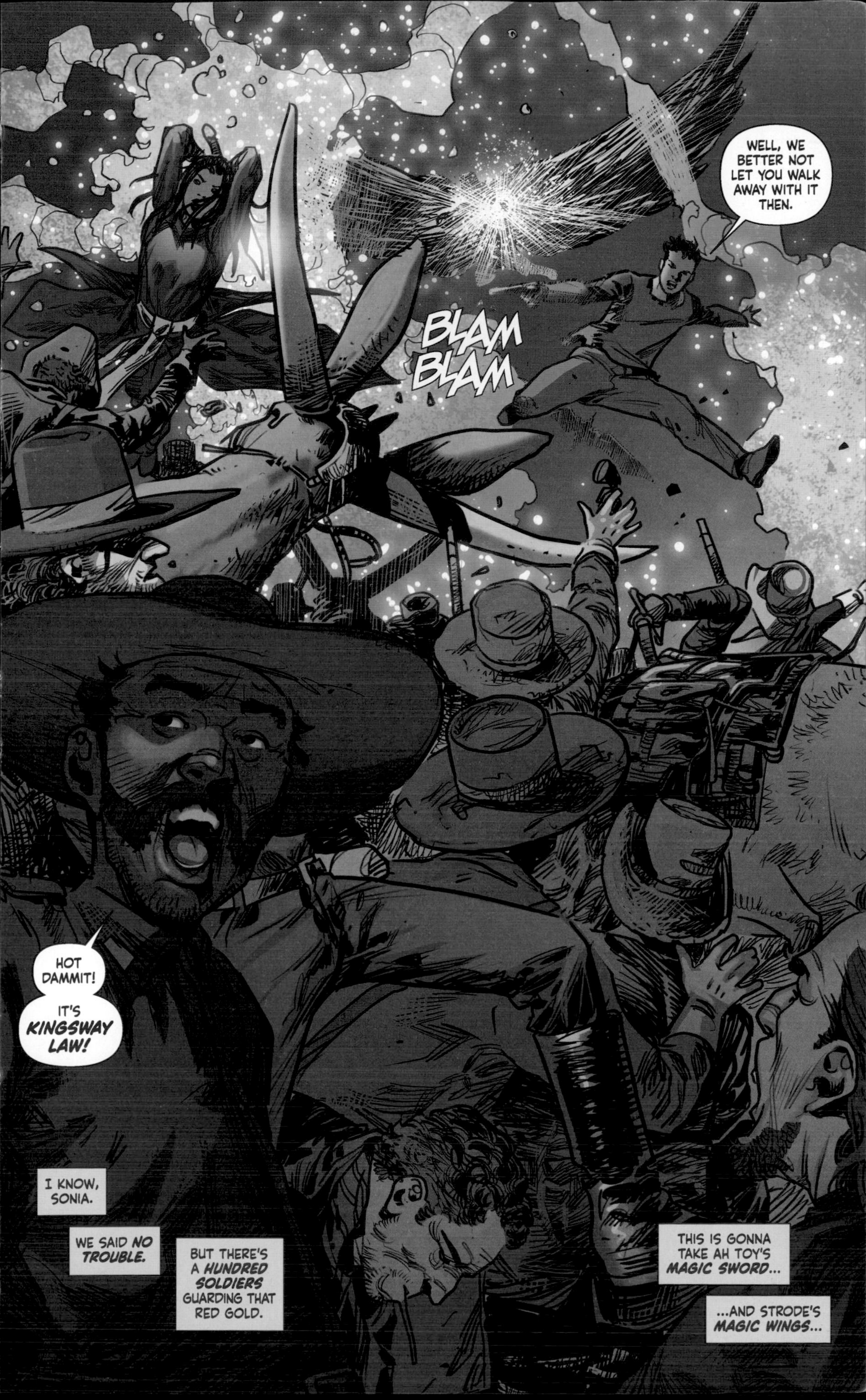
WELL, WE BETTER NOT LET YOU WALK AWAY WITH IT THEN.
BLAM BLAM
HOT DAMMIT!
IT'S *KINGSWAY LAW!*
I KNOW, SONIA.
WE SAID *NO TROUBLE.*
BUT THERE'S A *HUNDRED SOLDIERS* GUARDING THAT RED GOLD.
THIS IS GONNA TAKE AH TOY'S *MAGIC SWORD...*
...AND STRODE'S *MAGIC WINGS...*

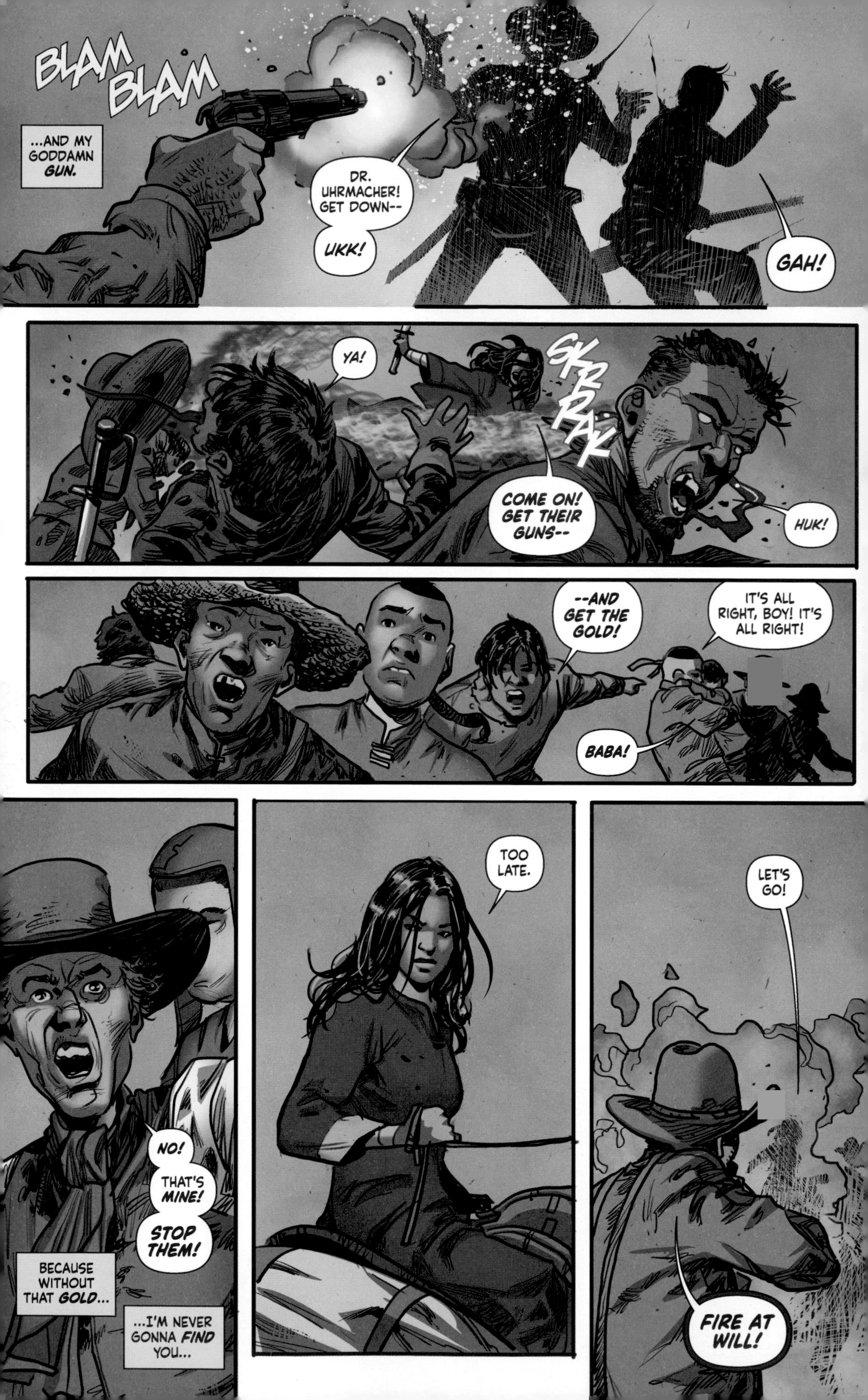
BLAM BLAM
...AND MY GODDAMN GUN.
DR. UHRMACHER! GET DOWN--
UKK!
GAH!
YA!
SKRRAK
COME ON! GET THEIR GUNS--
HUK!
--AND GET THE GOLD!
IT'S ALL RIGHT, BOY! IT'S ALL RIGHT!
BABA!
NO!
THAT'S MINE!
STOP THEM!
BECAUSE WITHOUT THAT GOLD...
...I'M NEVER GONNA FIND YOU...
TOO LATE.
LET'S GO!
FIRE AT WILL!

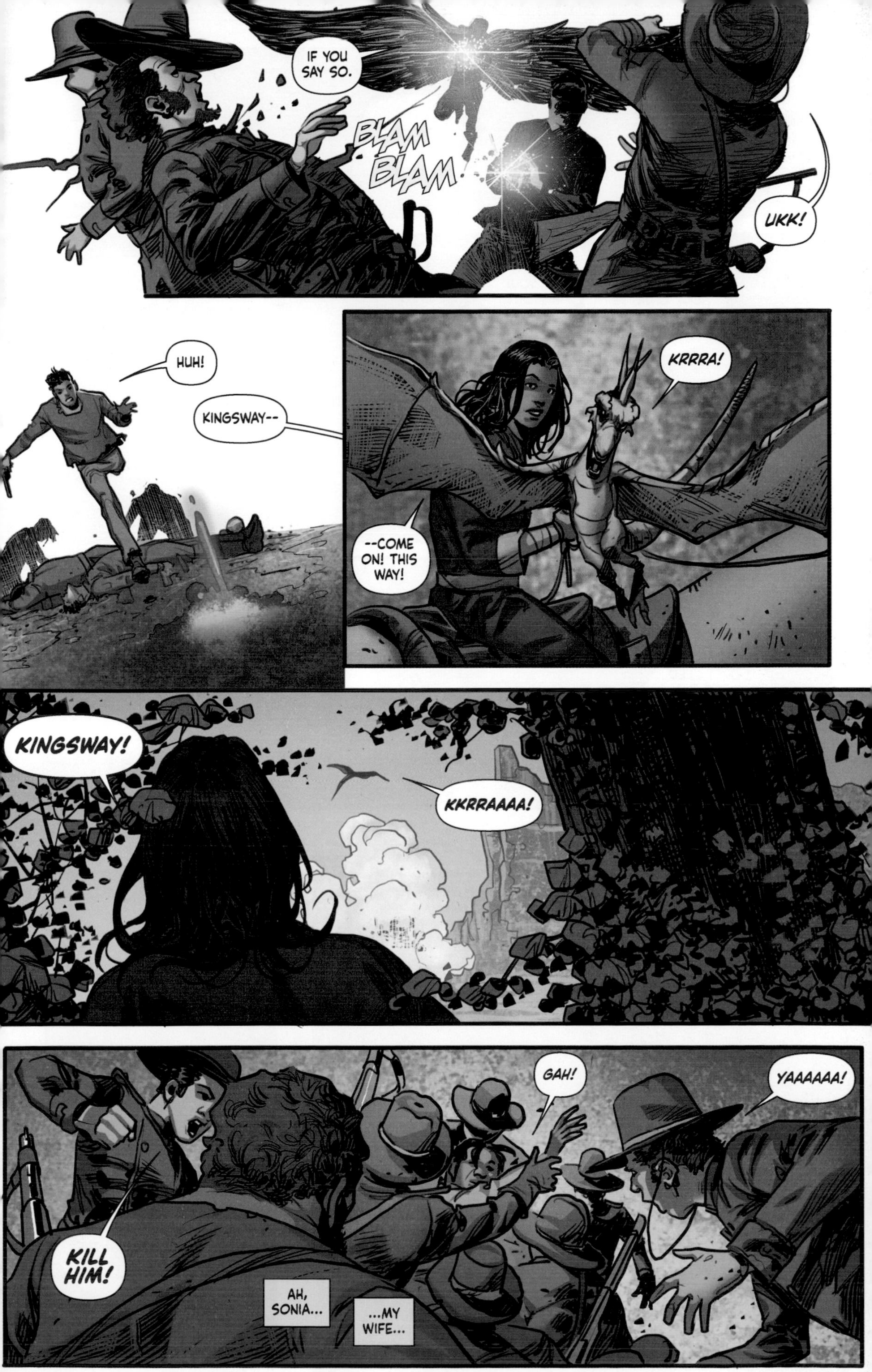
IF YOU SAY SO.
BLAM BLAM
UKK!
HUH!
KINGSWAY--
KRRRA!
--COME ON! THIS WAY!
KINGSWAY!
KKRRAAAA!
GAH!
YAAAAAA!
KILL HIM!
AH, SONIA...
...MY WIFE...

...I'M SORRY.

nnngh...

AH. YOU'RE AWAKE.

KINGSWAY LAW, CORRECT?

I'VE HAD MY *LIBRARIANS* IN *BROOKLYN* SEARCH OUR *CHINESE NEWSSHEET* ARCHIVE...

...SO I'VE GOT A LITTLE OF YOUR HISTORY.

GOLDEN CITY *WAR HERO* TURNED OUTLAW...

...*SCARRED* BY THE HORRORS OF *BATTLE*...

...SELF-EXILED TO THE *WILD.*

IF ALL THIS IS *TRUE,* I THINK WE MIGHT BE ABLE TO DO SOME *BUSINESS.*

I JUST NEED THE *RED GOLD* YOUR FRIENDS STOLE.

THEN I CAN STOP THE WARS THAT RUINED YOUR LIFE.

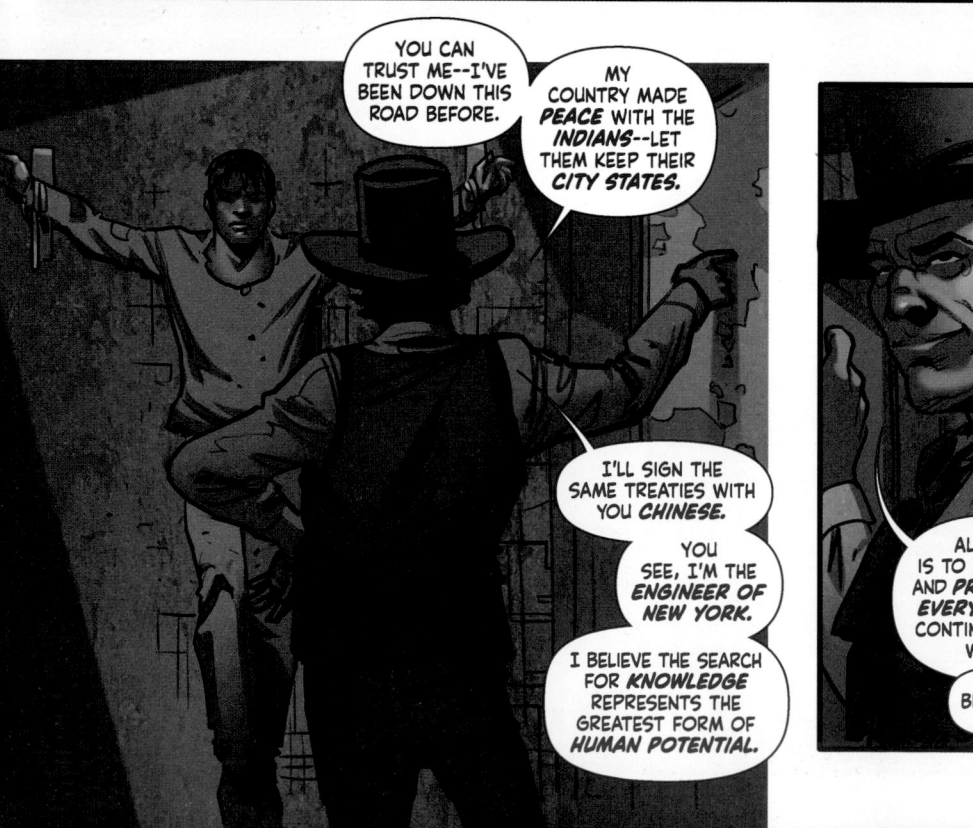

YOU CAN TRUST ME--I'VE BEEN DOWN THIS ROAD BEFORE.

MY COUNTRY MADE *PEACE* WITH THE *INDIANS*--LET THEM KEEP THEIR *CITY STATES.*

I'LL SIGN THE SAME TREATIES WITH YOU *CHINESE.*

YOU SEE, I'M THE *ENGINEER OF NEW YORK.*

I BELIEVE THE SEARCH FOR *KNOWLEDGE* REPRESENTS THE GREATEST FORM OF *HUMAN POTENTIAL.*

ALL I WANT IS TO BRING *PEACE* AND *PROSPERITY* TO *EVERYONE* ON THE CONTINENT SO THAT WE ALL--

BULLSHIT.

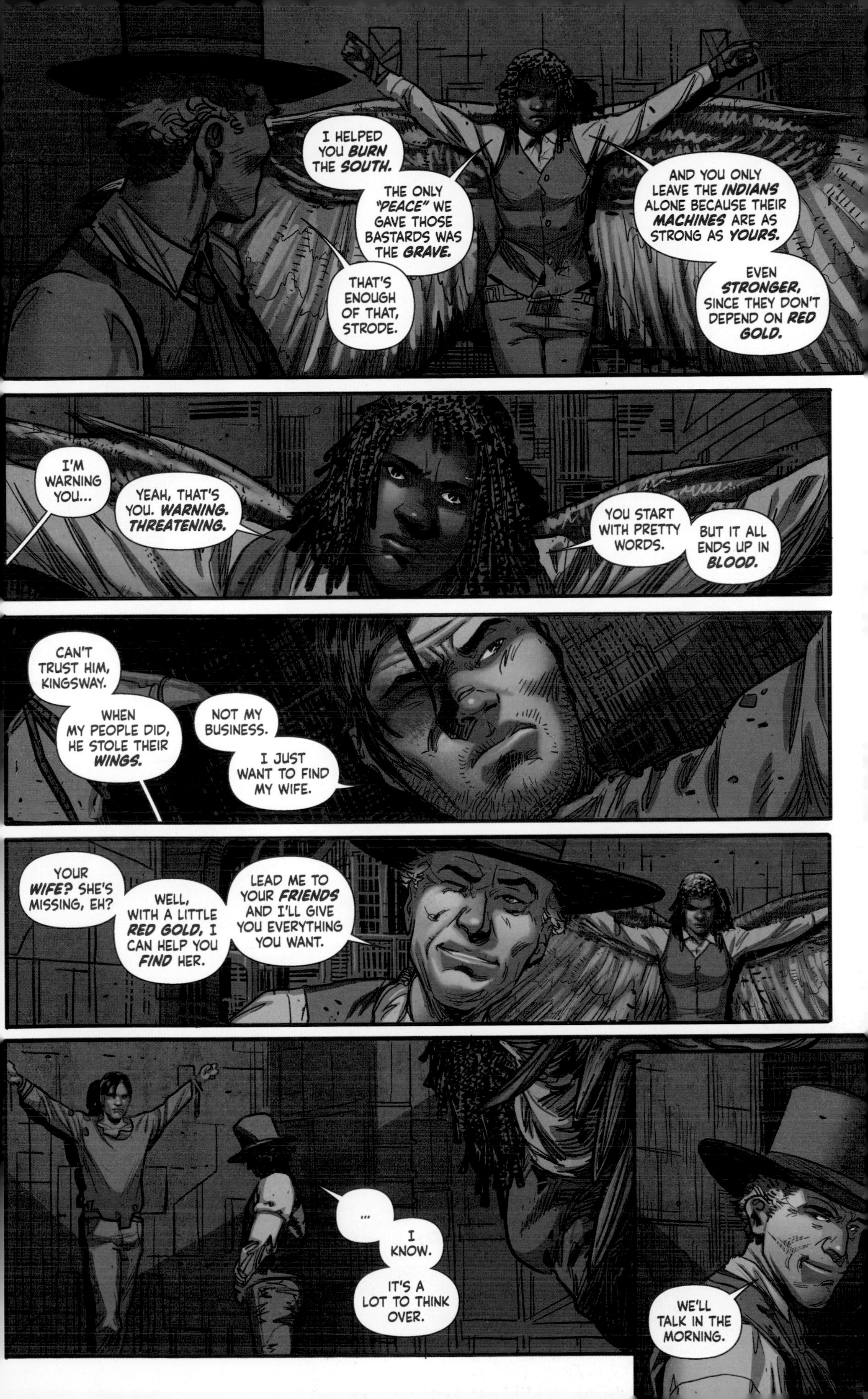
I HELPED YOU BURN THE SOUTH.
THE ONLY "PEACE" WE GAVE THOSE BASTARDS WAS THE GRAVE.
THAT'S ENOUGH OF THAT, STRODE.
AND YOU ONLY LEAVE THE INDIANS ALONE BECAUSE THEIR MACHINES ARE AS STRONG AS YOURS.
EVEN STRONGER, SINCE THEY DON'T DEPEND ON RED GOLD.
I'M WARNING YOU...
YEAH, THAT'S YOU. WARNING. THREATENING.
YOU START WITH PRETTY WORDS.
BUT IT ALL ENDS UP IN BLOOD.
CAN'T TRUST HIM, KINGSWAY.
WHEN MY PEOPLE DID, HE STOLE THEIR WINGS.
NOT MY BUSINESS.
I JUST WANT TO FIND MY WIFE.
YOUR WIFE? SHE'S MISSING, EH?
WELL, WITH A LITTLE RED GOLD, I CAN HELP YOU FIND HER.
LEAD ME TO YOUR FRIENDS AND I'LL GIVE YOU EVERYTHING YOU WANT.
...
I KNOW.
IT'S A LOT TO THINK OVER.
WE'LL TALK IN THE MORNING.

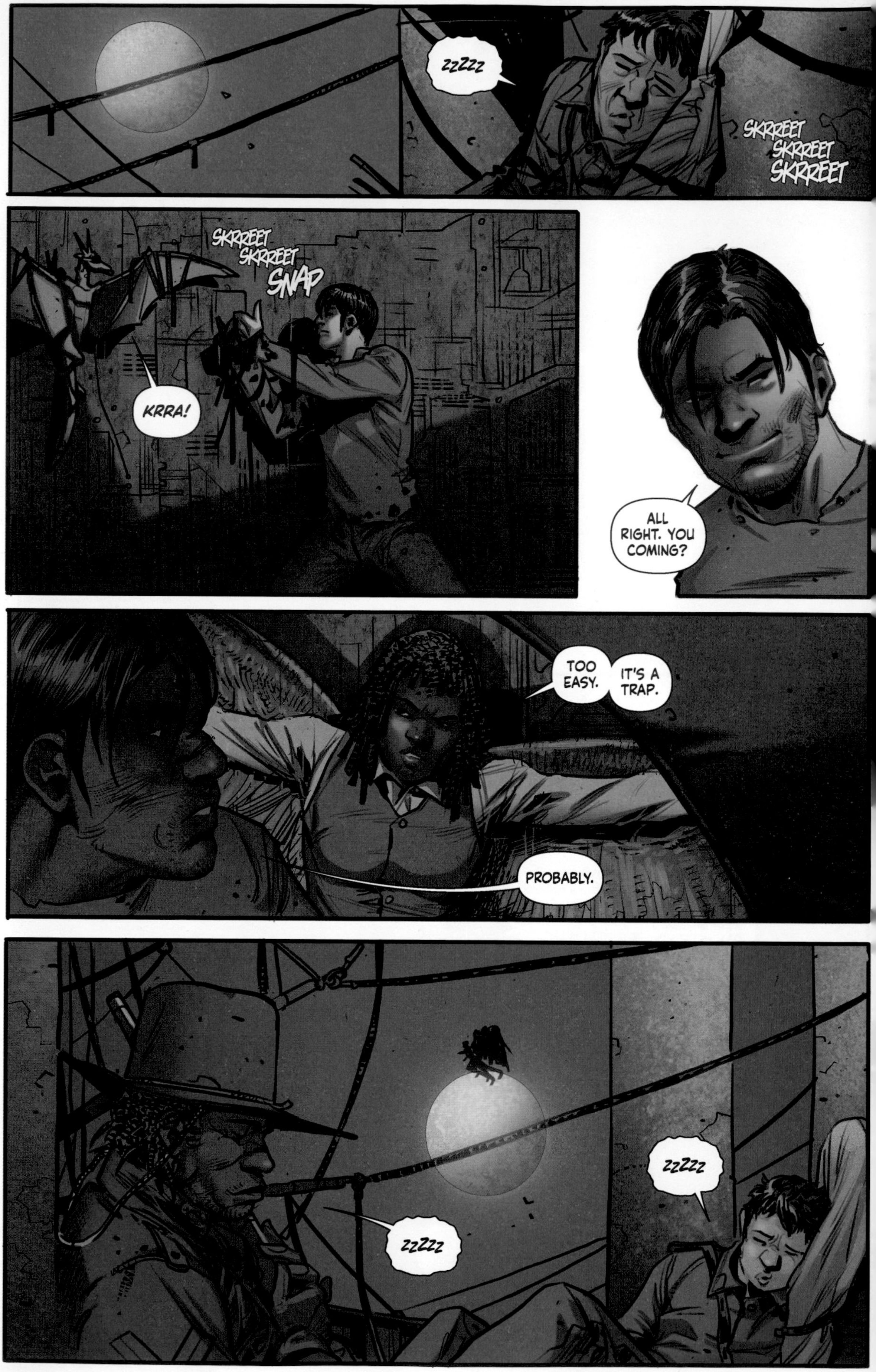
zzZzz
SKRREET SKRREET SKRREET
SKRREET SKRREET SNAP
KRRA!
ALL RIGHT. YOU COMING?
TOO EASY.
IT'S A TRAP.
PROBABLY.
zzZzz
zzZzz

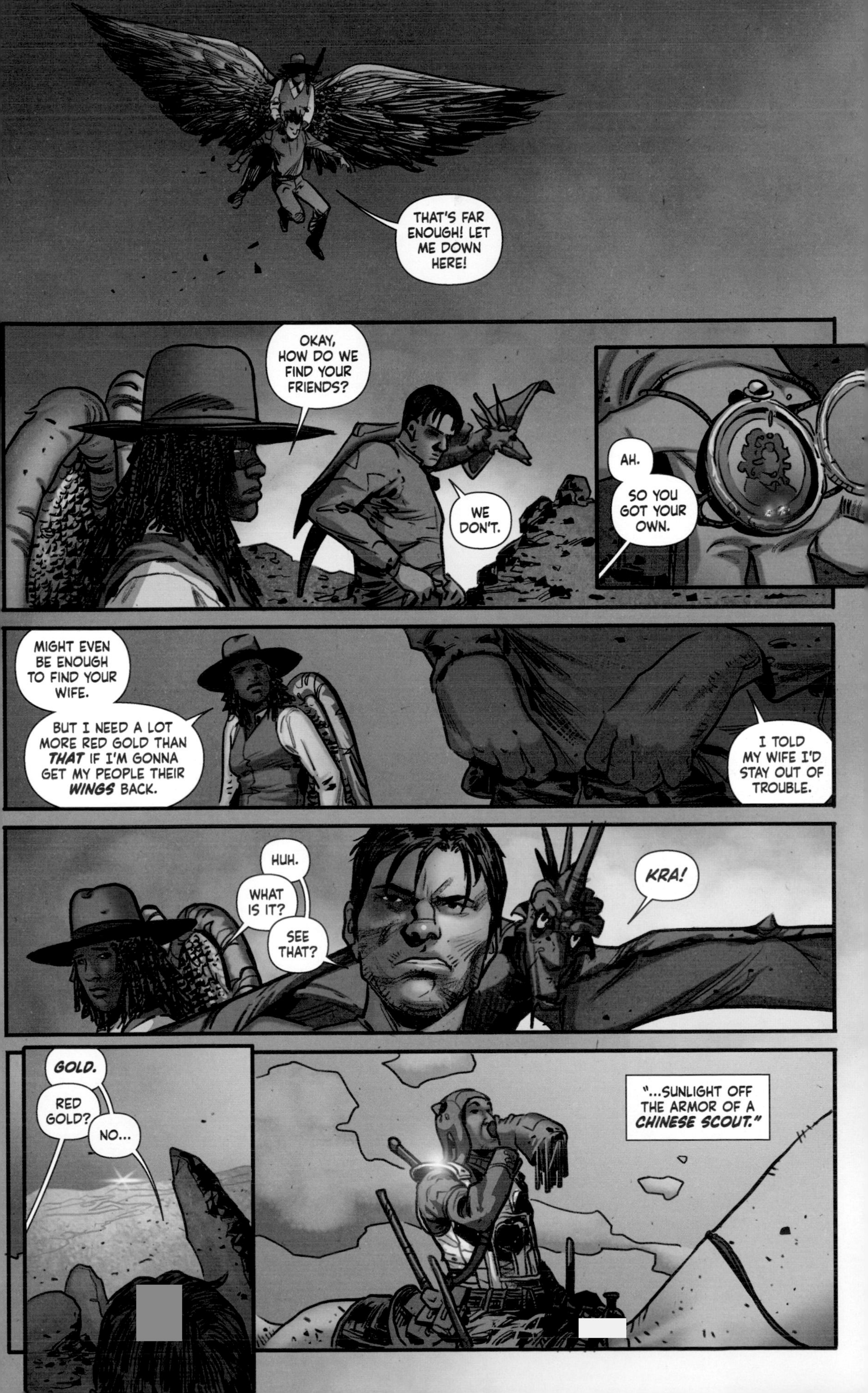
THAT'S FAR ENOUGH! LET ME DOWN HERE!
OKAY, HOW DO WE FIND YOUR FRIENDS?
WE DON'T.
AH.
SO YOU GOT YOUR OWN.
MIGHT EVEN BE ENOUGH TO FIND YOUR WIFE.
BUT I NEED A LOT MORE RED GOLD THAN *THAT* IF I'M GONNA GET MY PEOPLE THEIR *WINGS* BACK.
I TOLD MY WIFE I'D STAY OUT OF TROUBLE.
HUH.
WHAT IS IT?
SEE THAT?
KRA!
GOLD.
RED GOLD?
NO...
"...SUNLIGHT OFF THE ARMOR OF A *CHINESE SCOUT.*"

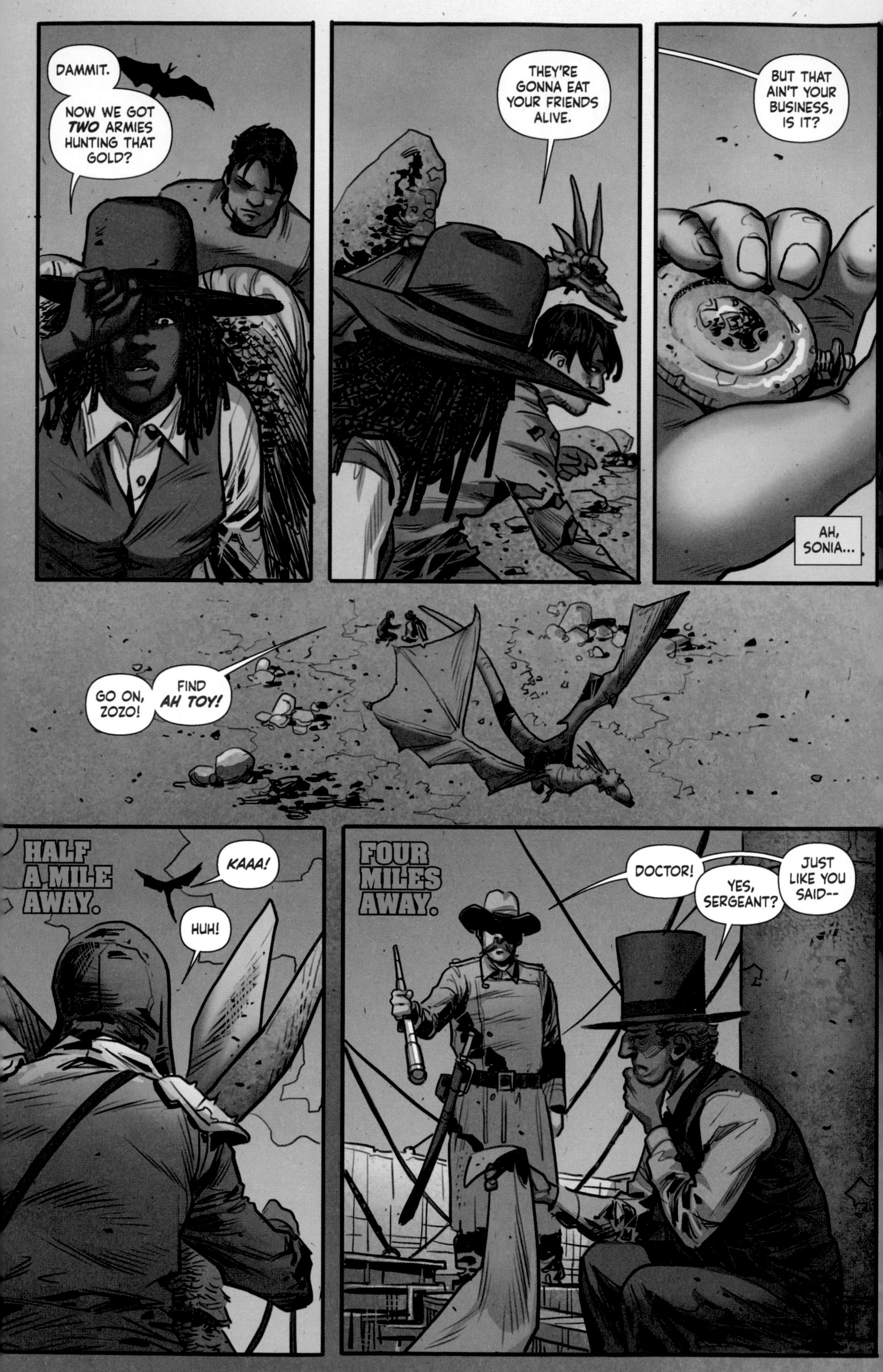
DAMMIT.
NOW WE GOT TWO ARMIES HUNTING THAT GOLD?
THEY'RE GONNA EAT YOUR FRIENDS ALIVE.
BUT THAT AIN'T YOUR BUSINESS, IS IT?
AH, SONIA...
GO ON, ZOZO!
FIND AH TOY!
HALF A MILE AWAY.
KAAA!
HUH!
FOUR MILES AWAY.
DOCTOR!
YES, SERGEANT?
JUST LIKE YOU SAID--

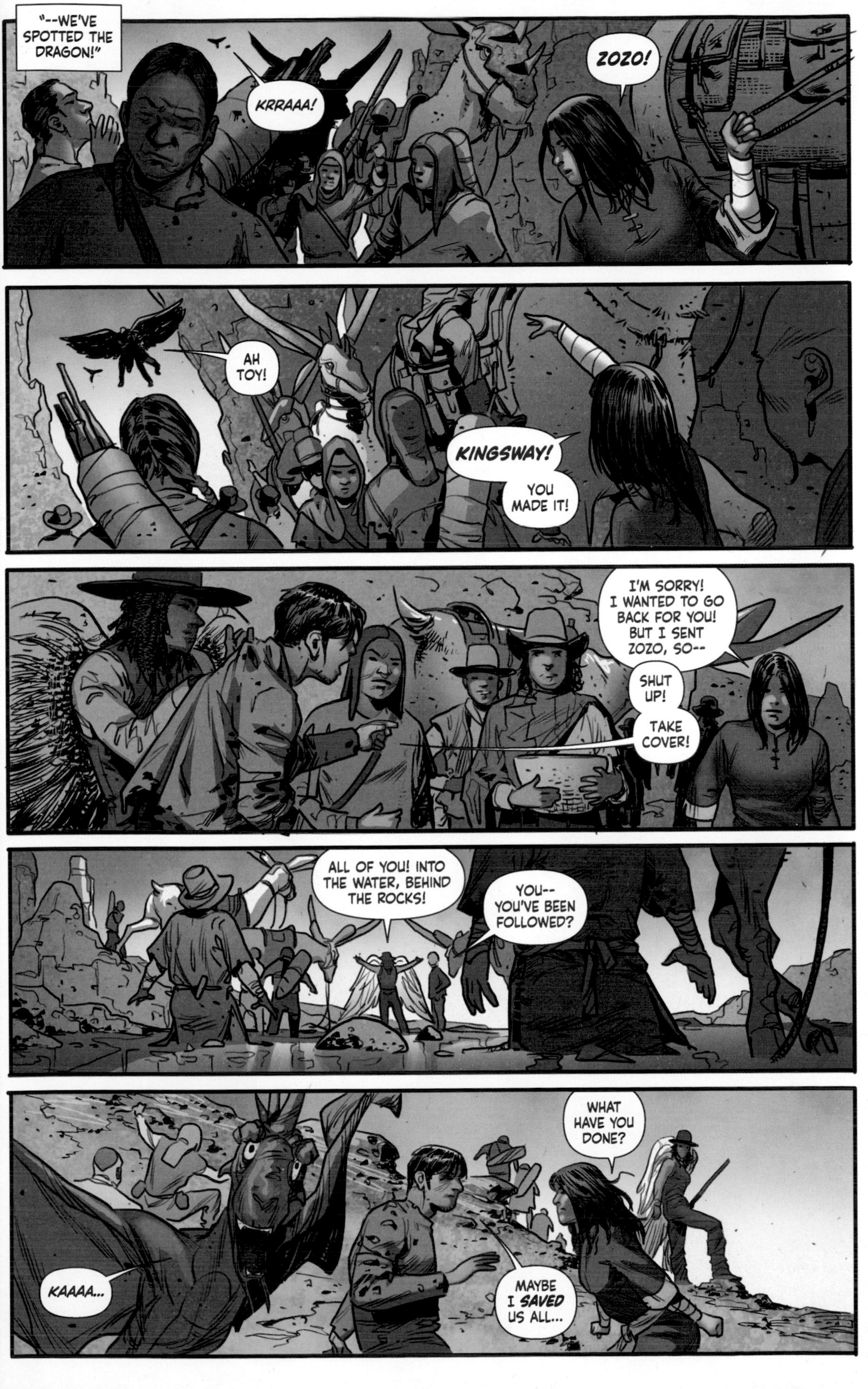
"--WE'VE SPOTTED THE DRAGON!"
KRRAAA!
ZOZO!
AH TOY!
KINGSWAY!
YOU MADE IT!
I'M SORRY! I WANTED TO GO BACK FOR YOU! BUT I SENT ZOZO, SO--
SHUT UP!
TAKE COVER!
ALL OF YOU! INTO THE WATER, BEHIND THE ROCKS!
YOU-- YOU'VE BEEN FOLLOWED?
WHAT HAVE YOU DONE?
KAAAA...
MAYBE I SAVED US ALL...

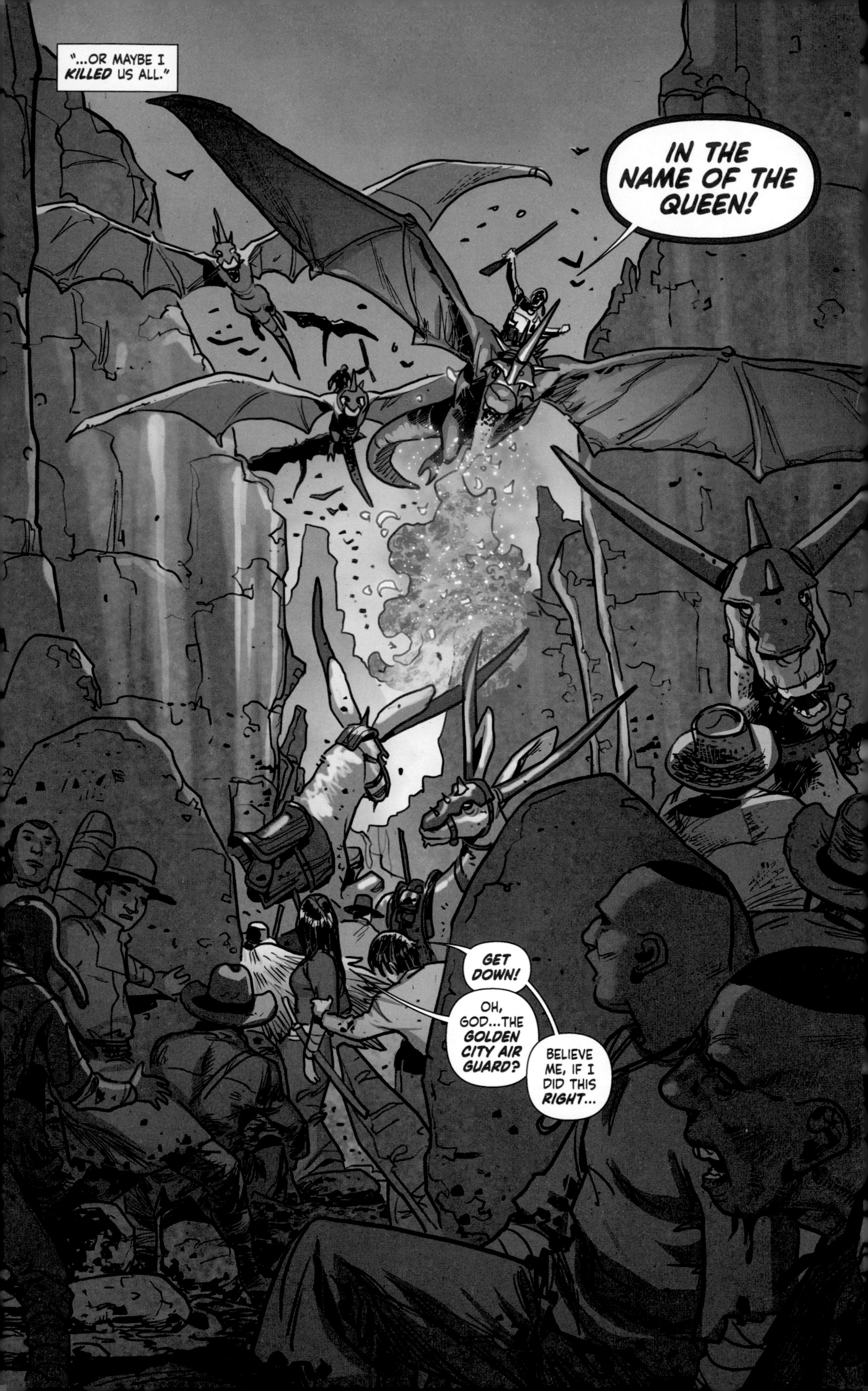
"...OR MAYBE I *KILLED* US ALL."
IN THE NAME OF THE QUEEN!
GET DOWN!
OH, GOD...THE *GOLDEN CITY AIR GUARD?*
BELIEVE ME, IF I DID THIS *RIGHT*...

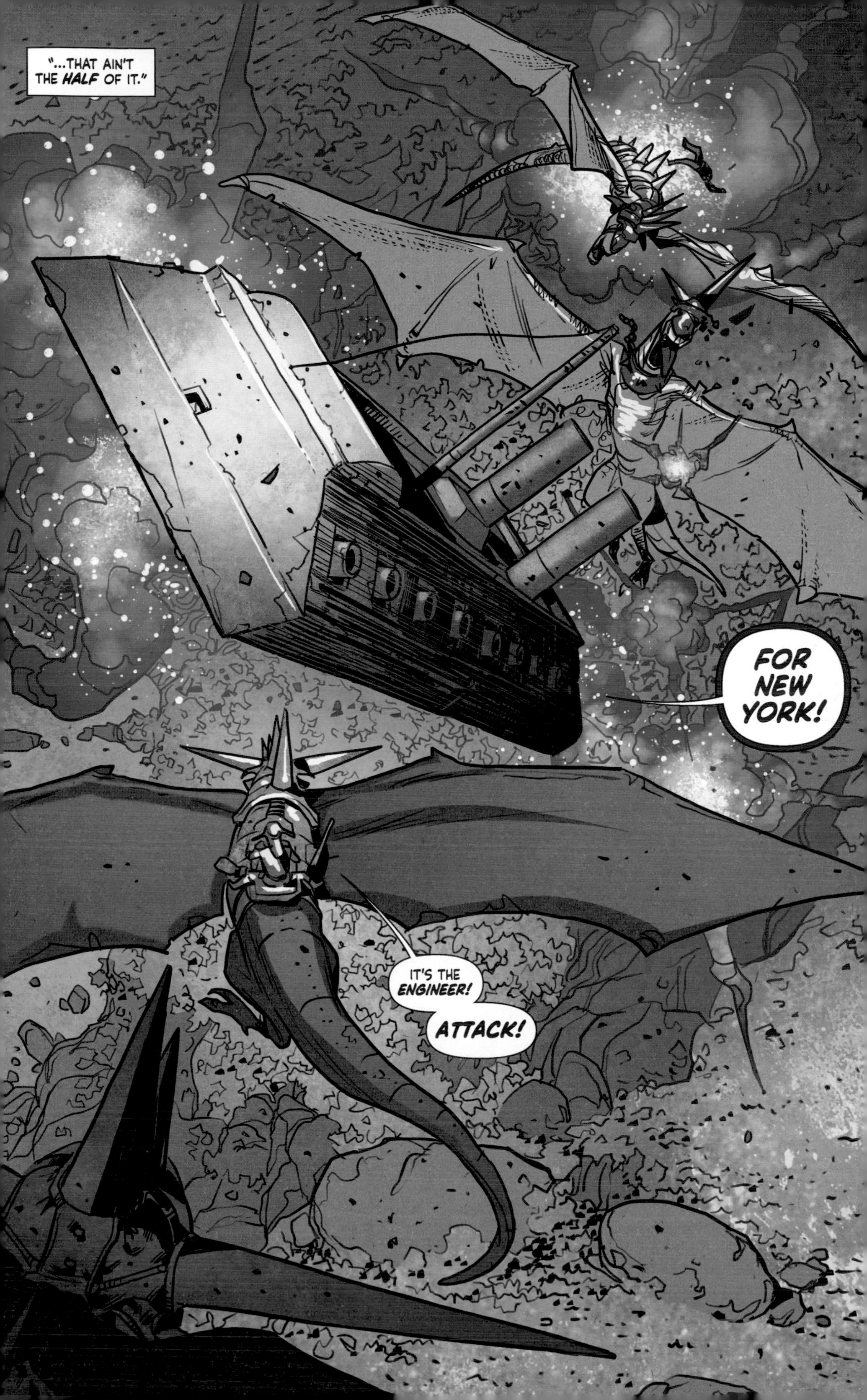
"...THAT AIN'T THE HALF OF IT."
FOR NEW YORK!
IT'S THE ENGINEER!
ATTACK!

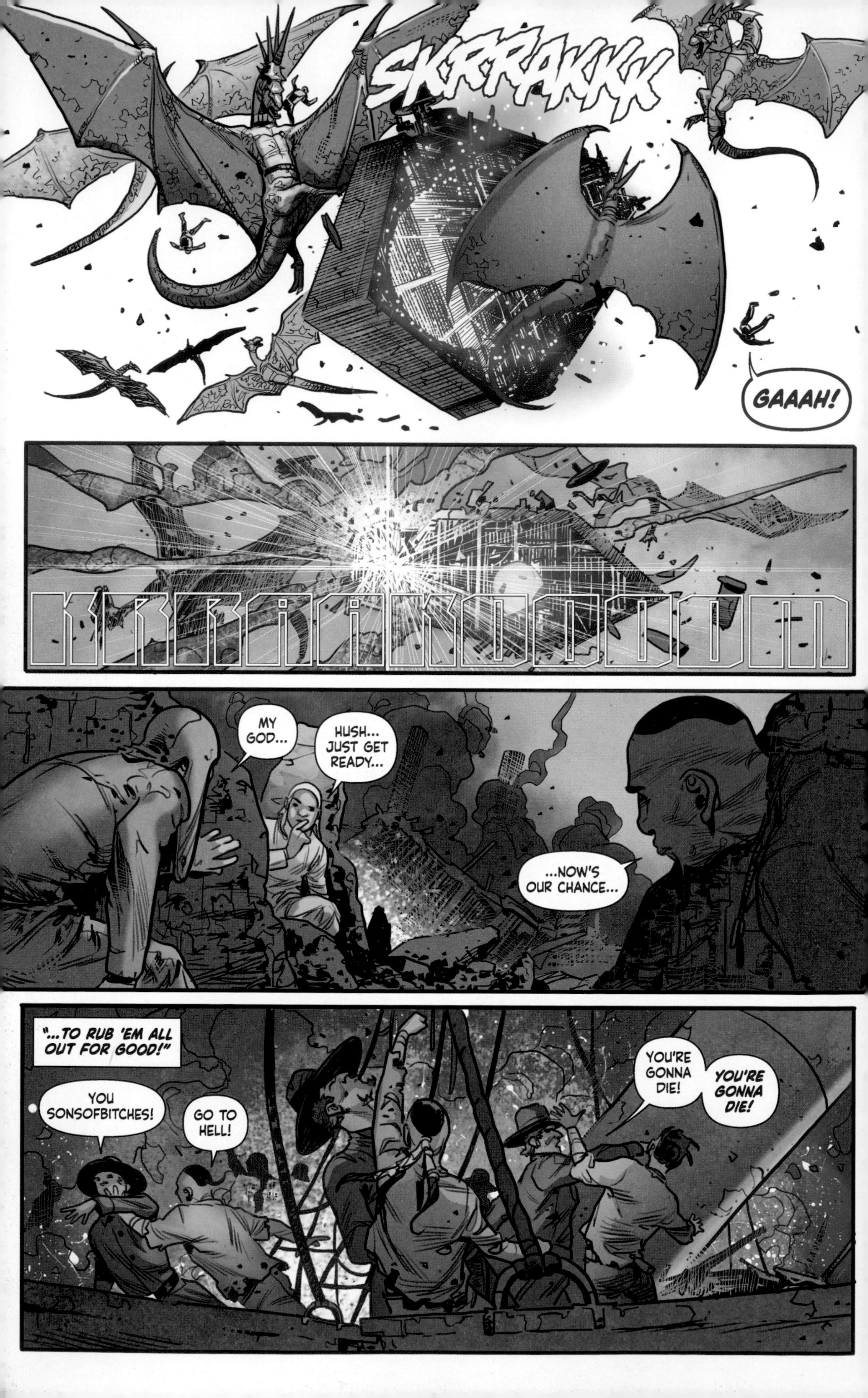
SKRRAKKK
GAAAH!
KRRBAAKBOOOOM
MY GOD...
HUSH... JUST GET READY...
...NOW'S OUR CHANCE...
"...TO RUB 'EM ALL OUT FOR GOOD!"
YOU SONSOFBITCHES!
GO TO HELL!
YOU'RE GONNA DIE!
YOU'RE GONNA DIE!

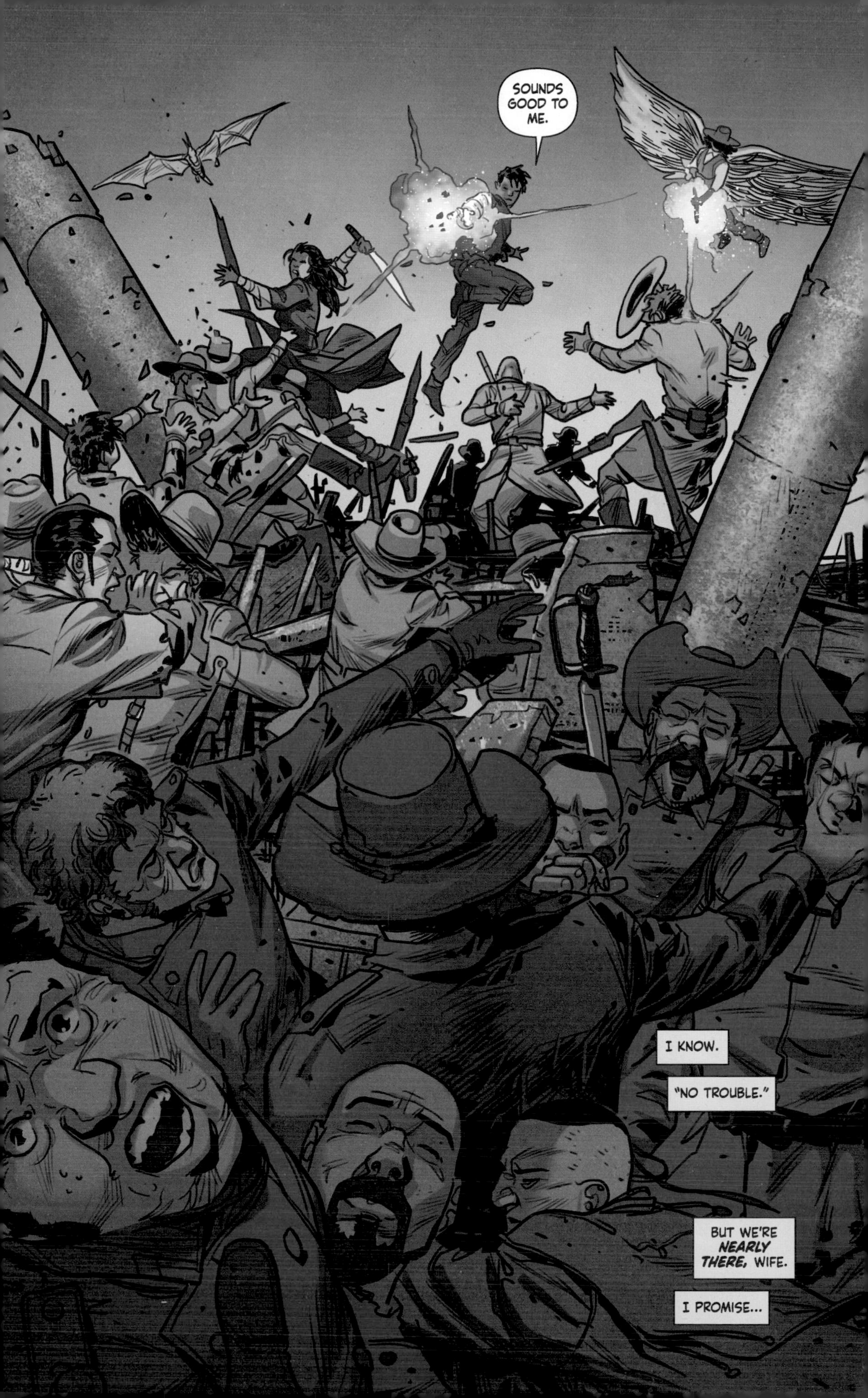
SOUNDS GOOD TO ME.
I KNOW.
"NO TROUBLE."
BUT WE'RE *NEARLY THERE,* WIFE.
I PROMISE...

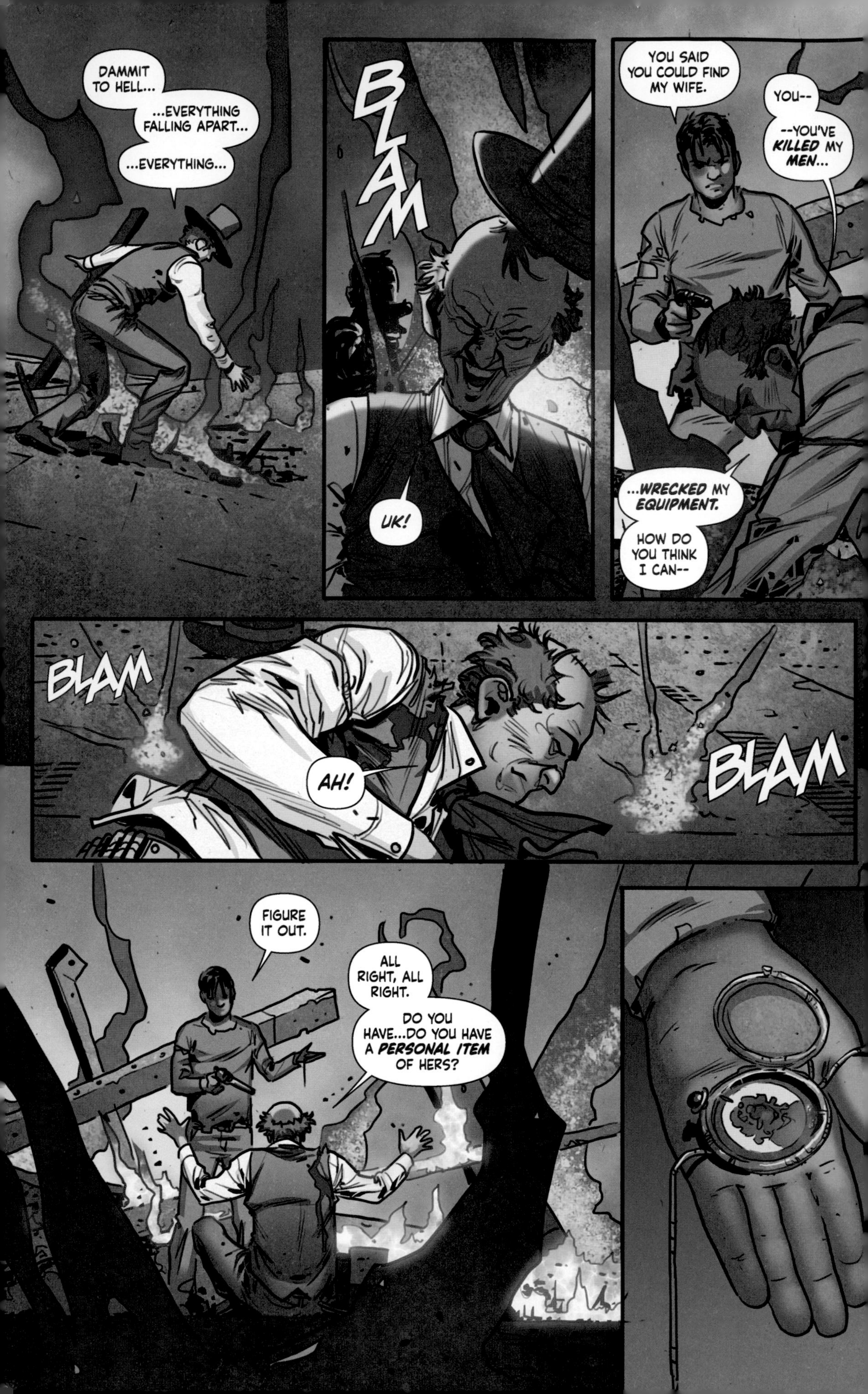
DAMMIT TO HELL...
...EVERYTHING FALLING APART...
...EVERYTHING...
BLAM
UK!
YOU SAID YOU COULD FIND MY WIFE.
YOU--
--YOU'VE *KILLED* MY *MEN*...
...*WRECKED* MY *EQUIPMENT.*
HOW DO YOU THINK I CAN--
BLAM
AH!
BLAM
FIGURE IT OUT.
ALL RIGHT, ALL RIGHT.
DO YOU HAVE...DO YOU HAVE A *PERSONAL ITEM* OF HERS?

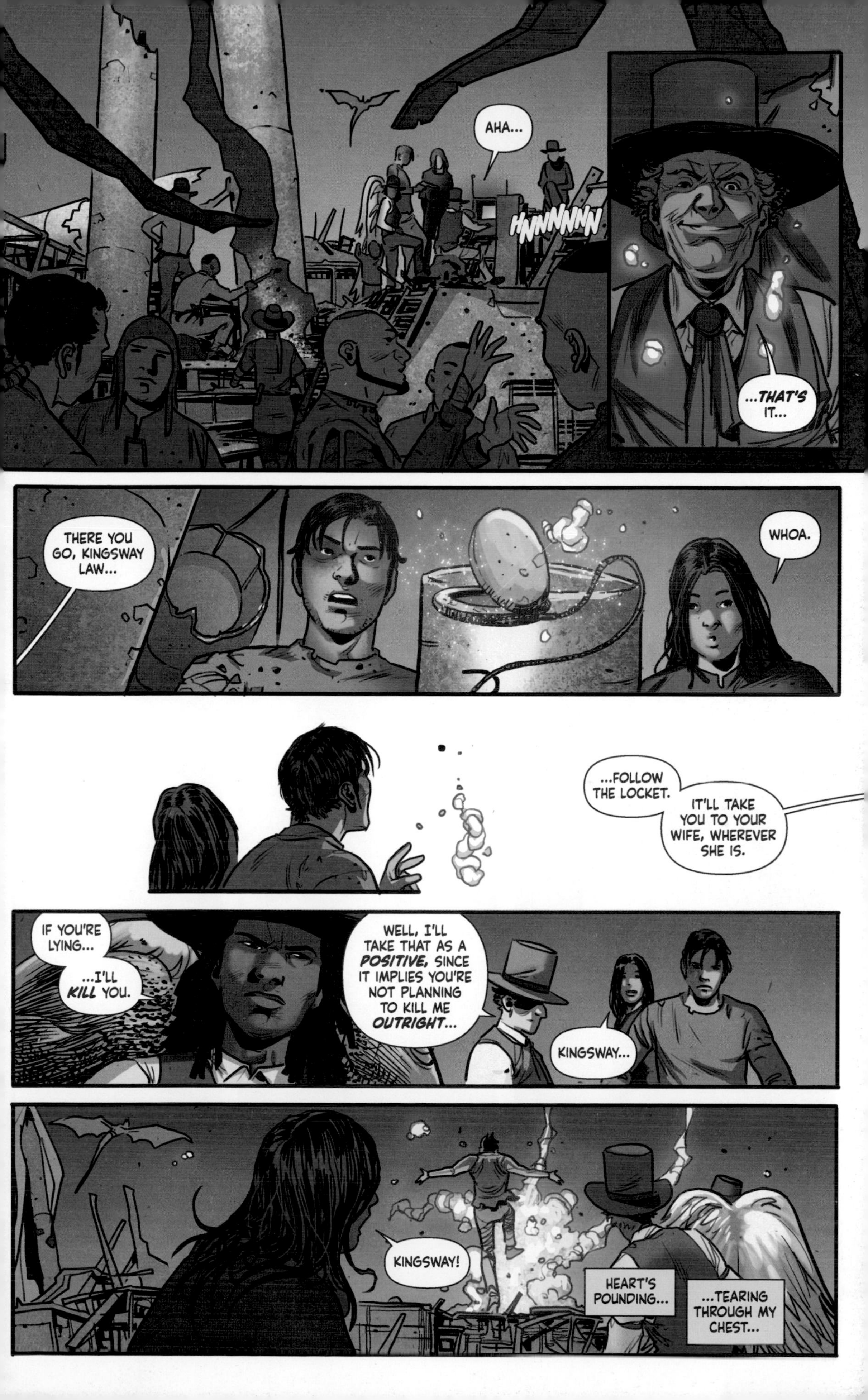
AHA...
HNNNNNN
...THAT'S IT...
THERE YOU GO, KINGSWAY LAW...
WHOA.
...FOLLOW THE LOCKET.
IT'LL TAKE YOU TO YOUR WIFE, WHEREVER SHE IS.
IF YOU'RE LYING...
...I'LL KILL YOU.
WELL, I'LL TAKE THAT AS A POSITIVE, SINCE IT IMPLIES YOU'RE NOT PLANNING TO KILL ME OUTRIGHT...
KINGSWAY...
KINGSWAY!
HEART'S POUNDING...
...TEARING THROUGH MY CHEST...

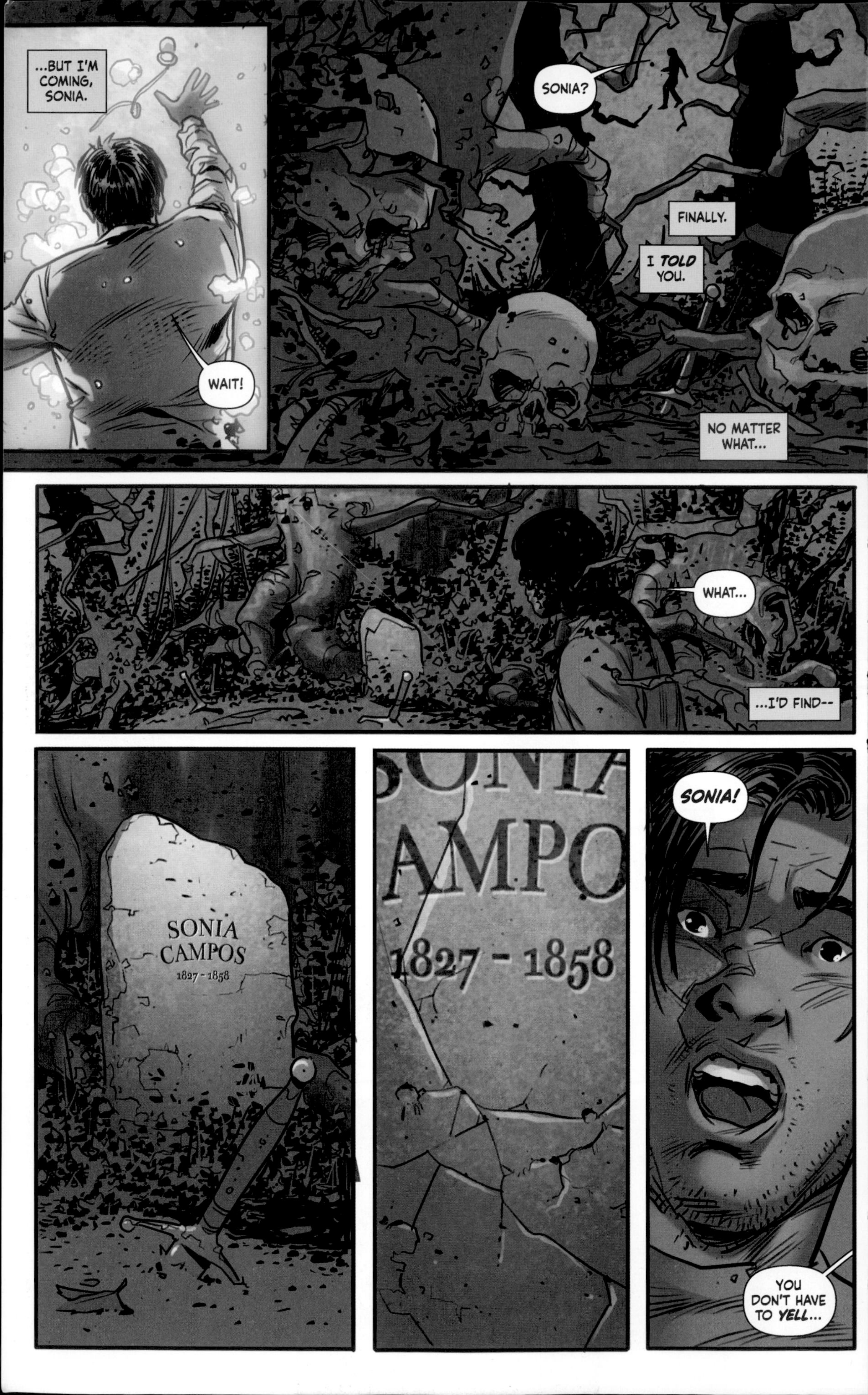
...BUT I'M COMING, SONIA.
WAIT!
SONIA?
FINALLY.
I TOLD YOU.
NO MATTER WHAT...
WHAT...
...I'D FIND--
SONIA CAMPOS
1827 - 1858
AMPO
1827 - 1858
SONIA!
YOU DON'T HAVE TO YELL...

...I'M RIGHT HERE.

YOU FOUND ME.

SONIA!

SONIA CAMPOS

YES! THAT'S ALL I--ALL I EVER--

BUT WHAT--WHAT'S GOING ON?

THIS... GRAVE...

YEAH. THAT'S WHERE MY BROTHER BURIED ME.

WHAT?

I DIED IN THE TERROR...

...WHEN GOLDEN CITY SOLDIERS MURDERED EVERY MEXICAN THEY COULD FIND AFTER THE BOMBING OF SAN FRANCISCO.

AND THEN I LAY HERE FOR FIVE YEARS.

SO COLD. SO LONELY.

SO ANGRY.

AND THEN YOU FELL AT MY FEET, SHOT IN THE SHOULDER.

I WAS JUST GONNA WATCH AND GRIN AS YOU BLED OUT.

BUT YOU...

...YOU WERE LIKE ME.

YOU'D HAD ENOUGH OF THE KILLING.

ENOUGH OF THE WAR.

ENOUGH OF BEING A MONSTER.

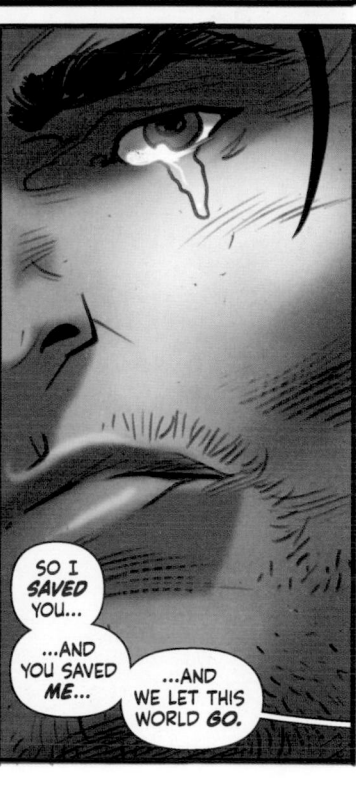

SO I SAVED YOU...

...AND YOU SAVED ME...

...AND WE LET THIS WORLD GO.

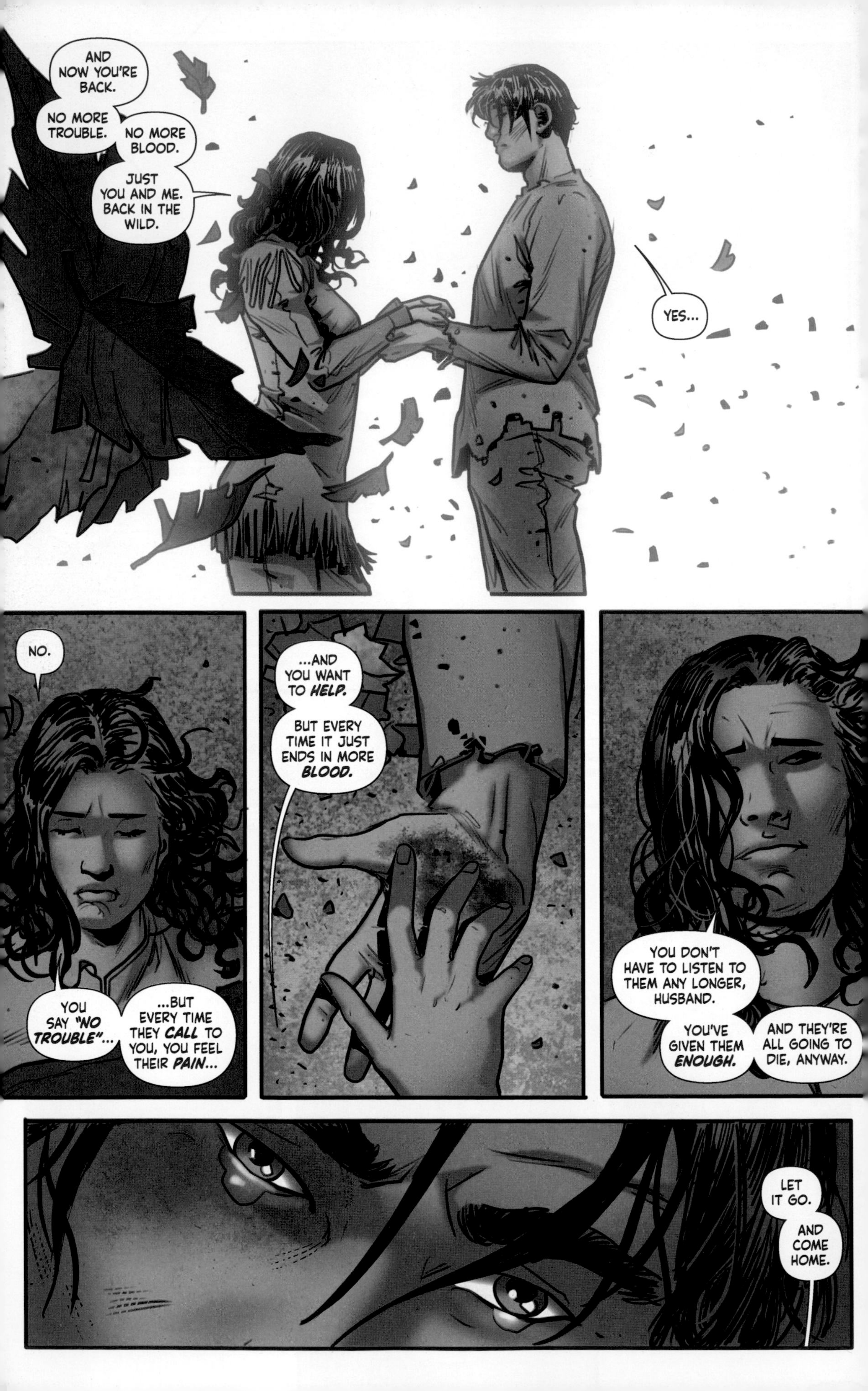
AND NOW YOU'RE BACK.
NO MORE TROUBLE.
NO MORE BLOOD.
JUST YOU AND ME. BACK IN THE WILD.
YES...
NO.
YOU SAY "NO TROUBLE"...
...BUT EVERY TIME THEY CALL TO YOU, YOU FEEL THEIR PAIN...
...AND YOU WANT TO HELP.
BUT EVERY TIME IT JUST ENDS IN MORE BLOOD.
YOU DON'T HAVE TO LISTEN TO THEM ANY LONGER, HUSBAND.
YOU'VE GIVEN THEM ENOUGH.
AND THEY'RE ALL GOING TO DIE, ANYWAY.
LET IT GO.
AND COME HOME.

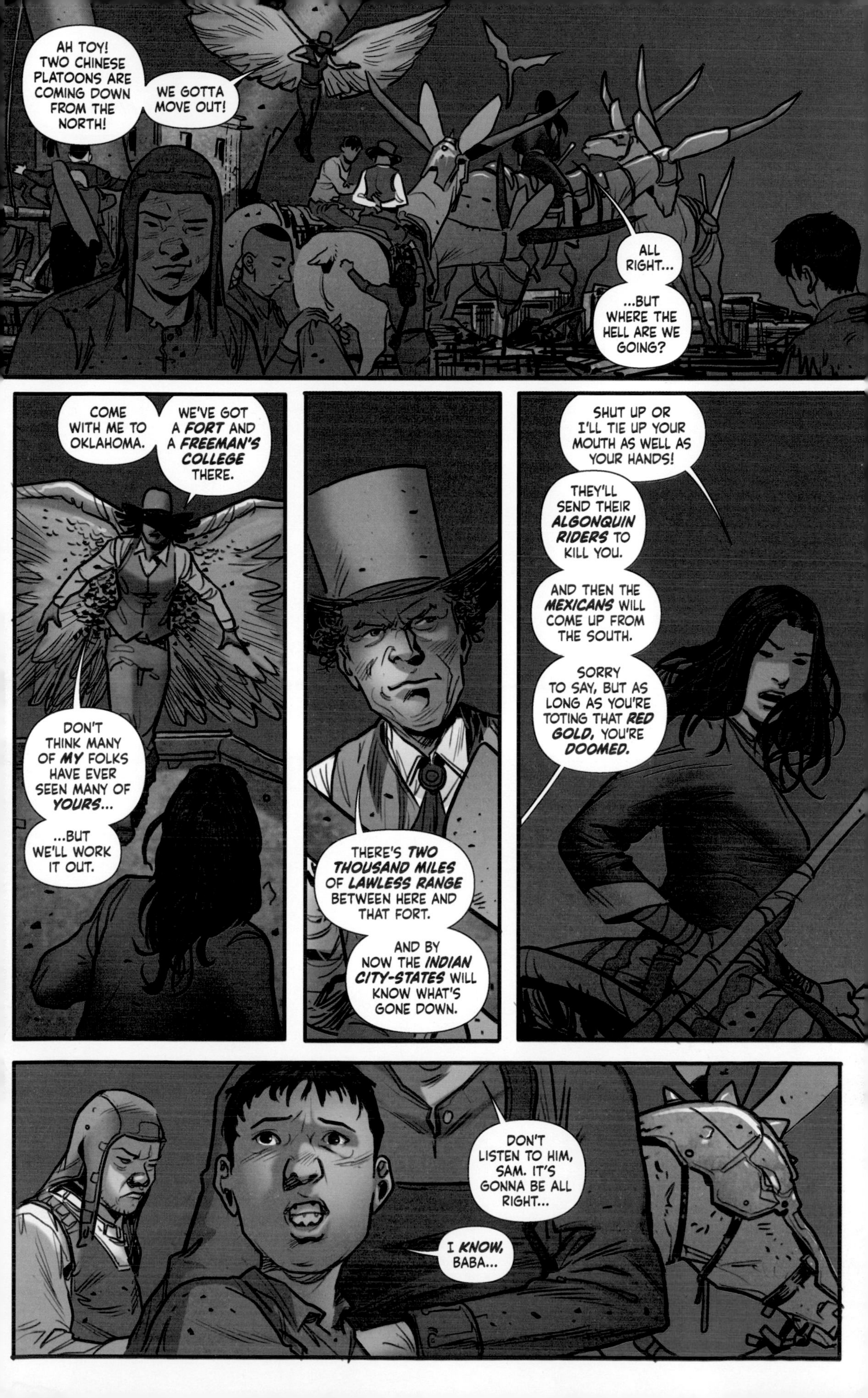
AH TOY! TWO CHINESE PLATOONS ARE COMING DOWN FROM THE NORTH!
WE GOTTA MOVE OUT!
ALL RIGHT...
...BUT WHERE THE HELL ARE WE GOING?
COME WITH ME TO OKLAHOMA.
WE'VE GOT A FORT AND A FREEMAN'S COLLEGE THERE.
DON'T THINK MANY OF MY FOLKS HAVE EVER SEEN MANY OF YOURS...
...BUT WE'LL WORK IT OUT.
THERE'S TWO THOUSAND MILES OF LAWLESS RANGE BETWEEN HERE AND THAT FORT.
AND BY NOW THE INDIAN CITY-STATES WILL KNOW WHAT'S GONE DOWN.
THEY'LL SEND THEIR ALGONQUIN RIDERS TO KILL YOU.
AND THEN THE MEXICANS WILL COME UP FROM THE SOUTH.
SORRY TO SAY, BUT AS LONG AS YOU'RE TOTING THAT RED GOLD, YOU'RE DOOMED.
SHUT UP OR I'LL TIE UP YOUR MOUTH AS WELL AS YOUR HANDS!
DON'T LISTEN TO HIM, SAM. IT'S GONNA BE ALL RIGHT...
I KNOW, BABA...

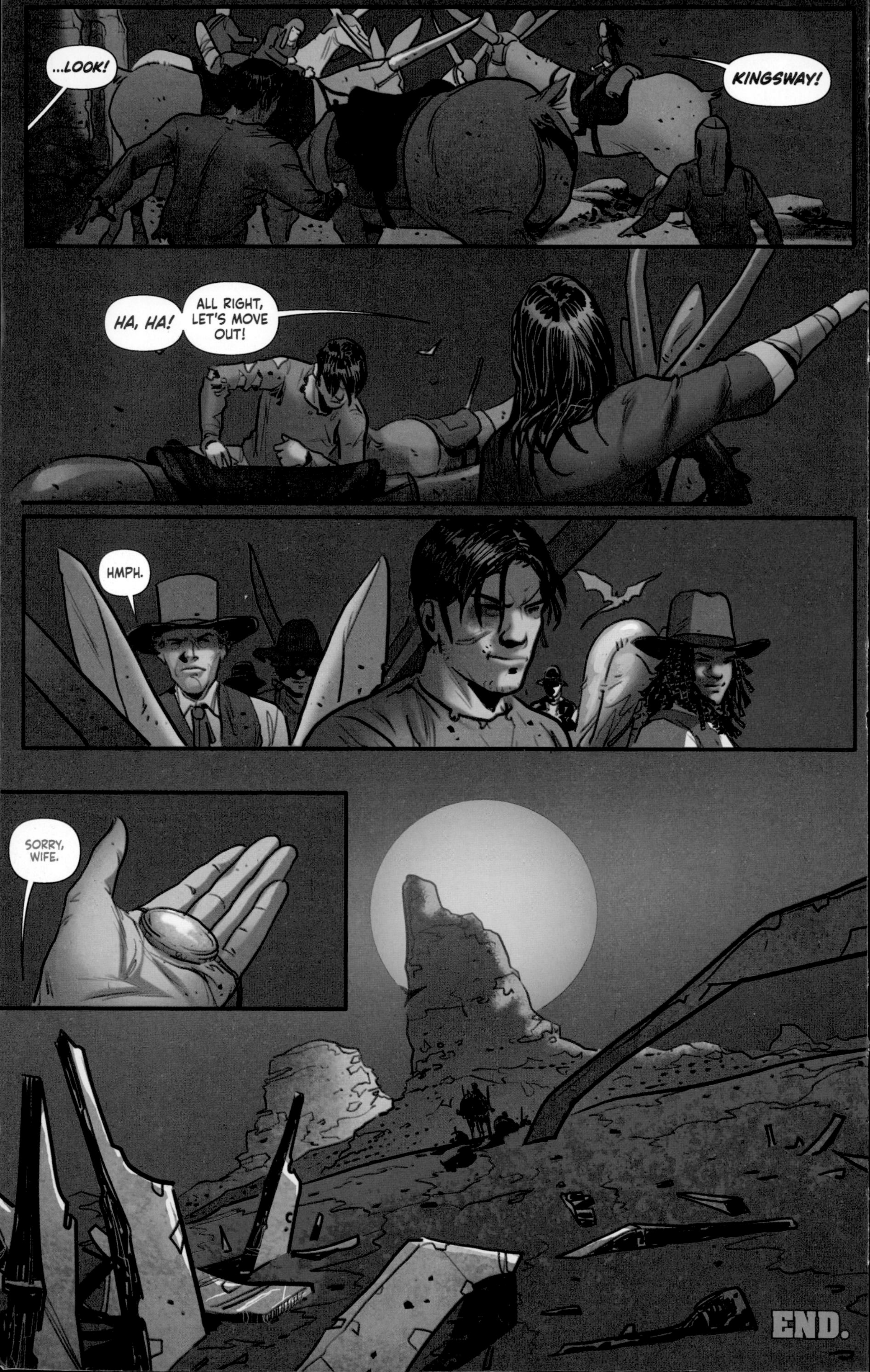
...LOOK!
KINGSWAY!
HA, HA!
ALL RIGHT, LET'S MOVE OUT!
HMPH.
SORRY, WIFE.
END.

I GREW UP AS A KOREAN AMERICAN BOY SCOUT in suburban North Dallas who loved outdoor adventure and westerns. So when I learned the true history of the Chinese in the Old West, my head nearly popped off. And ever since then, I've had a tall, lean Chinese gunslinger walking through my dreams.

I worked on multiple screenplays featuring Chinese gunslingers throughout film school at NYU and later wrote a couple of short comic book stories featuring a Chinese hero in the Old West that were illustrated by the great Ian Kim and Sean Chen.

And then a few years ago I teamed up with artist Mirko Colak and started talking with editor Jim Gibbons at Dark Horse Comics, who loved my pitch but asked if there might be something more that could take the story to the next level. Jim didn't say much more than that, but it started the wheels rolling.

I found myself thinking about all the different kinds of outdoor adventure I loved as a kid—and the strange way that Westerns and fantasy epics shared so many elements. And then a fantastical Old West started to take shape in my head, with a gold rush for magical red gold, monstrous bearfeet and windigos and jackalopes in the wilds, multiethnic empires vying for territory, and that tall, lean Chinese gunslinger in the middle of everything, just trying to find his wife.

Teaming up with artist Mirko Colak, colorist Wil Quintana, letterer Simon Bowland, and editors Spencer Cushing, Kevin Burkhalter, and Jim Gibbons to bring this world and these characters to life has been one of my greatest experiences in comics. Thanks so much for coming along for the ride.

Greg Pak
New York City
December 2016

SKETCHBOOK

The following pages feature some of artist Mirko Colak's earliest *Kingsway West* character designs, which show a few different stabs at the best kind of hat for our hero. (Hats are hard!) Also included are unused supporting character and villain designs and even a spectacular double-page spread that was cut from the final book. (Maybe we'll use it in the sequel . . . ?)

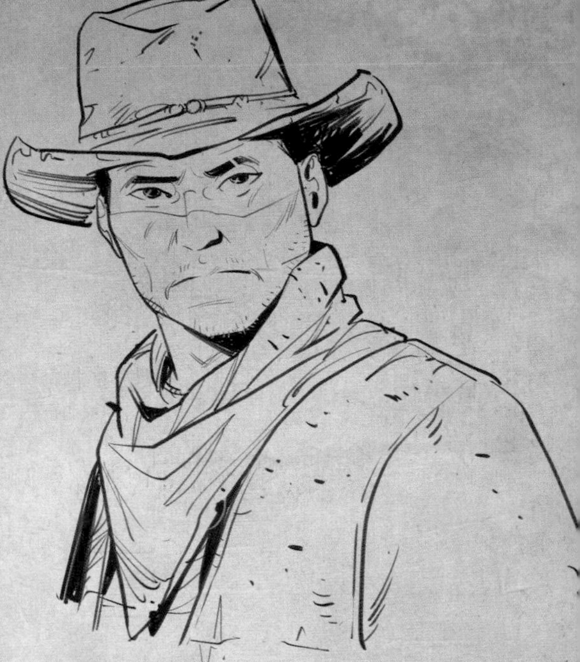

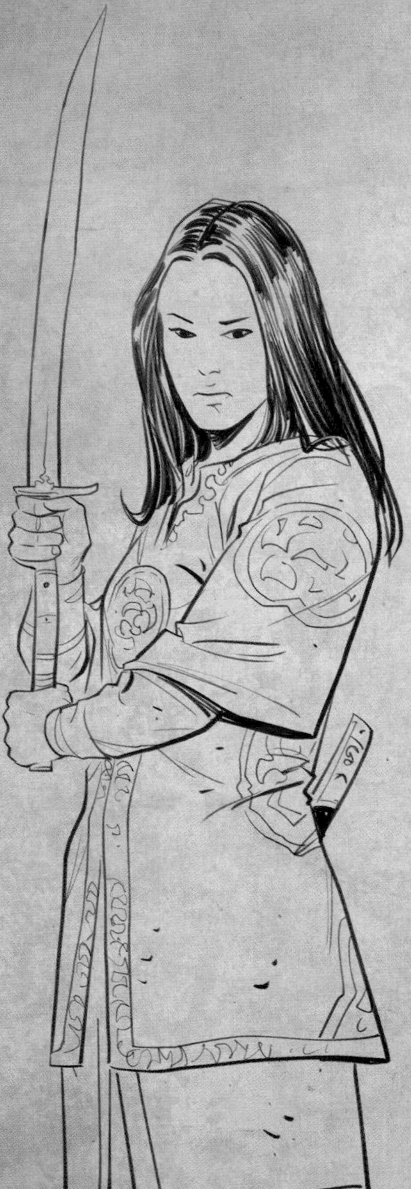

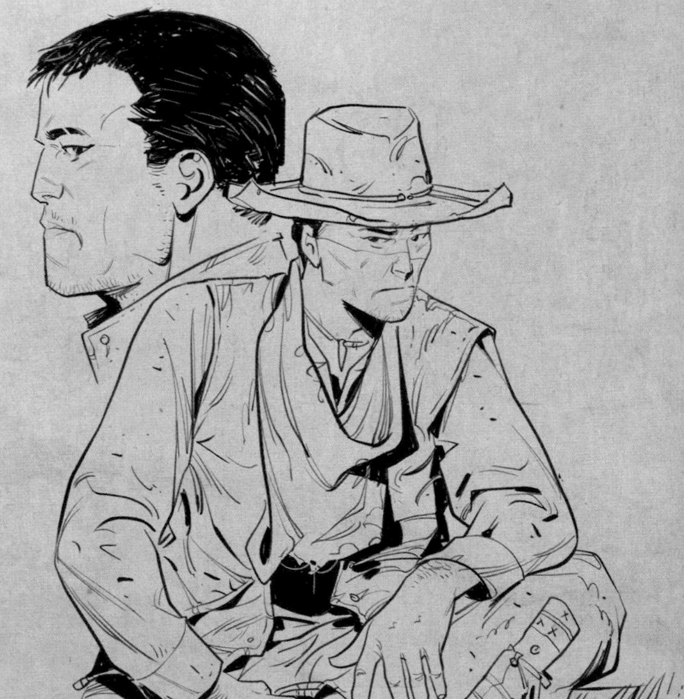

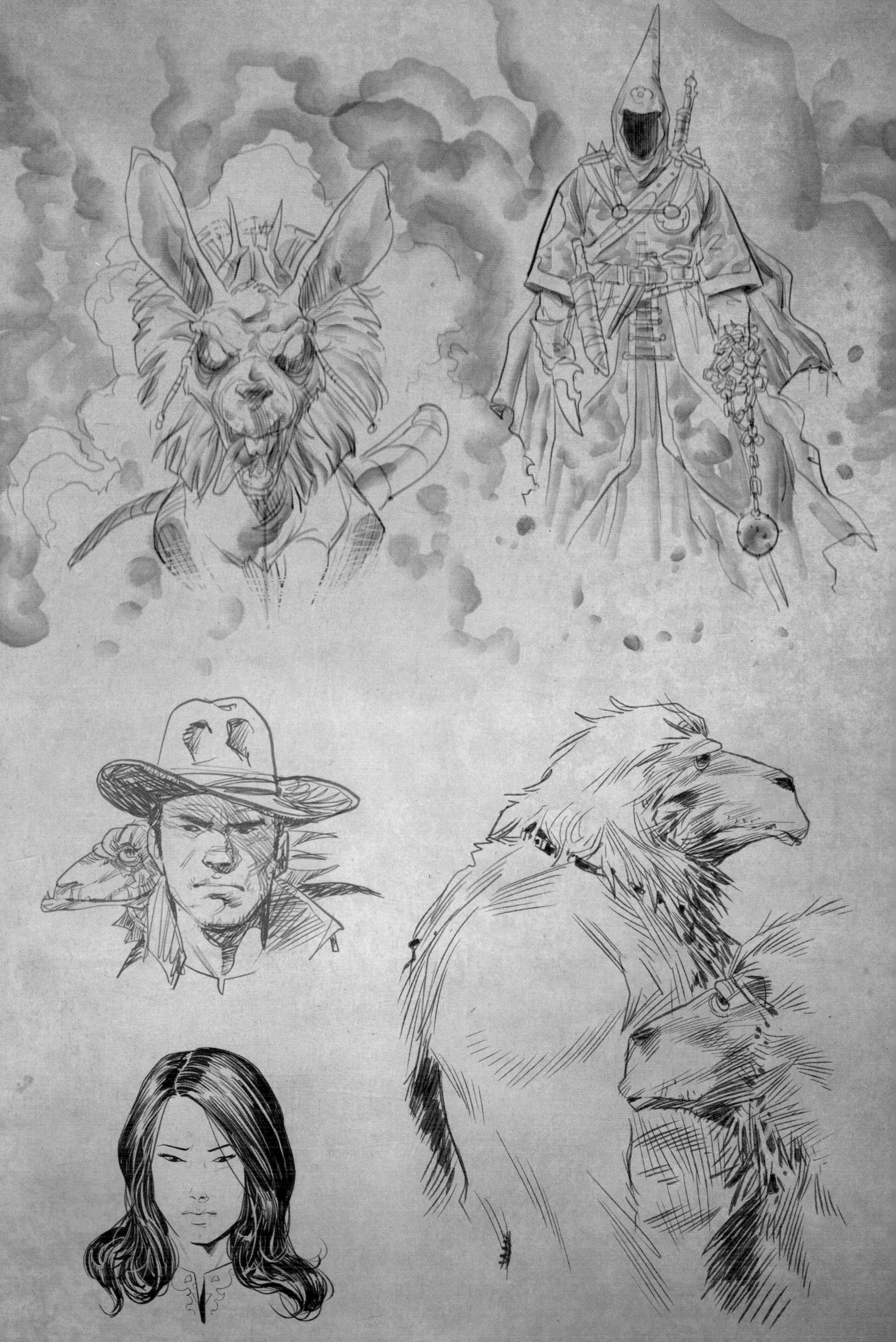

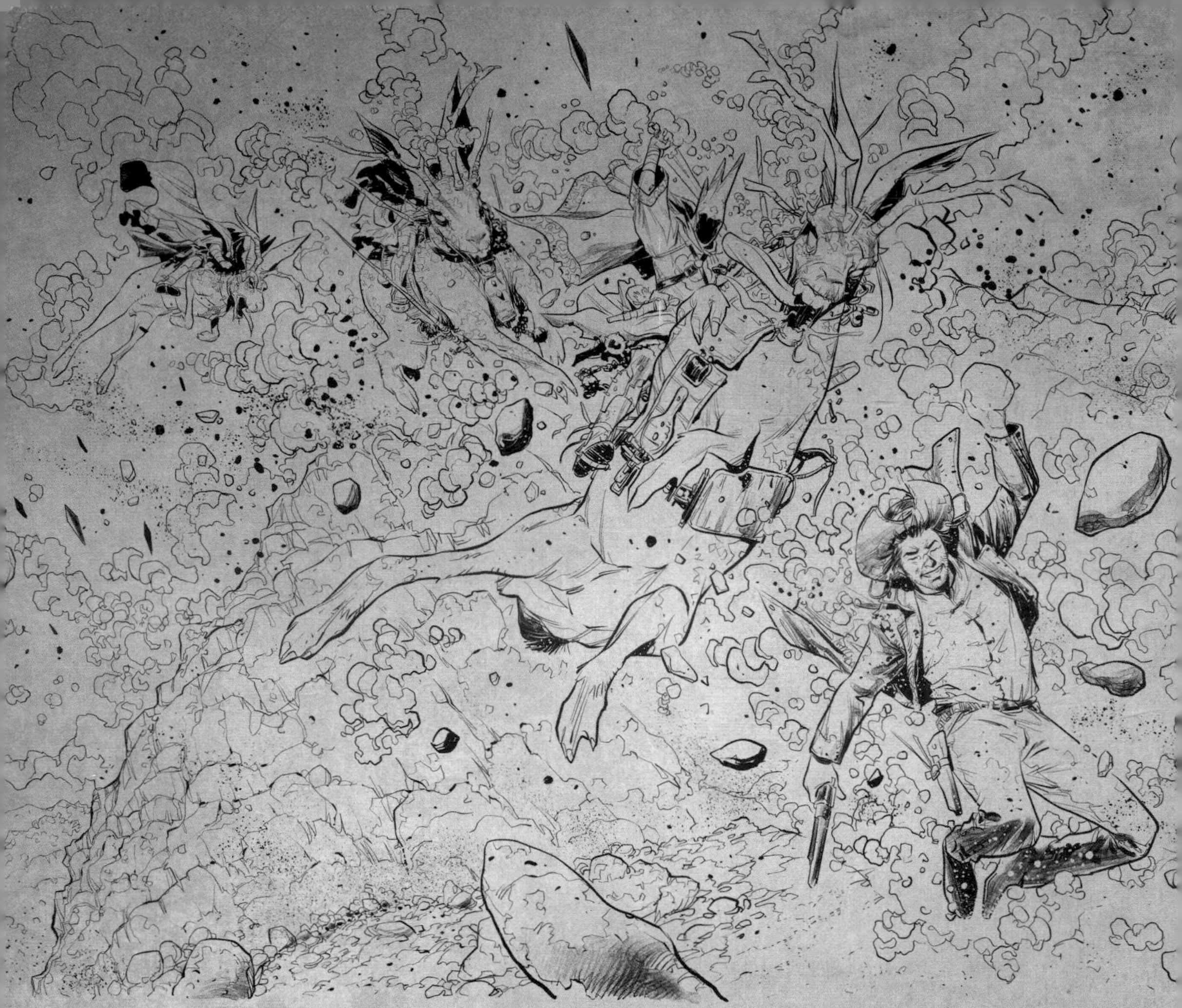

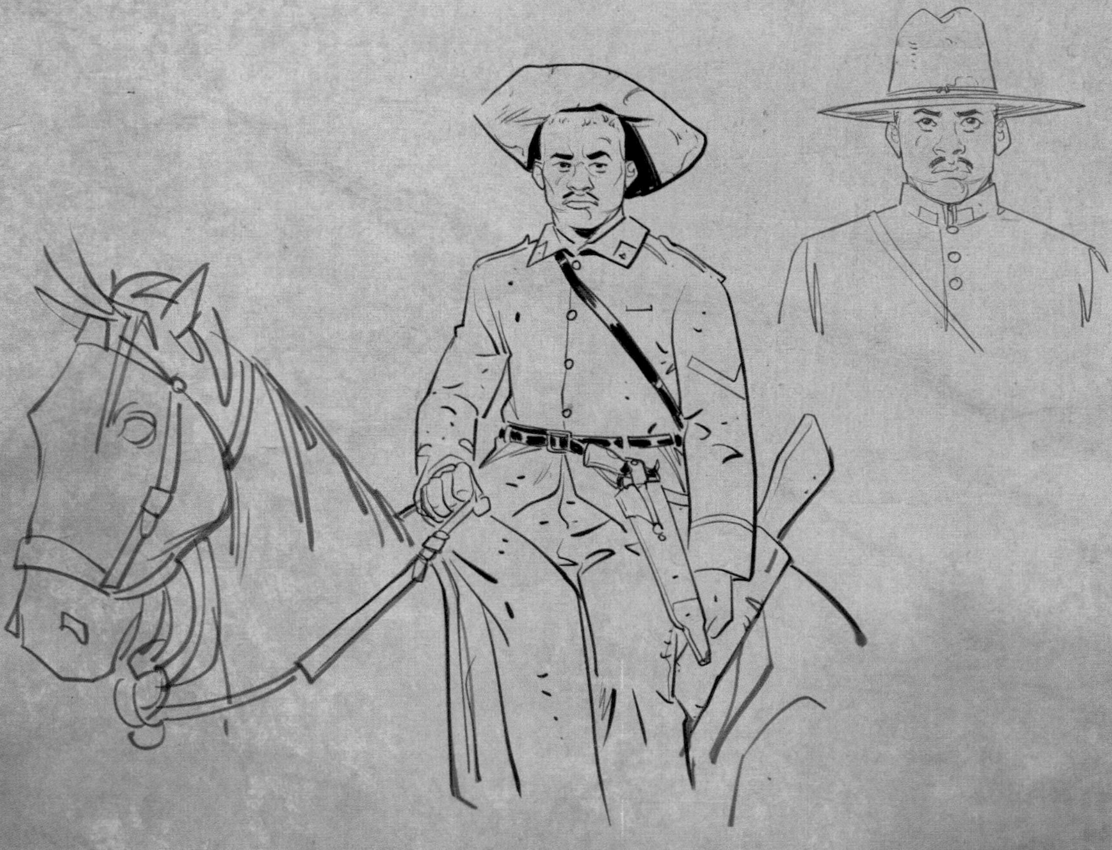